$2.95

JUVENILE DELINQUENTS

PATTERSON SMITH REPRINT SERIES IN
CRIMINOLOGY, LAW ENFORCEMENT, AND SOCIAL PROBLEMS

A listing of publications in the SERIES *will be found at rear of volume*

Publication No. 107: Patterson Smith Reprint Series in
Criminology, Law Enforcement, and Social Problems

JUVENILE DELINQUENTS

Their Condition and Treatment

BY
MARY CARPENTER

Reprinted with an Introductory Essay

Mary Carpenter and Reforms in the
Treatment of Juvenile Delinquents
By Katharine F. Lenroot

And with Index Added

MONTCLAIR, N. J.
PATTERSON SMITH
1970

Originally published 1853
Reprinted 1970 by
Patterson Smith Publishing Corporation
Montclair, New Jersey 07042
New material copyright © 1970 by
Patterson Smith Publishing Corporation

57375

SBN 87585-107-X

Library of Congress Catalog Card Number: 76-108224

This book is printed on three-hundred-year acid-free paper.

CONTENTS

MARY CARPENTER AND REFORMS IN THE TREATMENT OF JUVENILE DELINQUENTS, *by Katharine F. Lenroot, ix*

AUTHOR'S PREFACE, xxxvii

INTRODUCTION.

Relation of Juvenile Delinquents to Society as a whole, 1—7. Scope of the Question, 1—9. Analysis of the former volume on Reformatory Schools, 9—14.

CHAPTER I.

CHARACTERISTICS AND CLASSES.

Analogy between Physical and Moral Disease, 15—18. Examples, 15—23. Classes, 23—31. Poverty not the Chief Cause of Juvenile Crime, 31—35. Pickpockets, 35—39. Orphans and Neglected Children, 39—49.

CHAPTER II.

A SINGLE CAPTIVE.

Narrative of W. Thompson, 51—53. Ditto of R. Clarke, 54—59. Ditto of W. N., 59—64. Ditto of X., 65—72. A Contrast, in a Teacher's Record, 72—80.

CHAPTER III.

THE GIRLS.

True Position of the Female Sex, 81—83. Degradation of Delinquent Grls greater than that of Boys, 83—85. Reason of this, 85—88. Neglect of Mental Culture in Girls, 88—91. History of a Young Female Convict, 91—99. Training of Girls to Dishonesty, 99—104. Effect of the Present System on Girls, 104—113. Successful Efforts at Reformation of Girls, 113—117.

CHAPTER IV.

THE PARENTS.

General Character of the Parents of Delinquent Children, 119—122. Vagabonds, 122—129. City Vagabondism, 129—133. Intemperance, 133—138. Poverty not the Cause of the Existing Evil, 138—141. Individual Cases, 142—147. Children of Beggars, 147, 148. Social Condition of the Parents of Convicted Children, 151—155. Responsibility of Parents, 156—160.

CHAPTER V.

PRESENT TREATMENT.

Actual Treatment, 161—165. Its Effect in Rearing Adult Criminals, 165—168. A Prison School, 168—177. Effect of Imprisonment on Children, 177, 178. The Present System causes Impunity, 178—181. Lowers the Dignity of Justice, 181—187. Children Reared to Crime and Driven to it by the Poor Law System, 187—193. Principle of Fear as carried out in Parkhurst Prison, 193—198. Illustration, 198—202. Suicide of a Child in Gaol, 203—205.

CHAPTER VI.

AMERICAN EXPERIENCE.

Principles Developed, 207, 208. "Common Schools" do not Reach the Criminal Class, 208—213. Boston Farm School Society, 214—216. New York Reform School, 217—220. House of Refuge in Philadelphia, 221—223. Westboro' Reform School, 223—225. Baltimore House of Refuge, 225, 226. Report of Commission from Canada, 226—229. Law for Truant Children, 230—233.

CHAPTER VII.

CONTINENTAL EXPERIENCE.

French Agricultural Colonies, 234, 235. French Law respecting Children, 236—242. Organization of the Colonies, 243—246. Wurtemburg Farm Schools, 245—248. Belgian Farm Schools, 248—251. Swiss Farm Schools, 252—255. Mr. Fletcher's Opinion, 256, 257.

CHAPTER VIII.

INDIVIDUAL EXPERIENCE.

The Rauhe Haus, 258—282. Reformation of London Thieves, 283—291.

CHAPTER IX.

PRINCIPLES OF TREATMENT.

Childhood considered Physically, 293—295. Spiritually, 296—298. Family System, 299, 300. Qualifications in Instructors, 301, 302. Kind of Instruction, 303, 304. Agricultural Labour, 305—307. Labour must be Voluntary, 308—312. Recreations, 312—315. Discipline, 315—319. Age, 320. Length of Residence, 321. Admission of both Sexes to the same School, 321—323.

CHAPTER X.

APPLICATION OF PRINCIPLES.

Delinquents Convicted and Not Convicted, 325, 326. Select Committee of the House of Lords, 327, 328. Birmingham Conference, 329—334. Memorial of Conference Committee, 334—337. What a Ragged School cannot do, 338—340. Objections Considered, 342—363. Principle of Punishment, 363—369. Responsibility of Society, 369—371. The Common Law of England, 371—376. Principles stated, 376—379. Legal Enactments needed, 379—381.

APPENDIX, 383. INDEX, 389.

MARY CARPENTER AND REFORMS IN THE TREATMENT OF JUVENILE DELINQUENTS

By Katharine F. Lenroot

DEAN Roscoe Pound of the Harvard Law School, writing in 1949 on "The Juvenile Court in the Service State," pointed out that all legal history shows "a constant fluctuation between reliance on rule and justice administered in accordance with established norms or patterns of conduct and of decision, on the one hand, and reliance on discretion and unfettered judgment of judge or magistrate in molding his decision to the case in hand and the parties individually, on the other hand." He added that "The nineteenth century, following an era of personal government and of judicial discretion in the rise of the court of chancery, turned to rule and pushed discretion into a corner. The present century by a like reaction turns back again to discretion."[1]

Yet well before the end of the nineteenth century, first mainly in America and on the Continent and then in Great Britain, the theory of individualized treatment of juvenile offenders in "refuges,"

---

[1] Roscoe Pound, "The Juvenile Court in the Service State," in *Current Approaches to Delinquency,* Yearbook of the National Probation and Parole Association, 1949 (New York: The Association, 1950), p. 27.

industrial schools or reformatories had been widely accepted, and substantial progress had been made in a number of places in putting it into practice. Criminal procedure had been modified in some degree, to permit court commitment to such institutions, and a probation system had been put into operation in the state of Massachusetts. Through developments such as these a strong foundation had been laid for the juvenile court movement, which originated in the United States in the final year of the last century and soon spread to Great Britain, the Continent, and other parts of the world.

Turning to the present century, before twenty years had passed after the publication of Dean Pound's paper, the rate of political, legal, and social change in our country had accelerated so sharply as to hasten the beginning of a turn toward more formal and prescribed procedures affecting juveniles. This turning point was signalized by the *Gault* decision, in which for the first time the United States Supreme Court considered the constitutional rights of children in juvenile courts.[2]

The Concept of "Individualized Justice" for Juvenile Offenders

For achieving in Great Britain, at the midpoint of the century, epoch-making reforms which had been

---

[2] Alan Neigher, "The Gault Decision: Due Process and the Juvenile Courts." Reprinted from *Federal Probation* 31 (December 1967): 8-18. (Washington, D.C.: U.S. Department of Health, Education, and Welfare, Social and Rehabilitation Service, Children's Bureau).

under consideration without result for several decades, chief credit is due to our author. The daughter of a non-conformist minister in Bristol, Mary Carpenter for some years had engaged in local educational and social service undertakings. In 1846 she opened a "ragged school" in one of the worst districts of that city, and from that time on gave her full devotion to the cause of the children of the "perishing and dangerous classes," as she called them. Although she did not use the term "individualized justice," now commonly employed to describe juvenile court proceedings and treatment methods for juvenile delinquents, this concept was the core of the principles which she, with other leaders, worked out and championed, and which influenced greatly developments in her own and other countries. She has been described as being more than a half-century in advance of her time in her theory of treatment based on individual need rather than punishment for the offense committed.

In examining the origin and growth of this concept, consideration must be given not only to changing legal theory, but also to ethical, religious, and philosophical beliefs and motivations, and the social conditions of the time. Before the middle of the nineteenth century, in England and Scotland, considerable segments of the population, including many Irish who had migrated to England in the hope of bettering their condition, had been subjected to drastic changes and upheavals in their place of abode, accustomed ways of living, earnings, and regularity of employment. These changes had given rise both to increasing social protest and to rising social concern shared by persons from all classes of society. Their consciences had been aroused and personal efforts inspired by the great Evangelical movement then sweeping the Realm.

Among the earliest objectives of social reform were amelioration of the grave evils of child labor at very young ages, and extension of educational opportunity to the great majority hitherto almost entirely unreached by formal schooling. The cause of homeless, neglected, exploited, vagabond, and delinquent children was coming to public attention with growing insistence. The chief agencies for meeting the special needs of such children were the "ragged schools" — Sabbath, evening and weekday schools for children too ragged, hungry, and forlorn, and too accustomed to street life, to take advantage of the British and National Schools, for which at that time small fees were charged. Under the "Ragged School Union," which was formed in 1844, a variety of programs and organizations developed, including day industrial schools and emigration programs.

Measures beyond these were required for children who had violated the laws, upon whom the same legal penalties as those inflicted upon adults were imposed, subject on occasion to suspension on ground of "legal incapacity" due to tender age. As early as 1748 the great prison reformer, John Howard, had asked, "What can be done with the young offenders in our jails?" More than sixty years later, in 1811, the first parliamentary inquiry into the matter was instituted. Its report condemned the imprisonment of twelve and thirteen-year-old children. Another inquiry in 1819, and a Royal Commission appointed in 1834, took cognizance of this problem. The latter's report was followed by a House of Lords Committee appointed in 1835, which took a mass of evidence and laid down the principle that juvenile offenders demanded different treatment from that which then prevailed. Finally, in 1838, a "penitentiary" solely for juvenile offenders was established at Parkhurst, on the Isle of Wight. Essentially a prison, and characterized as a "gigantic failure," Parkhurst was the only reformatory recognized and supported by the State during the next fifteen years.

In 1847 a Select Committee of the House of Lords was appointed to inquire into the execution of the Criminal Law, especially respecting juvenile offenders and transportation. Its report, based on voluminous and expert testimony, emphasized the necessity of establishing "reformatory asylums" for young offenders wherein reformation, not punishment, and industrial training, should be the main features of their programs.

With amazement Miss Carpenter learned that the Committee's report was not receiving wide attention, and that no action had been taken on its recommendations. Concluding that the facts must be made known, she consulted with leaders having first hand experience with children in jails and penal institutions, reviewed experience on the Continent and in the United States, and published in May, 1851, her book, *Reformatory Schools, for the Children of the Perishing and Dangerous Classes, and for Juvenile Offenders.* Not content with writing this book, the author talked with advocates of reformatory principles in London and the north, paving the way for the "Conference on Preventive and Reformatory Schools," held in Birmingham on December 10, 1851. A Conference Committee was set up to work for the requisite parliamentary enactments and to try to secure a fair proportion of the parliamentary grant for education for ragged schools and free day schools for the destitute, including industrial schools.

In harmony with the first objective, a Committee of Inquiry Into the Condition of Criminal and Destitute Juveniles was appointed by Parliament. Miss Carpenter testified before this committee, in spite of the pain she felt in being brought into any degree of notoriety; "but I must speak for I have to tell a solemn truth which has not yet been clearly told."

Purpose and Scope of Juvenile Delinquents

In preparation for a second conference on the same subject, held in December, 1853, and hoping that the work of the Committee of Inquiry would lead to definite action, our author wrote her book *Juvenile Delinquents,* published in 1853. She undertook this task because of the general recognition of the importance of adopting some mode of dealing with juvenile delinquency very different from that pursued by the State, and with the purpose, as the Preface stated, "to throw as much light as possible on the actual condition of these children, and on their position in relation to the rest of society; to ascertain the results of the system adopted in other countries; and to evolve from all these sources principles for the regulation of institutions in our own country similar to those which have been elsewhere successful."

In her first book, the author demonstrated the need for governmental measures to supplement and strengthen educational and industrial training for children remaining in the community who were in a condition of neglect or committing petty offenses. She called, also, for a different system of treating juvenile offenders which had been successful, she believed, in other countries, and also to a limited extent in Great Britain. She entered into a much wider field of inquiry in her second treatise, which, she hoped, would remove many difficulties and answer many objections.

In the Introduction and first four chapters it was shown that juvenile delinquents were *perishing* from lack of knowledge, lack of parental care and all that should surround childhood, and in a condition of grave "moral disease" which not only threatened their own souls but was dangerous to society. By no means confined to the impoverished and the destitute, it was found among those abounding in this world's goods and holding "a respectable position in society." In the latter group, however, the protecting care of parents could shield their children from a treatment which would be their inevitable ruin. Children who had no effective parental care and protection might, even when very young, be "seized by an officer, carried before the magistrates, introduced to the prison, for the theft of a few halfpence." For them a moral hospital, providing treatment guided by the highest wisdom, was needed.

According to Miss Carpenter, similar modes of treatment should be applied to both physical illness and moral disease. Careful study of all the symptoms and circumstances relating to the disease, even going back to the history of the parents and remote relatives, should be followed by a consideration of what the best treatment would be.

The characteristics and classes of youthful offenders were analyzed and detailed histories of several young delinquents were given, together with discussions of the general character and social condition of the parents. Striking differences in personalities, character, behavior, and general situation were shown. But no symptoms were found, in the opinion of the author, which should "make us pronounce them as incurable."

Three chapters dealt with methods of treatment in Great Britain, and with American and Continental experience. Raising the question of how in Britain the State corrected offenders when they became its children, she answered that the jail continued to be the only infirmary provided by the

State's parental care. To it all her young criminals were assigned indiscriminately, without regard to the degree of their guilt, all sharing the same treatment, for the length of time arbitrarily fixed, and coming back again and again, unreclaimed. In contrast, farm schools for neglected and delinquent children were being developed on the European Continent, and some houses of refuge and reform schools for delinquent children had been established in the United States. This experience offered, the author believed, promising precedents for British reform in accordance with the principles of treatment and their application which form the subject matter of the last two chapters.

Principles of Treatment

In considering the principles developed by Miss Carpenter almost 120 years ago, we must bear in mind that at that time the professions of child psychiatrist and clinical psychologist had not been thought of, nor had intelligence tests been conceived; Sigmund Freud had not been born and the term "psychoanalysis" had not been invented; there was no professional training for social work, nor was the term in general use; and teacher-training schools were in their youth. Theories of the causes of crime often emphasized hereditary factors, and in some instances linked crime with physical characteristics. No methods of scientific study of the child, his development, and the growth of his personality, had been conceived, except as philosophers and educational reformers, notably Rousseau and Pestalozzi, dealt with principles of child training.

Nearly all the British pioneers in what has been called "child-saving" work were inspired by religious motives and committed to the principles of the Evangelical Movement. They held that the first objective of reformatory work was the growth in the child of faith and trust in God and in those having him in charge. The latter would be developed in response to the love—by no means of a sentimental nature—which they had for him and manifested toward him, and the former through religious training. Such faith and trust in God would lead the child to love of God and of his fellowmen.

Schooling was ranked next in importance in a day when most of the children of the destitute classes had little or no formal education. Along with schooling, and often surpassing it in the value attributed to it, was the child's labor and his training in vocational skills. Many of the schools or reformatories which had been established were farm schools. To farm work was added instruction in trades related to farming or carried on in towns, given chiefly by means of the learner working with and under the direction of a master workman associated with the school for this purpose. Training in a craft often led to apprenticeship to a master when the child was ready for discharge. Girls were prepared mainly for domestic pursuits.

Miss Carpenter held that two other features were of very great importance in reformatory schools:

(1) the combination of voluntary and governmental effort, with the operating responsibility in private hands but under the supervision of the State, which would approve or certify the schools and aid them through grants from the Exchequer; and (2) continuing parental responsibility for contributing to the child's maintenance, even after his commitment to an institution. If parents were not able to contribute, the parish should be required to do so.

To make these principles effective, a sufficient number of reformatory schools must be established, as stated in Miss Carpenter's first book, and carried on under the guidance of enlightened Christian benevolence, sanctioned and mainly supported by government inspection and aid. Magistrates and judges must be empowered to send all convicted children to such schools, whose masters would be authorized to retain them as long as needful for their reformation.

In *Juvenile Delinquents* the author entered into fuller consideration of the premises and methods to be employed in treatment. Her discussion reemphasized the importance of founding the system adopted on God's laws, the relationships of masters and teachers to children "springing from a deep fountain of love in the heart." The period of care must be determined only by the degree to which the remedies employed produce their effect on the patient. In order that these values and objectives might be realized as near an approach as possible to the family plan of organization should be made in all reformatory schools. Unless the population was so small as to constitute only one group, they should be divided into small units, each housed in its own building. Boys and girls should be cared for in the same school, with appropriate safeguards.

Her more detailed comments emphasized strong individual influence as the key to success. The recommendations included enlistment of the child's will; voluntary labor, the main feature of the plan, helping the child to *feel,* what no reasoning could make him comprehend, his true relation to the world around him; recreation on an informal basis, with the master associating with the children in their sports; little or no corporal punishment, with punishment to be perceived by the child as the natural and inevitable effect of transgression; and, through giving him property of his own, inculcation in the child of a feeling for individual property and respect for the property of others.

The last chapter included a plea for efforts looking toward prevention, as well as treatment, of juvenile delinquency. Free Day Schools, based on the experience of the ragged schools, should be greatly expanded. They should be under voluntary auspices but should receive government aid. Industrial Feeding Schools—day schools for children having subjected themselves to police interference by vagrancy, mendicancy, or other offenses—should be generally available. They should be supported by legislation conferring on magistrates power to enforce attendance and require payments for the maintenance of the children, by the parents if practicable, or the parish. An educational grant from the Government should aid in meeting expenses of instruction.

As for correctional schools, it was recommended that legislation be enacted based on the principles outlined, authorizing the establishment of Penal Reformatory Schools for children convicted of a felony or such misdemeanors as involve dishonesty, and conferring on magistrates power to commit such offenders to these schools instead of to prison. The magistrates, in exercising the right of the State to assume, "so to speak, a parental relation towards the child," should have power to consign the care of him to those who could discharge the duty satisfactorily, subject to strict State inspection.

The book closes with this plea: "Let each one who 'knows these things,' respecting the condition and treatment of our poor young delinquents, earnestly endeavour to 'do them;' let each strive to rouse others to partake in the work."

Legislation and Progress in the Last Half of the Century

The work done between 1850 and 1853 gave such impetus to the whole question that the period was looked upon as "forming an epoch in the progress of reformatory science." In 1854 Parliament enacted a Reformatory Schools Act for Great Britain and an Industrial Schools Act for Scotland. Amended and supplemented in several succeeding and later years, and consolidated in 1866, they incorporated substantially the principles stated in Conference recommendations and Mary Carpenter's books. By December 31, 1870, the number of reformatory schools in Great Britain had increased to 64, and the number of industrial schools—for younger, mainly homeless, destitute, or neglected children—to 91. Nearly all of these had been established under voluntary management, with State aid; most had adopted the family, rather than the congregate, system of organization.

In the United States, where a few such institutions had been founded between 1825 and 1849, several more under private or local public auspices came into existence in 1850 or a few years later. The provision of institutions for juvenile offenders, however, was accepted, increasingly, as a function of the State. From 1850 to 1900, more than sixty juvenile reformatory or industrial schools had been established, most of them State supported and operated.

When Miss Carpenter came to the United States in 1873, she found several of these schools a great disappointment. As Grace Abbott said, writing in *The Child and the State,* "The ideal of experiment in treatment had gone and the dreary, prison-like reformatories were certainly not institutions in which progress was being made." Yet they were better than police stations, jails, and prisons, in which large numbers of children were still detained while awaiting trial, or to which they were committed for short or sometimes long sentences.

Twentieth-Century Outcomes: The First Fifty Years

As nineteenth-century reforms in the treatment of juvenile offenders began with reformatory schools, twentieth-century efforts began with juvenile courts, the first having been established in 1899 under statewide law, in Cook County (Chicago), Illinois. The movement soon spread almost around the world. Great Britain enacted its first juvenile court legislation in 1908. In the United States before 1910 thirty-four states, the District of Columbia, and Hawaii, and by 1921 every state but two, had such legislation.

Juvenile courts were the natural outgrowth of the slow but steady movement of the preceding century toward "individualized justice," expressed mainly through institutions, but involving certain modifications in court procedure. In the United States the philosophy underlying the statutes and high court decisions holding them to be constitutional derived mainly from English Chancery law, under which the principles of equity were applied to cases in which the rigid rules of law alone would not result in justice. The State, under this doctrine, acted as *parens patriae* in behalf of children needing the substitution of its guardianship for that of parents or others, the object being, as stated in the case of Commonwealth v. Fisher (Pennsylvania, 1905), not the punishment of offenders but the saving of children.

Probation work developed as an indispensable arm of the court, as did detention homes for children. The first child guidance clinic in the country was established in 1909 under the Cook County Juvenile Court. From that time on, great emphasis was placed on "scientific study of juvenile delinquents," carried on by clinics which were usually under community, not court, auspices, and available mainly in urban centers. In many places community child welfare resources were lacking or very limited in scope, leaving the court as the only agency available for developing a variety of services. The first state-wide mothers' aid legislation (for mothers with dependent children) was an outgrowth of the work of the Chicago court, and was court-administered; a number of other early child welfare programs were administered by juvenile courts.

With the establishment in 1912 of the United States Children's Bureau, whose mandate for studies and reports included juvenile courts and whose first Chief, Julia C. Lathrop, had been one of the moving spirits in the passage of the Illinois law, national leadership in the movement became available. This was carried on in cooperation with many agencies—including the National Probation Association, and later, the National Council of Juvenile Court Judges. Among the activities undertaken were studies, reports, and monographs by leading experts; committee and conference work; development of juvenile court standards and statistics; promotion of improved standards and methods of institutional care, and encouragement of programs of training personnel.

The mental hygiene movement and the newly emerging profession of social work contributed greatly to the understanding of the child's personality development and the social, as well as the psychological and emotional, factors in delinquent behavior and its treatment. Juvenile courts and training schools for delinquent children increasingly availed themselves of these resources.

By the third and fourth decades of the twentieth century, as in the case of the industrial and reformatory schools of the preceding century, there arose a considerable amount of disillusionment concerning the results of the work of juvenile courts and their associated agencies, and the state schools for juvenile delinquents. Many children were still detained in jails. New resources had been made available to the courts, however, through the development, with some federal aid, of broader and more effective state and local child welfare programs. From time to time questions of possible realignment of the functions of the juvenile courts and administrative agencies arose, to recur with great force in the present day.

In Great Britain and on the Continent some of these problems seemingly had not developed to the same extent as in this country. "Children's villages" in some countries had retained some of the excellent features described by Miss Carpenter, while, at the same time, incorporating new principles and methods. The Scandinavian countries, believing that children should not be tried in courts at all, gave to administrative councils responsibility for determining questions relating to the care, custody, and treatment of delinquent children.

Challenges and Dilemmas of the Present Time

For many years a general attitude of "permissiveness" in the rearing and training of youth has prevailed in many quarters, accompanied by a lessening of parental, community, or institutional controls. The unprecedented rapidity of social change, markedly accentuated in recent decades, has been associated with social unrest, mounting social protest, mass demonstrations, and violent confrontations. There has occurred, also, a marked increase in the prevalence and gravity of individual juvenile delinquency and youthful crime. The resources of juvenile courts and related community programs and state services, already gravely inadequate, have been seriously overtaxed in many instances, and the value of their services greatly impaired.

These conditions may have contributed to the acceleration of a trend toward the questioning of what has seemed to many to be arbitrary powers exercised by the police and juvenile courts in respect to children faced with charges of juvenile delinquency.

On May 15, 1967, the United States Supreme Court, in the *Gault* case, considering for the first time the constitutional rights of children in juvenile courts, ruled that such courts must grant to children many of the procedural protections required by the Bill of Rights in criminal trials. Among these are notice in writing of specific issues to be met at the hearing; notification of the child's right to be represented by counsel (if financial conditions require, counsel to be appointed for him); notification of the child's right to remain silent; certain requirements relating to admissions or confessions by the child; and, in the absence of a valid confession, support of a finding of delinquency or commitment for any length of time, by confrontation and sworn testimony of witnesses available for cross-examination. In commenting on the probable effects of this decision, a member of the Office of the General Counsel, Department of Health, Education, and Welfare, predicted that it would prove to be a prologue for further decisions extending the constitutional requirement of due process to other aspects of juvenile court proceedings. The fact that the Court refused to accept the non-criminal label attached to such proceedings constituted, in his opinion, the decision's greatest significance.

Thus our highest court has challenged directly the underlying philosophy of the juvenile court movement, as stated in the early statutes and decisions of state courts. In comments on the effect of the decision, however, it has been affirmed that it will neither frustrate the purpose nor destroy the concept of the juvenile court, but will generate the action which has long been needed to improve such courts, including a proper balance between "individualized justice" and constitutional rights.

Some of the protections referred to in the decision are incorporated, in part at least, in state statutes and court practices, and in national standards prepared for the guidance of legislatures, courts, and receiving institutions. Since the *Gault* decision a number of proposals have been made for alterations in juvenile court jurisdiction, realignment of court and agency functions, changes in policies and procedures, and restructuring of the organization of both courts and administrative agencies.

Although efforts such as these are long overdue, it is this writer's opinion that great care should be taken lest children, particularly those under the age of fourteen or fifteen years, and their parents, become confused, extremely anxious, and perhaps frightened and overwhelmed, by the complexity and formality of the proceedings, the numbers of persons involved, and the delays which may occur, in some cases at least, in arriving at a determination. Not only the legal profession, but also those concerned with the psycho-social study and treatment of disturbed, aggressive, and delinquent children, should participate in the review of these matters. Recently a number of suggestions have been made that in the realignment of functions it should be possible to reduce greatly the numbers of children coming before the courts by clearer differentiation than now exists between cases requiring judicial determination and those which can be disposed of by administrative agencies, with the free consent of all concerned, and enlarged provision of services of the latter type. These possibilities merit serious consideration.

Many other issues confront those concerned with the prevention and treatment of deviant behavior in children and youth. Among these are shifts in theories of personality development and their incorporation in treatment programs. In therapy, less emphasis is being placed by some on the exploration of the child's earliest experiences and relationships in family life, and more on opening up opportunities, suited to the child's stage of growth, for developing feelings of adequacy, competence, self-reliance, and personal worth, leading to purposeful living and the progressive acceptance of responsibility. Among programs directed to the latter objective are remedial or "compensatory" education; expanding opportunity for post-secondary education of various types; aesthetic and cultural experiences; job-counseling, training, placement, and advancement; work with "peer groups" and street gangs; home, neighborhood, and community improvement and development programs; and involvement in the wider concerns of social and political life.

In planning services, a strong dose of common sense and an effort to assign priorities and develop policies with such logic and consistency as characterized Mary Carpenter's work, may be helpful. Certainly there is need for expanding and greatly improving programs designed to afford avenues of opportunity for all children and young people, keeping in mind the whole spectrum of variations in their personalities, capacities, needs, and aspirations. At the same time the necessity of more extensive and better programs for children in special need of care and treatment, for their own sake and the safety and welfare of society, cannot be ignored. In the process advantage must be taken of the insights afforded by different philosophies and theories, and the understanding, knowledge and skills developed in the various professions involved.

The objective in revamping court and treatment programs for juvenile delinquents should include not only improving the fairness and quality of such services, but extending their availability, as rapidly as feasible, to all children who need them, wherever they may live. This will require statewide planning and organization to encourage, aid, and supplement community services, with stimulation and assistance from national agencies. It should result in strengthening and developing local and regional resources for treatment, including smaller and differentiated training schools and other treatment centers, which are more accessible to the communities from which the children come and which should be used as far as possible as substitutes for large, central state institutions. Under such plans consideration must be given, also, to differentiated deployment of professional and auxiliary personnel, economizing, so far as possible, in the use of highly specialized experts in very short supply for expanded services. Perhaps the analogy of neighborhood or community health stations or centers, having access to specialized personnel at a city-wide or regional base, might be helpful in working out plans. Firsthand study of certain

European programs might also be useful.

Surpassing in importance all such considerations is recognition of the fact that the ills of children are largely a reflection of the confusions and disorders of society as a whole. Strong commitment by the adults responsible for the child's rearing and training to values and standards which give guidance in personal living and social relationships alone will provide a foundation for the child's developing within himself some sense of security and stability, some framework of values and standards, and some commitment to purposes and ideals which seem to him valid, with hope for their more complete realization.

Princeton, New Jersey
April, 1970

References

General

Abbott, Grace. "The State and the Child Offender." In her *The Child and the State,* 2: 323–489. Chicago: University of Chicago Press, 1938. Includes a paper prepared by Mary Carpenter on the Care of the Neglected and Criminal Children of the United States, *Proceedings of the Conference of Charities Held in Connection with the General Meeting of the American Social Science Association, 1875.*

Lundberg, Emma Octavia. *Unto the Least of These: Social Services for Children.* New York and London: D. Appleton-Century Co., 1947.

Platt, Anthony. "The Rise of the Child-Saving Movement: A Study in Social Policy and Correctional Reform." *The Annals of the American Academy of Political and Social Science* 381 (January 1969): 21–38.

Nineteenth Century

Carpenter, J. Estlin. *The Life and Work of Mary Carpenter.* 2d ed. London: Macmillan, 1881.

Carpenter, Mary. "Ragged Schools; the Duty of Government to Aid in the Education of Children of the Perishing and Neglected Classes." In *Transactions of the National Association for the Promotion of Social Science, York, 1864.* London: The Association, 1865.

———. *Reformatory Schools, for the Children of the Perishing and Dangerous Classes, and for Juvenile Offenders.* 1851. Reprinted as Publication No. 106, Patterson Smith Reprint Series in

Criminology, Law Enforcement, and Social Problems. Montclair, N. J., 1970.

―――. "Suggestions on Reformatory Schools and Prison Discipline Founded on Observations Made during a Visit to the United States." In *Transactions of the Third National Prison Reform Congress, Saint Louis, Missouri, May 13–16, 1874.* New York: The Association, 1874.

Montague, Charles J. *Sixty Years in Waifdom; or, the Ragged School Movement in English History.* 1904. Reprinted as Publication No. 108, Patterson Smith Reprint Series in Criminology, Law Enforcement, and Social Problems. Montclair, N. J., 1970.

Morgan, William. "The Reformatory Enterprise: Its Pioneers and Principles." In *Proceedings of the Annual Congress of the National Prison Association of the United States, Boston, July 14–19, 1888.* Chicago: Knight & Leonard Co., 1888.

Peirce, Bradford Kinney. *A Half Century with Juvenile Delinquents: The New York House of Refuge and Its Times.* 1869. Reprinted as Publication No. 91, Patterson Smith Reprint Series in Criminology, Law Enforcement, and Social Problems. Montclair, N. J., 1969.

Turner, Sydney. Paper included in *Report on the International Prison Congress of London, July 3–13, 1872.* Washington, D. C.: Government Printing Office, 1873.

Twentieth Century

Aichorn, August. *Wayward Youth.* With a foreword by Sigmund Freud. Revised and adapted from the second German edition. New York: Viking Press, 1935.

Flexner, Bernard, and Oppenheimer, Reuben. *The Legal Aspect of the Juvenile Court.* United States Children's Bureau, Publication No. 99. Washington, D.C.: Government Printing Office, 1922.

Healy, William. *The Practical Value of the Scientific Study of Juvenile Delinquents.* United States Children's Bureau, Publication No. 96. Washington, D.C.: Government Printing Office, 1922.

Kahn, Alfred J. "Social Work and the Control of Delinquency: Theory and Strategy." *Social Work* 10 (April 1965): 3–13.

Lundberg, Emma Octavia. "The Juvenile Court as a Constructive Social Agency." Reprinted from *Proceedings of the National Conference of Social Work, Forty-Ninth Annual Meeting, 1922.*

―――. "Juvenile Courts—Present and Future." Reprinted from *Proceedings of the Annual Congress of the American Prison Association, Jacksonville, Florida, October 28–November 3, 1921.*

Moynihan, Daniel P. *Maximum Feasible Misunderstanding: Community Action in the War on Poverty.* New York: Free Press. 1969.

Neigher, Alan. "The Gault Decision: Due Process and the Juvenile Courts." Reprinted from *Federal Probation* 31 (December 1967): 8-18. Washington, D.C.: U.S. Department of Health, Education, and Welfare, Social and Rehabilitation Service, Children's Bureau.

Plant, James S. *The Envelope: A Study of the Impact of the World upon the Child.* New York: Commonwealth Fund, 1950.

―――. *Personality and the Cultural Pattern.* New York: Commonwealth Fund, 1937.

Sheridan, William H. "The Gault Decision and Probation Services." Reprinted with permission from

Indiana Law Journal 43 (Spring 1968). Washington, D.C.: U.S. Department of Health, Education, and Welfare, Social and Rehabilitation Service, Children's Bureau.

———. "Juveniles Who Commit Noncriminal Acts: Why Treat in Correctional System?" Reprinted with permission from *Federal Probation* 31 (March 1967): 26–30. Washington, D.C.: U.S. Department of Health, Education and Welfare, Social and Rehabilitation Service, Children's Bureau.

———. "New Directions for the Juvenile Court." Reprinted with permission from *Federal Probation* 31 (June 1967): 15–20. Washington, D.C.: U.S. Department of Health, Education, and Welfare, Social and Rehabilitation Service, Children's Bureau.

———. "Structuring Services for Delinquent Children and Youth." Reprinted with permission from *Federal Probation* 31 (September 1967): 51–56. Washington, D.C.: U.S. Department of Health, Education, and Welfare, Social and Rehabilitation Service, Children's Bureau.

United States Children's Bureau. *Institutions Serving Delinquent Children: Guides and Goals.* Publication No. 360. Prepared in cooperation with the National Association of Training Schools and Juvenile Agencies. Washington, D.C.: Government Printing Office, 1962.

———. *Standards for Juvenile and Family Courts.* Publication No. 437. Washington, D.C.: Government Printing Office, 1966.

AUTHOR'S PREFACE

THE importance of adopting some mode of dealing with Juvenile Delinquency very different from that now pursued by the State, appears to be generally acknowledged by all who have directed their attention to the subject. Whatever views may be entertained respecting adult criminals, all agree that *reformation* is the object to be aimed at with young offenders; nor is it doubted that the GAOL is not a true Reformatory School, though at present the only one provided by our country; since thousands of young children annually committed to it come forth not to diminish, but to swell the ranks of vice.

The appointment of a Parliamentary Committee to inquire into the condition of "criminal and destitute juveniles," gives hope that some new system will, ere long, be adopted towards these unfortunate children. It behoves, then, all who feel a deep and stirring interest in the question, to throw as much light as possible on the actual condition of these children, and on their position in relation to the rest of society; to ascertain the results of the system adopted in other countries; and to evolve from all those sources sound principles for the regulation of institutions in our own country similar to those which have been elsewhere successful.

It is the object of the present work to offer a full and clear picture of the actual condition of Juvenile Delinquents, to consider their various characteristics, to trace out their mode of life, to see their homes, and thence to learn their early influences. Our attention will next be directed to the course at present adopted by society towards them, and having in a former work, shown the utter inefficacy as well as costliness of the prison system, we shall endeavour to point out other evils which arise from it. The mode of treatment will then be considered which has been of late extensively adopted, with excellent results, in the United States, in France, Belgium, and Germany, with the principles on which it is founded.

It is not presumed that any thing new will be offered to those whose official position or voluntary devotion have brought this subject but too painfully under their notice, and whose own experience will have anticipated the principles here developed. But the public in general know but little of it. The mass of society are better acquainted with the actual condition of remote savage nations, than with the real life and the springs of action of these children, whose true nature is less visible to the public eye when collected in a Ragged School, or swarming in by-streets, than is the state of little heathen children as exhibited in the Reports of Missionaries. Hence the general apathy to their moral danger;—hence the difficulty with which hundreds only are wrung out of the already overtaxed benevolent few, to support institutions for the reclamation of our own young heathens, while thousands are offered with a lavish hand to convert those in foreign lands;—hence the ignorance which exists of the means devised by enlightened philanthropists for their rescue, and of the principles which guide them. May this volume stimulate some to work in this sacred cause,—sacred, for it is the work of the Redeemer, " to seek and to save them that are lost."

Since the commencement of its preparation, one has been called from his labours in this world, to whom the author desires here to express her warm and grateful acknowledgments;—to the late Joseph Fletcher, Esq., she feels deeply indebted for the friendly encouragement and wise counsel, by which, as one of Her Majesty's Inspectors of Schools, he aided efforts made to raise the degraded class hitherto unassisted by the grants for public education, and directed the attention of the Privy Council to the importance of making a permanent provision for these children;—the amount of valuable information which he collected in reference to important principles will be increasingly prized as the subject is more studied, while the deep and earnest conviction with which he called attention to a wise treatment of pauper and criminal children, will command more serious attention when uttered from the grave. May the removal of so devoted a labourer from this neglected vineyard only excite others to more zealous work, and may the Divine blessing rest on this and all faithful exertions.

BRISTOL, *November*, 1852.

JUVENILE DELINQUENTS.

INTRODUCTION.

If we regard society as a whole, we may at once divide it into two great classes, those who live, or profess to live, under regard to law, human and divine,—and those who do not. These are grand moral divisions, which are irrespective of physical condition in society; for among the first class may be found those who hardly know where they shall obtain their daily bread, who have barely sufficient for their needful shelter and clothing; while among the second are those who abound in this world's goods, and who are usually regarded as holding a "respectable position in society." There are, indeed, certain outward and visible signs of the inward condition, whereby the two classes are distinctly indicated to the experienced eye; but poverty and destitution alone cannot be regarded as the sole criteria; they are not in themselves the cause, though often the consequence of the spiritual condition of the second class. Yet the line of demarcation between the two classes is as certain in its existence as is that line, invisible to the eye, with which the astronomer, who views the earth in its relation to the heavenly bodies, divides the northern from the southern hemisphere.

In every grade of society the existence of this line is felt, if not openly acknowledged. In the higher ranks it does not cause the distinct separation that it does in the lower, because the conventional restraints imposed by established usage prevent that open violation of the rights of others which exposes the offender to the interference of the law; but as we descend in the social scale, the moral distinction becomes more and more obvious, until in the lowest, where all regard to public opinion is discarded by persons whose only law is that of their own will, there is a deep gulf fixed between those who fear God and those who do not; and the first may not associate with the last, except at peril of moral destruction.

The truth of this will be acknowledged by all who have viewed society morally and spiritually. Sin against the laws of God, and offence against the spirit, if not against the letter, of the laws of man, is confined to no class of society. But in the higher classes it is so sheltered by those of the same caste, and controlled by public opinion, as not to be frequently the subject of legal interference; while as we descend, it becomes more gross, less controlled, more hurtful to society,—which consequently interferes to defend itself by such means as it is able to employ. Hence these form a distinct class, living in antagonism with society.

Now, it is only occasionally that the law actually takes within its grasp individuals of this class,—the class of persons who habitually live regardless of God and duty. When it does so, it brands them as well as punishes them; they are termed delinquents, felons, and the like; and the amount of crime in England is computed by the number of annual convictions. Such statistics show, indeed, the number of *detected* offences against the laws, but they by no means show the amount or degree of actual criminality, for the greatest criminals often go unpunished for a length of time, and an offence which, in legal language, is a very serious one, may, in the circumstances of the case, be no crime at all; the skilful and gentlemanly swindler may defraud honest industrious persons of thousands of pounds, and go forth from the court unscathed, save by a flash of indignant denunciation,—while the individual convicted of the high offence of housebreaking, and sentenced accordingly, may be a poor houseless, starving, orphan child, who took a morsel of oatmeal to stop the cravings of nature. Such anomalies bear the name of *Justice* in our days!

But while delinquents, *i. e.*, offenders against human laws, will be found in every grade of society, they will not, for the reason above stated, occur so frequently in the higher as in the lower classes; in these last also greater temptations exist to commit those overt acts of dishonesty, to which their more easy circumstances present no allurements in the former. Hence, whatever moral delinquency exists in the higher and middle classes of society, the avenging hand of the law falls almost exclusively on the lower, and a gigantic array of learned judges, recorders, gownsmen, benched magistrates, vigilant police officers, with their numerous subordinates, is compelled to wage a close and interminable warfare with a degraded class ;—these, nevertheless, go on and flourish in our very midst, living in idleness and luxury on the spoil of the industrious and frugal, until, undeterred by the detection of their companions, they too are taken prisoners; still, though in durance, they live on the toil of their countrymen, until again at liberty to pursue the same mode of life with greater circumspection, with unconverted hearts! If such is the painful truth in reference to adults, how much more fearful is it as regards youthful criminals! We do indeed find occasional instances in which such glaring violations of law are committed by adults who move in the higher circles of society, as compel justice to assert its dignity, and to pour a fearful retribution on the offender's head. Our own day has not witnessed a more atrocious murder than was committed lately, even by one who, as a professor, should have been the instructor of youth; no influence, no regard to station or to talents, no outward show of morality, sheltered his cool, hardened guilt from the legal punishment. But when do we hear of a child being brought to trial for his offences from the higher classes of society? When do we see the children of parents of respectable character appear before the magistrates?— When do we find fathers who live honestly bringing their sons up for punishment for thefts committed on themselves? Yet every magistrate exercising his duties in a large town, can testify how often such cases appear before him from among the pariah class. Why is this? Is it that dishonesty does not occur among the higher ranks of society? We know the contrary, and that even children of noble parents have been found as regardless of the property of others as those of the poor. But in these higher classes the young have a protecting care to shield them from a treatment which would be their inevitable ruin;—in the "perishing and dangerous classes," the child is, almost from infancy, exposed in his immatured, inexperienced, and untaught condition to face the dangers and share the treatment of *a man!* In the more favoured portion of society, parental love shelters like a guardian angel tender childhood, defending it from physical want, from spiritual danger; nor is the care relaxed, but rather increased, when independent boyhood would fain be freed from parental control, for then even greater dangers may assail him, and he still needs for his guidance the firm authority of a father, the yet more powerful check of a mother's love. How can the law grasp him? Is it to him or to his father that men complain when he has proved a nuisance to them? Is it from him or from his father that they claim indemnity, for losses sustained from him? Our courts of law can bear testimony. But these poor pariah children, these "moral orphans," who watches over them with tender care through their early years? The streets their nursery, an elder brother or sister already well versed in crime their nurse, sometimes driven almost from their mother's breast to seek their own living, knowing a father often only by hearing his curses, or bearing his drunken brutality, defying in the earliest years a parental authority which has been used but to abuse them, they have at twelve, perchance even at eight or nine years of age, the determined will, the violent passions, even the knowledge, in crime, of a man; why should not the law treat them as such? *And so it does!*

Why should it not? Because there is another law besides the law of man,—the law of nature, of Christ, of God; a much higher one, infinitely higher, to which the human law must bow, however much with its whips and scourges, its bolts and bars, it may defy the law divine. True Christian men will never obey any human authority, if by doing so they disobey their Master. Why do we not find those who are defrauded by a high-born child, delivering him up to the magistrates? Why do we not hear of those whose gardens are assailed by constant attacks from the sons of gentlemen in a neighbouring school, pursuing the thieves and handing them over to the next justice of the peace? Why do we not read of pious parents carrying to a court of law their children who have practised on themselves or their neighbours serious thefts, and as a religious duty delivering them up to be dealt with as the law directs? The answer is self-evident. Because society is fully assured that such a course pursued towards a child would brand him for life, would not reform him, but would almost certainly ruin his character; it is equally certain that it is to parental authority that the child ought to be consigned. Why, on the other hand, do we hear of a young child being seized by an officer, carried before the magistrates, introduced to the prison, for the theft of a few halfpence;—boys sent for three months to Bridewell for stealing three apples;—parents having their children sent to gaol for robbing themselves? Because society, though equally assured that such treatment will but harden, and probably corrupt the child, is actuated towards him only by a desire of self-protection, and too often also a spirit of revenge;—because there is no parental authority to which the child *can* be consigned.

What then is to be done? The answer is here also most plain. Christian men and Christian women must become the fathers and mothers of these "moral orphans." They must restore them to the true condition of childhood, give them a home, open their souls to good and holy influences, if need be correct them, but with a loving severity, and so under God's blessing restore them to society, prepared to fill well their station in it, and to pass honourably through this life, always striving to attain to a better.

But how can these Sisters of Charity, those Brothers of Mercy, obtain the trust which they so much covet, which their hearts long for; if they are poor in this world's goods how shall they feed the large family whom they have adopted in loving obedience to the Saviour's command? The parents have a legal hold on the children, and will not give it up, for they cannot discern their children's true good; the law has laid its grasp on them, and so long as they remain in its custody it may not yield them up, for they are the " children of the State;" or the child, already independent, knows how to claim the privileges of manhood, and "the liberty of the subject" must not be interfered with, even to save him from destruction. The legislature only can take from the parent the authority which he has abused, still binding him to the duty which nature has imposed, the maintenance of his child; the legislature only can delegate to authorized agents the care of the " State children," as a parent intrusts his offspring to an instructor in whom he confides; the legislature only can authorize magistrates to take from the vicious boy the liberty which makes him a bane to society, and consign him, for such length of time as may be needful, to persons who can and will watch over him with parental anxiety; providing at the same time for his maintenance from public funds, and when practicable from the resources of his lawful guardians.

Here, it is conceived, lies the scope of the whole question, and if these principles are understood and conceded, none can say, on the one hand, that reliance is placed in government to do that which individual devotedness alone can truly accomplish; or, on the other, that it is proposed for private persons to do what can be achieved only by government.

It will be presumed that the reader is acquainted with the former work by the same author, "Reformatory Schools for the Children of the Perishing and Dangerous Classes," and it will therefore be unnecessary to do more than incidentally allude to the facts there stated; it may, however, be useful here to make a brief recapitulation of the general subject of that book.

Having given some faint idea of the actual amount of juvenile crime in our country, as estimated by official criminal returns, and of the absolute ignorance of these criminal children, irrespective of the actual amount of education they had received, a picture was presented of the "children as they are;" and some of the principles were considered which should guide in all attempts to reform them. These attempts were then reviewed. The first great movement to raise from spiritual and physical degradation the little heathens of our own land, was that of Sunday Schools, which in its origin was directed to the very class which we are now considering; and then, as now, religion was the moving spring, and Christian influence brought to bear on the outcasts, effected wonderful transformations. But religious teaching *alone* proved insufficient for the elevation of the " perishing and dangerous classes," and the institution of Sunday Schools, where religious instruction was communicated by voluntary teachers, gradually became applicable only to a higher class of children, those of the labouring poor, to whose weekly secular education this was supplementary. This work of Sunday-school teaching, has always been a *purely voluntary one*, neither soliciting nor receiving any aid from public educational funds; it has always been felt that government aid and inspection would be fatal to what must be a heartless labour, if not a labour of love and Christian zeal. The Ragged School movement originated in the same way and with the same objects, and its voluntary teachers still gladly bring their offering of time and unwearied effort in the hope of imparting to these destitute ones the religious treasures they possess; they too jealously shrink from government aid, accompanied as it must be with inspection. But a Sunday evening's lesson is utterly inadequate to change the whole nature of a child, and to counteract six long days of evil instruction. Other evenings were added, but these also were insufficient; the little light which these attempts threw on the condition of these children, only revealed the appalling darkness of their condition, without dispelling it. It was perceived that there must be daily teaching, but it was not understood that an ill-paid and illtrained teacher was not calculated to raise the condition of children requiring peculiar knowledge, peculiar skill, peculiar zeal and patience to produce any real and abiding effect upon them. It is not generally understood yet; and therefore we so often find the supporters of these schools satisfied, if they have been able to obtain a teacher at a very low salary, who will undertake to manage some 200 children, and to make them go through a certain examination at an appointed time. But if a Free Day School is to be adapted to the peculiar wants of this class, it must, as was shown by example, be a very expensive one, and yet it is unable to meet the government requirements for educational grants, which are adapted to a higher class of schools. If then education is to be brought within the reach of a class below that attending the National and British Schools, it must be by enlisting the zeal both of paid teachers and of voluntary workers, aiding and directing it by government grants proportioned to the necessary expenditure of the school; the inspection being directed solely, as in the Dissenting schools at present, to the general management and the secular education, the religious instruction being left entirely to the managers and teachers.

But, were such schools so extensively established as to meet the wants of all below the existing pay schools who would attend them, there is a large class, and that most requiring aid, who neither can nor will attend them. They cannot, by reason of extreme poverty, which obliges even the young children, to seek in some way how to satisfy the cravings of nature;— they will not, because they prefer liberty, and their parents prefer their unlawful gains. To feed and clothe them, as well as teach them, will not effect the end of obtaining from these children a regular attendance, and will besides encourage culpable neglect in the parents, thereby encouraging pauperism and vice. Liberty must be resigned if charity is accepted; and the law must here interfere, and oblige such parents as neglect to send their children to any school, (thus allowing them to be a nuisance to society,) to send them to an Industrial School, where a certain amount of work shall be rewarded with the needful supply of food. This principle has been fully developed and amply tested at Aberdeen;—it needs but for the government to give magistrates authority to enforce such attendance, and to the parishes to pay in such cases to the School rather than to the parent any allowances to which the child has a claim. The educational grants having been adapted to the Free Day School, will supply part of the instructional expenses, and the zeal of voluntary workers will do the rest, as has been sufficiently proved in many large towns. But the next class, the delinquent children, are become the "children of the State," and for them she therefore provides a school, the Gaol. An inquiry was made into the adaptation of this school to erring children;—it was found to be most costly, most inefficacious for any end but to prepare the child for a life of crime. But how can benevolent effort reach these children? *It cannot, as the law now stands.* Yet, in other countries, the State intrusts delinquent children to those who with Christian devotion will take on themselves the parental charge of them. Such establishments were examined, founded by the zeal of ardent lovers of the lost and perishing; in these the spirit of a Christian family infused into the children produced effects which arise from no prison discipline or mercenary teachers. Mettrai is a powerful contrast to Parkhurst, which is a prison rather than a school. In England the experiment has also been tried whether children, even after numerous convictions, may not be made good and useful citizens; it has been proved that they can be so; in these establishments also a religious spirit and individual influence, have been the moving springs of the institutions;—they have only wanted legal power of detention, and funds;—magistrates and judges have wanted power to commit children to them under due security;—authority has also been required to oblige parents, while deprived through their criminal neglect of the care of their children, still to contribute to their maintenance.

It is hoped that these points were all fully proved;

but when preparing to carry them into practical operation in our own country, many difficulties arise, which a fuller knowledge of the class for whom we desire legislation, might remove;—many questions occur as to what kind of discipline is the most truly reformatory;—many objections are made by those who, viewing the subject in different aspects, see it in a different light;—above all, scepticism exists as to the possibility of really reforming children who have once entered the lists of vice. A very wide field of further inquiry is thus opened, part of which we shall now attempt to explore.

CHAPTER I.

CHARACTERISTICS AND CLASSES.

JUVENILE DELINQUENTS! The very term is an anomaly, and should startle us as something monstrous and fearful; something which should lead us to think, "How can this be? And if it be so, what can each one of us do to remove so dreadful an evil?" For we are speaking of children,—of young beings but recently come from the hands of their Maker, of whom the Saviour has said, that " of such is the Kingdom of Heaven," and that unless we be converted and become as such, we can in no wise enter therein;—Children of whom he declared, " Whosoever shall receive one of such in my name receiveth me," and the care of whom as his "lambs" he committed with twice repeated injunctions to that apostle whom he appointed to be the rock on which his church should be built. Yet these are called, perhaps are, delinquents; not only *perishing* from lack of knowledge, from lack of parental care, of all that should surround childhood, but they are positively become *dangerous;* dangerous to society, which rises in formidable array to defend itself against them, and in a condition most dangerous to the world around, to succeeding generations, to their own souls! And of what worth is every immortal soul! Such a condition is one of grievous moral disease; it needs a moral hospital, and requires a treatment guided by the highest wisdom of those who have learnt the art of healing from the Physician of souls.

A strong analogy may be traced between spiritual and physical disease, and no dissimilar mode of treatment should be applied to both. Now when a skilful and an experienced physician undertakes the treatment of a new and complicated case, he not only notes carefully all the symptoms of the disease, comparing them with those usually attendant on it, but he investigates into the ordinary habits and manners of his patients, and the tendencies both of mind and body which appear natural to him; he ascertains how far his present complaints arise from his original constitution, or are occasioned by accident, and thus forms some opinion respecting the deep-seated causes of the malady, which must be removed before any but a temporary cure can be anticipated. Nay, more; our philosophic practitioner inquires into the history of the parents and even remote relatives, to ascertain whether the disease is one transmitted from generation to generation as an ill-omened heirloom, and showing some unfortunate conformation which is likely to be a never-ending source of evil until the whole race is exterminated, or whether these tendencies have developed themselves in disease only in peculiar cases, and under injudicious treatment, but are susceptible of being turned to good account, and rendered compatible with a healthy state of the system under wise management. All this having been ascertained, he will consider what will be the best treatment of the case. Such a course we shall now pursue in reference to juvenile delinquents. They are a sadly diseased set of patients, whom some, in desperation, would gladly exterminate, if they could. Fortunately they cannot; indeed, it would be of little use to themselves or to others if they were able, for abundance of other poisonous weeds would be continually springing up with a rank growth, in a soil filled with all sorts of impurities;—they cannot sweep those poor diseased children away—we must try to cure them, and to eradicate the seeds of the complaint.

Let us note the symptoms of these youthful patients, and then consider what should be their treatment.

When juvenile offenders are spoken of, young thieves are usually intended; for an examination of the annals of crime will show that varied as are the offences of adults, those for which children are arraigned in a criminal court are almost invariably thefts more or less trivial; as thieving is that particular kind of delinquency which is most inconvenient and annoying to society at large, so one branded as a thief is usually regarded with as much repugnance and fear as if he were known to have a contagious disease. There are many other forms of juvenile delinquency, not less dangerous to the individual, or ultimately injurious to society; but these do not come under the cognizance of the law, which so scrupulously abstains from interfering with the liberty of the subject; we cannot therefore at present speak of these.

We will take a few examples of these different cases.

V. is a steady energetic boy; no one who sees him working vigorously and cheerfully in the shoemaker's class of an Industrial School, with an open intelligent look, would place him in the class of young thieves; still less would any one have felt any fear of him who saw him a little time since actively and usefully engaged in a respectable bookseller's shop. There was no dishonesty found in him there; he was discharged from a change of arrangements being made in the business; he did not succeed in getting another place, was thrown among idle and bad associates in the streets, was detected in thieving, and sent to gaol for some months for this, his first offence,—has now a prison brand upon him, and cannot get work.

The visitor to a Ragged School, who expects to find many thieves among the scholars, would probably not select that fine intelligent monitor who is skilfully managing a young class. P. came out of Bridewell that very morning, and went straight to his teacher to ask counsel and help. He said that he had been driven to stealing by absolute want of food. He had been deserted by his mother, and the relatives who gave him a lodging could not supply his needs. His teacher was aware that he had been in prison two or three times before from a similar cause, but yet, from a knowledge of his character, felt a confidence that he might be trusted, and *was not mistaken*.

Nor would that green-grocer's errand-boy, G., be suspected to be of the pariah caste. He is earning in the neighbourhood of London 12*s*. per week, and the customers congratulate themselves on having so active, regular, and well-conducted a lad to serve them. One morning he offered the cook in a family he attended to change a half-sovereign for her, and she gave him one which she had just received from her mistress, and which both had happened to remark as peculiarly new and bright. In the evening he brought back one evidently a counterfeit, much rubbed, and showing the base metal. He asserted that this was the one he had received in the morning, that his mistress on trying it had discovered it to be bad, and that he should himself be at the loss of it unless it were changed for him. Inquiry was made of his mistress, when it was discovered that the whole was a tissue of falsehood, and no doubt remained, after the investigations that were made, but that he was an accomplice of coiners.

None would imagine that that well-dressed, respectable youth belonged to the class we are considering. Nor did the benevolent founder of the "Place of Repentance" for thieves, when this young man came as a visitor, and spent some hours with him in friendly conversation, expect that, in conclusion, he would request admission for himself! He was told that the establishment was not for such as he. But the next morning he appeared before the master in old and worn attire, confessed by what means he had hitherto lived, and expressed his determination henceforth to maintain himself only by what he earned by the sweat of his brow.

Juvenile thieves must not, then, all be classed together, any more than all those patients who are brought within the walls of an Infirmary; nor would even an experienced eye be always able to detect those who are now to be numbered among them; many fine open-looking boys who really belong to the felon class, as the law now stands, would pass without suspicion, while many wretched half-starved creatures, who would naturally be placed in it by most, may prove to have committed no greater offence than seeking, in ways which to their view were quite innocent, to obtain their daily bread by mendicancy.

Even in prison we may find many who would appear most undeservedly its inmates. That youth X., gentle, earnest, serious, working diligently in his solitary cell, and thankfully availing himself of the means of instruction offered him, had been uninstructed and untrained until he committed the offence for which he was sent to Parkhurst; then he was very miserable, and at last, in a sort of desperation, endeavoured to escape. For the *crime* of housebreaking committed in the attempt, he was again condemned to transportation. Now his spiritual nature has been awakened; he feels, as he says, that he has begun a new and better life; he submissively, and even happily, bears his punishment, and if he were at large, there is every prospect that he might become an honest and respectable man.

Some, however, do at once reveal themselves in their true character. The experienced eye readily detects the elder S. as an old offender, though still young, by his determined independent manner, his dress so different from that of a hard-working lad, and a certain indescribable air which at once points him out as the associate of rogues. His little brother at eight, has the resolute gait of a man, and the rapid movements of his fingers reveal him as an experienced thief; the older one has escaped detection, while his associates have been imprisoned or even transported; the younger has been more than once in Bridewell, but that does not inspire him with such terror as school; though kindly treated there, and offered a warm fire and even dinner, he prefers shivering in the streets to resigning his liberty.

That clever, self-indulgent-looking lad, R., has never worked in his life; he left an easy place which was provided for him in a few hours; he has found a readier means of supporting himself; though his only parent regrets his way of life, she has no power to curb him; he has entered on a way of life which he will probably continue if not checked.

There can be no doubt respecting that wretched lad, A.; crime is written on his countenance in characters that cannot be mistaken, and yet his miserable, ragged, barefooted aspect shows that he is not reaping, like S., the reward of his iniquity, and leads one to ask where is that poor boy's home. *He has no home,* he has recently sought in vain admission to the poor-house; its guardians concern themselves not for him more than to drive him from them unrelieved, undirected where to go; and society waits to give him an abode until he has qualified himself by overt crimes to become one of the " children of the State;" then he will be again provided with one with which he is already familiar—the Gaol.

These two lads may tell their own short but heart-stirring tale, as recorded in the journal of a London Ragged School Teacher:—" Two miles from this place all round," says D., " I don't think I could stand on any spot, and be out of sight of places I have robbed. If the houses could speak, one or two or more would say, you have robbed us." " I have broken into many houses," says another youth of sixteen, " and gone all over them at dead of night, and have taken things off the bed where they have been asleep." "Suppose they had awoke," said the master. "It would have been best for them to have kept quiet; they would not have been the first we have settled with the neddy (life preserver)."

All of these are classed by the law among juvenile delinquents, and all of them have, indeed, transgressed the law of God and of man, yet we do not perceive in most of them at a cursory glance, or even on close communication with them, anything which need separate them from others as afflicted with a contagious disease, still less do we discover any symptoms which should make us pronounce them incurable. There are, however, striking differences in them which may suggest a division of the whole into the following classes:

The *first class* consists of daring, hardened young offenders, who are already outlaws from society, caring for no law divine or human, perhaps knowing none; they live notoriously by plunder; their hand is against every man, and every man's hand is against them. That such exist in our civilized land is a disgrace to it, and betokens a strange apathy to evil, or a strange want of power to grapple with it. But they do exist. Such are the two lads from the London Ragged School who, in youth, have the unblushing audacity of villains of maturer years. One of them has even been dismissed from the school at the request of the scholars themselves, wild and bad as most of them probably were. Such boys will generally be deemed incurable, from whom nothing is to be expected in after life, but to be a plague to society as long as they are at large. We need hardly ask what has been their previous history; it is certain that they have led an undisciplined childhood, over which no moral or religious influence has been shed, and which has been untrained to any useful, industrious habits. What are the means by which even such as these have been subdued?—these very lads themselves will appear hereafter.

The *second class* is, if possible, more dangerous to society than the first, because more systematic in their life of fraud, and often less distinguishable by their external appearance and manner. These are youths who are regularly trained by their parents or others in courses of professed dishonesty, some as pickpockets, others as coiners, or in such varied modes of depriving their neighbour of his property as their peculiar circumstances may suggest. The condition and character of the professed pickpockets will receive full consideration hereafter; such was probably the well-dressed youth who, happily, was led to a place of repentance, for they not unfrequently have the semblance of young gentlemen. The greengrocer's lad, G., is an example of a young coiner; here a boy of apparently good dispositions and talents which might enable him to gain an honest livelihood, is already an artful adept in crime, and likely to become even more injurious to society than the preceding class, because practising dishonesty in a way which can be less guarded against. Sergeant Adams, in his charge to the grand jury of the county of Middlesex in 1849, gives the early history of one of this numerous class of young offenders, referred to, also, in his evidence before the Lords' Committee, in 1847. [*Vide* "Reformatory Schools," p. 255.] In November, 1837, a boy of twelve years of age was sentenced to twelve months' imprisonment with hard labour in the house of correction, in Cold Bath Fields; and the Sergeant obtained the following particulars of his past history. "He is the son of a coiner, and a boy of quick and lively parts, rather diminutive in his person, but of high courage, and apparently good temper. *Until he was ten years old, he was employed to watch when his father was at work, and he was then promoted to the higher office of uttering the base money his father had coined.* He and his father used at night to go out together. The father would give him a base shilling, and remain at a short distance, whilst the boy went into some small shop, and bought a pennyworth of tobacco, onions or the like. The father would then receive the change from the boy, give him another shilling, and continue the traffic seven or eight times in a night. To my question, 'What used your father to give you for doing this?' His answer was, ' Plenty of victuals, and a penny a-day if I did well, and a good hiding if I did not.'" We shall not yet inquire what the present treatment of juvenile offenders did for this poor boy,—but we will ask, which was the offender in the sight of God, and according to the dictates of plain, unsophisticated moral sense,—the quick, lively, courageous, good-tempered child of ten, who was obeying " the first commandment with promise,"—or the man who, having the natural and legal control of his son, wilfully, knowingly, and perseveringly employed it to train him to break the laws of God and man? The law as it now stands punishes the obedient child, and lets the disobedient parent go free!

A *third class*, and perhaps a still more numerous one, consists of children who are not hardened and daring as the first, or *trained* to crime as the second, but who, from the culpable neglect of their parents, and an entire want of all religious or moral influence at home, have gradually acquired, while quite young, habits of petty thieving, which are connived at rather than punished by their parents, and which will, *unless effectually stopped*, lead ere long to daring violations of the law. Such is the younger S., a skilful thief at ten, yet possessing various good traits of disposition, united with strength of character, which, if developed, might make him a valuable member of society: such is R., whose unchecked idleness and selfishness have now led him to learn from the vicious company he has frequented adroit methods of stealing. Both of these boys have had a school open to them for many years; they have been repeatedly urged to attend it regularly, but their own will was not strong enough in a right direction to lead them to persevere in submitting to restraint, and they have not attended with sufficient regularity to reap any permanent benefit. Into this class are thrown numbers who would seem to be led into dishonesty only by that love of enterprize and daring so common among boys of all classes; let them be actively employed, with their energies well exercised and directed, and there is no tendency to dishonesty in them, while the very spirit which led them into mischief will be developed for good. V. did not show the least inclination to steal when he was an errand boy in a bookseller's shop, nor does he now that he is engaged in industrial occupation at school, and he is frequently employed by his master on confidential errands. Z. was the plague of the neighbourhood, from his mischievous and thievish propensities, until he got a place of work, when such practices were quite relinquished, and he was even sent to the bank by his master for money, without ever betraying his trust. In the higher classes of society, robberies of this kind committed by boys at school are deemed by many "capital jokes," "harmless pranks," "proofs of spirit;" in the lower ones, they subject a boy to imprisonment, even to transportation, a prison brand being affixed for life to the unfortunate children. Many, too, are enlisted in this class who are the children of the respectable labouring portion of society, but who, from some want of parental care, from early uncontrolled desires, leading to an association with vicious companions, have fallen into a first crime, and most probably become for life the associates of the unprincipled and worthless. What might not each of these have been made had he been rescued in time! But unrescued, unchecked, thousands of them infest all our large towns, a few of whom are, from time to time, arrested by the hand of justice, scarcely to thin the ranks of crime, not at all to deter those that remain.

In these three classes, actual destitution is scarcely even the alleged inciting cause of crime; if these children are poor, it is a poverty caused directly by vice. But our *fourth class* will consist of those who have been actually driven into crime by their utter destitution, by their being thrown on the world without any to care for them, while their claims on support from the National Poor Laws have been either passed by unnoticed, or rejected by the administrators of those laws. The *Ragged School Magazine* furnishes numerous and touching examples of this class, of which there will always be multitudes, who will and *must* lapse from poverty to vice, unless cared for, not only by public charity, which often slumbers, and gladly escapes from its charge, but by the watchful guardianship of Christian love.

Such is the boy A., who is now leading, in the city of Bristol, a wild and certainly not an honest life, after being refused admission to the Union, or even temporary help. In every large city there must be numbers of these uncared-for children, whose honesty we must admire if they abstain from supplying the cravings of nature from the property of others; for, as Dickens well remarks in a recent article in his *Household Words*, "Lambs to be Fed," "they in fact seem to hop about like wild birds, pilfering the crumbs that fall from the table of the country's wealth. It seems difficult to see how they can have any higher relation to the moral view of crime than blackbirds among currant bushes. They certainly have no higher notion of what we call justice, than blackbirds have of nets, scarecrows and guns."

How completely ignorant these poor children are of the needs of their spiritual nature, how incapable they therefore are of a voluntary and wise effort for their own improvement, may be illustrated by the following anecdote:

"A few days ago," says a teacher in a Ragged School, "I met a little sweeper whom I had frequently endeavoured, but in vain, to induce to attend the school. He was assured of my friendly intentions, for he had recognised me 'as the lady who brought us buns when the school was opened in the little room;' and working upon this pleasing recollection, I had often since begged him to attend, enforcing my admonitions by a halfpenny. Promises were always made to comply with my wishes, and as soon forgotten. On the present occasion, as soon as he saw me, he exclaimed, 'I shall go to school this evening.' Suspecting the motive of his promise, and perceiving the uselessness of my former bribery, I determined to take a different course, and the following conversation ensued between myself and the poor little urchin and his brother. 'Well! but what good will it do *me* for *you* to go to school?' 'You likes little boys to go to school.' 'But why do I like them to go; what good does it do me?' 'You likes 'em to learn to read.' 'But why do I like them to learn to read? they do not read for me!' 'No, they reads to the master.' 'But it does not do the master a bit of good; to whom does it do good?' The poor little fellows seemed sadly puzzled, and at last exclaimed, 'God!' 'It cannot do good to God, but He is pleased to see little boys do right. To whom does it do good?' 'To our Saviour!' 'It cannot do him good, though he is pleased to see children good.' The poor lads seemed completely at fault, evidently trying to make out my meaning, but unable. At last a bright idea struck the younger of them, and he exclaimed, 'Moses!' 'No, Moses has nothing to do with it; now do think again.' But he had evidently exhausted his thought. At last, the elder made the great discovery—'To *ourselves!*' 'Yes, we wish to do good to yourselves, and we cannot do you good while you are running wild about the streets. I know two boys who were as wild as you, and as ragged, and we got them to come to school and be steady, and now they are apprenticed to shoemakers and doing well.' 'O! I know who they are, Charley and George.' 'Yes, but you never see them now with the wild ones, and how tidy they look. We want you to be like them.' So we parted; the little fellows seemed to have a new light burst on them, and did not ask me for a halfpenny. They came to school, and though I did not observe them, being otherwise occupied, they did not try to attract my attention. They had, however, the pleasure of a bath, which left a visible effect upon them when I saw them three days afterwards They seemed then to have quite a different feeling towards me from what they had had before. I was not only the lady who gave them buns and halfpennies, but one who had roused a consciousness of a better nature."

An equal degree of ignorance is frequently shown of the nature of crime and its consequences. The Hon. Miss Murray, who for many years devoted much time and attention to the Hackney Wick Institution for girls connected with the Children's Friend Society, records the case of an orphan child

CHARACTERISTICS AND CLASSES. 31

of 11, who was confined in the Milbank Penitentiary for a year, for stealing sovereigns. On inquiry, it appeared that the child did not know the difference between sovereigns and shillings; "I saw," she said, " a great deal of money in a drawer, and I took some sovereigns; a man asked me where I got the money, *and I told him.*" Surely this child acted "sans discernement."

Our *fifth class* live, both parents and children, in a condition of squalid poverty, and yet with a profession of gaining an honest livelihood, for they are hawkers, merchants of small wares, and indignantly repel any who should interfere with them, young as they are, in the exercise of their lawful calling. And what indeed is there wrong in selling matches, sticks, freestone, and the like?

Yet this is the testimony on the subject of one who has been an experienced thief. The following description, given by a convict in Preston Gaol, to the Rev. J. Clay, (*vide* Report for 1851, p. 43,) will be recognised as most true, not only of one town, but of most populous cities.

" There are hundreds of poor children in Liverpool and other large towns training up as thieves. But Liverpool I select, having had numerous opportunities of observing them, which I have done for days together. I will select a few streets in the same locality, namely, Marybone, and Little Ireland, as it is called. They are inhabited principally by the lower class of Irish; and the children are sent out in the morning with watercress, chalk-stones, cocoa-nut husks (for scrubbers), &c., &c., and at night with firewood. The whole of these children are very dirty, ragged, and without covering for the head or feet. *They must bring home a certain sum or value, whether obtained by selling, begging, or stealing, is immaterial.* Nothing comes amiss to them; bits of iron, copper, brass, anything from the docks, warehouses, door-mats, if left exposed, and hundreds of miscellaneous articles always to be found in a sea port. These boys, some of them only six or seven years of age, have their own markets in the streets above mentioned, where, in some of the cellars, they dispose of their 'swag,' and away out again to look for more. *I firmly believe that these boys are never washed, except when they are sent to gaol.*"

These children infest large towns; in the more agricultural districts of the south of England, there is a *sixth class* who seem to be born to a sort of hereditary calling, that of thieving. "We were born *travellers*," say two brothers under sentence of transportation; "my parents and two sisters are travellers now." This name cloaks almost every sort of vice; the unhappy children who are constantly rising up to perpetuate the class, live from infancy in an atmosphere of the most degrading iniquity; though not so early trained in audacious thefts, and skilful evasion of detection as the town children, they grow up with an equally hardened wickedness of spirit, and become eventually bold housebreakers and robbers. Seven members of the notorious "Frimley gang," convicted of the burglary at Uckfield, and transported for life, were removed to the Preston gaol for probationary discipline:—Mr. Clay ascertained that all of these, with only one exception, "belonged, *almost from infancy*, to one of the most daring and profligate divisions of the dangerous class,—the division known as 'travellers;' who,—both men and women, perambulate every part of the country in parties more or less numerous, and maintain themselves by begging and imposture, or by robbery of every kind,—from trifling, but frequent petty larcenies, to carefully planned and cruelly executed burglaries." It is evident that children thus born and brought up can be rising to maturity only to perpetuate a distinct class in society ready for almost every species of crime;—it requires, with the preceding one, some peculiar and distinct action for its suppression.

It is generally imagined that poverty and destitution are the great causes of juvenile crime. But facts carefully considered will lead to a very different result,—at any rate with respect to that crime which is indicated by conviction and punishment. The condition of the most hardened and vicious juvenile delinquents may be fairly represented by that of the convicts at Parkhurst, for they are boys "of a character so depraved that they would be sentenced to transportation if that prison did not exist."

Now in the Report of Parkhurst for 1844, is a table showing the amount of schooling received by each convict who had been in the establishment. [*Vide* " Ref. Sch.," p. 30.] From this it appears that of the whole number, 957, only thirty had never been at school, and 732 had been attending day schools longer than a year; the average period of schooling received by these was no less than three years and ten months, as many as 163 having had five years' instruction or more. Now as all the schools enumerated in that table were pay schools, except in the case of twenty-seven who had been in workhouse schools, it follows that only a very small proportion of these boys belonged to the class admissible to Ragged Schools, from being unable, through destitution or loss of character to attend the Pay Schools; still less did they belong to the three classes of juvenile thieves, who may allege poverty as an inciting cause to crime. Other, and important inferences, are derivable from the same table, but we confine our attention at present to this alone.

Similar results are arrived at from the records of the Reformatory School at Stretton-on-Dunsmore. [*Vide* "Ref. Sch.," pp. 341, 342.] Boys are received into this institution who have been convicted of crime in the county of Warwick, and whose sentence has, in many instances, been shortened with a view to their admission to it. The Register of that Asylum from Jan. 1, 1847, to May 1, 1852, gives the following striking results :—Of forty-nine boys admitted during that period, three only had no professed employment; one had been in the workhouse; of the rest, five were employed as servants or errand boys, the rest had regular occupations, most of them requiring skill. With respect to education, sixteen only professed to have had none, but only five were able to read and write well, the others being entered as "imperfect." There were only fourteen of the forty-nine who were orphans; and it is remarkable that only one of these had received no education; except in one case, *where both parents had been transported*, all the parents had regular occupations;—most of them were mechanics, one a jeweller, another a grocer and druggist! It cannot be said then that it was destitution which caused the necessity of establishing this Asylum, and supporting it at a great annual cost, to save the country a still heavier expense, and society the infliction of a great amount of crime, as well as to snatch a brand from the burning. The following is a specimen of the entries, being the first six in the list, together with the workhouse-boy.

Age	Education.	Employment.	Crime.	Sentence.	Parentage.	Trade of Parents.
14	None.	None	Stealing shoes.	7 days	None.	..
16	None.	Labourer	Stealing coal.	7 days	Father & Mother	Labourer.
14	Read Imp.	Boating ..	Robbing his master of £5.	1 month ..	Father & Mother	Bridle-maker.
14	None.	Glass-blowing.	*Stealing bottle of gin.*	4 days	Father & Mother	Engine-fitter.
15	Read.	Nail-cutting.	Picking pockets	7 days, 3rd conviction	Father & Mother	Bricklayer.
14	Read, Write.	Casting.	Stealing pigeons	14 days, 2nd conviction	Father & Mother	Bricklayer.
16	Read, Write.	In the Workhouse.	*Stealing loaf of bread.*	9 months (Sentence commuted.)	None.	..

It is remarkable that though the offences of three of these six indicate considerable progress in criminality, they have very short, and merely nominal imprisonments, while the workhouse boy, for taking a single loaf (a strange theft indeed, where it is sup-

posed that abundance of food is provided,) is sentenced to nine months in the House of Correction.

The following extracts from the Inspector's Report of the Liverpool Borough Gaol in 1845, confirm the same truth, that it is not physical destitution, nor even want of education, which is the cause of crime in the most bold and hardened young offenders, but moral destitution, arising from want of early training, and parental neglect. Records of twelve boys were made by the Inspector, who were not selected, but taken accidentally, as they happened to be placed. All exhibit the same general feature, and from them the following are selected as fair specimens.

"A. aged 14. Been here three times. Came from —— with his father, a crucible maker; has no mother; been in the Corporation School for seven months; could read when he came in, but not write. First came to the gaol about twelve months since, for stealing a box of cigars, for which he was sentenced to ten days' solitary confinement. His father ran away from his mother, and is now living with another woman, who was always beating him. Has lived at a lodging-house when away from home; goes out of prison on Monday next; has heard the woman has left his father, and intends to go home. This boy is getting on both in reading and writing. [March, 1846. Re-committed in seven days for three months; discharged, and re-committed in three days. Now in prison under another name.]

"B. aged 14. Been in gaol five times; mother alive; step-father; living at home. Has stopped away three weeks at a time. Went to a lodging-house. Has been six times at the Amphitheatre play-house. Attended parish school, and could read before he came to gaol; he reads well, is learning to write, and knows the commandments. [Re-committed for three

CHARACTERISTICS AND CLASSES. 37

months: removed from school as incorrigible in two months; re-committed Feb. 14 for one month; April 18 for one month. Transported in July, 1846.]

" C. aged 14. Father dead; mother alive; ran away from her and lives anywhere; his mother is good to him, and came after him when he ran away, but he would not go back with her. Has been about thirty times to the Amphitheatre; went to a Catholic school; could read imperfectly when he came to gaol, but not write; he is improving and learning to write; says he intends to go home on being discharged, but I fear he is incorrigible. [Re-committed Feb. 14 for one month; April 18, one month. Transported for seven years July, 1846.]

" H. aged 16. Seven times in gaol. Father alive, a boilermaker; step-mother beat him, and he left home. Has been staying at a lodging-house; men and women are there all together, about six men and six women. Father taught him to read. Has been at the Queen's theatre, but only three times. This boy reads very well, but does not write. [Out seven days, and re-committed for three months; discharged Jan. 26, and re-committed Jan. 30 for three months.]"

It surely needs not to go through this melancholy record; these four cases are but ordinary specimens of what is the usual condition of the young offenders.

The cases we have cited give a general idea of the juvenile thieves of the first three classes mentioned, where entire want of early training and parental control, with exposure to temptations and the influence of bad example are generally the causes of crime; yet the pickpockets as a class, show, even at an early age such peculiar audacity and skill in evading justice, that they require especial notice, for extraordinary vigilance and care should be taken early to arrest their career.

The Rev. John Clay, in his 27th Report of the Preston House of Correction, has given full and most painful particulars of the cases of the Manchester pickpockets referred to in "Reformatory Schools," p. 52, and from them we may derive important information respecting the real condition of young persons of this class, and the effect which the present administration of the law has upon them. The gang respecting which Mr. Clay gives his information, consisted of fifteen persons, of whom two were women; six of the gang were then under his care; seven were lying under sentence of transportation; five were still at large. All of them began their career of crime between the ages of ten and fifteen; five of the gang who were among the most daring and experienced, were members of one family, and had been the means of drawing on many others into the same dishonest calling. Mr. Clay gives in his Report the autobiographies of the six pickpockets then under his care. They all present the same features. Each one at about the age of 14, freed himself from parental control, led a life of plunder and vicious indulgence, and after numerous imprisonments, which were quite ineffective in checking his career, was then lying under sentence of transportation. One of them, then only 28 years of age, had led a life of crime for fourteen years. He had been first "coaxed to it," and became the "slave" of his employers, being forced to yield up to them all his gettings. "I kept them in style," he says, "and thought myself well off if I got a shilling or two for pocket-money. But, getting older, I kept my own share, although it did me no good, for I lost it by tossing with my companions." On two several occasions he got £200 at once, and from a detailed account of all his thefts, Mr. Clay computes that during these fourteen years, he could not have robbed the public of less than £5,800. From this may be deducted something for the time he spent in prison, but this sum does not include the expenses of his various apprehensions and trials; he had been apprehended and discharged from want of evidence, about fourteen or fifteen times; imprisoned about seventeen times; he had been twice tried and acquitted, and only twice tried and convicted, receiving each time a sentence of twelve months' imprisonment. The remainder of his imprisonments were under summary convictions as a reputed thief. It is a remarkable feature of our English law, that those persons whose known guilt is such that they have a legal reputation and designation amounting to a conviction, should be allowed to be at large pursuing their unlawful avocations with *no attempt effectually to stop them.* And if not arrested in their career by some means which will meet the evil at its early commencement, the number of these juvenile pickpockets must inevitably increase with fearful rapidity. This last-mentioned experienced thief states, from his own knowledge, that "there are at this time, at least ten times as many boys 'wiring' (picking pockets) as when I was young." Nor is this to be wondered at; many circumstances connected with the progress of civilization present not only increased temptations, but facility for this kind of theft, "while," adds Mr. Clay, "the rapidity and ease with which they reach by the trains, any place which they think worth 'working;' the facility, the impunity with which they *do* 'work' the railway carriages and stations especially, these are circumstances demanding effective means of counteraction." But besides this, young boys and girls become a prey to experienced pickpockets who teach them their trade at a very high premium, viz., their whole earnings, besides making "slaves" of them, both body and soul. "Kelly," says the same witness, "who has been up to everything for twenty years, trains these boys. He has pointed to a lad, and said to me, 'There's one of my bringing out!'" And this finished master of every branch of his profession, had then reached only the age of thirty! "The men that go about with dog-carts are gamblers, and are up to all kinds of roguery. They have not courage to rob, themselves, but they will often set on *a little lad* who has got anything by thieving, and make him give it all up." How valuable the services of these boys must be to those sinful employers is shown by the fact that when "a boy named O'Brian, alias 'Slaver,' was caught," says Mr. Clay, "in the attempt to pick a lady's pocket in Preston, his accomplice, a man who had trained him, escaped, and reached Manchester in time to secure the professional services of a rather celebrated attorney, who came to Preston to appear for 'Slaver,' and extricate him from his dangerous position. The boy's skill as an *apprentice* pickpocket made it worth his *master's* while to incur the expense (probably £10) of hiring the 'best professional aid;' 'Slaver' was convicted however as a regular vagabond, and sentenced to three months' imprisonment, and for that time his master was deprived of the income obtained through the boy's thievish skill." His career then was only beginning! Such then are the boys of whom perhaps thousands are at large in England; for be it always remembered, that the circumstance of detection by no means proves the lad who is taken to be worse than others, and that he could not have arrived at the skill which entitles him to the designation of pickpocket, without a number of previous and successful attempts of the same kind.

The *fourth class* of delinquents present features similar to the first three, and their moral condition is much the same; they are distinguished from the others only on the following ground. In the classes already spoken of, the delinquency of the child is directly traceable either to the viciousness of the parent, his culpable neglect, or his inadequacy to fulfil the charge assigned him of the guardianship of the child. The parent is in these cases the party from whom society should demand an account of the child. But in this class there is no parent. *Society must fulfil the parental duty, or suffer for the neglect or ill discharge of it.* Two cases were mentioned in " Reformatory Schools," pp. 284, 285, the one of a poor child who perished miserably after a life of suffering, shame and sorrow, because society had passed him by, caring not to bear his burden; the other of a boy now living a vicious life, hardened in sin, because the guardians of the poor, who could not pass him by, since he confronted them face to face, *refused* to give him bread and lodging; if he took it for himself unlawfully because it was not given him lawfully, and he could not earn it, *the gaol was open to him*, that was his concern; what was that to them? Numbers fall into this condition, simply because no one " careth for their souls." "Let a boy," says Sheriff Barclay,* " tell his own story, taken at random from many similar ones to be found in the prison reports. [*Inspector's Eleventh Report, Glasgow*, p. 8.] 'My father and mother died soon after each other, when I was twelve years old. *No one looked after me.* At first I went about carrying gentlemen's luggage, but sometimes I could get no job, and had nothing to eat. *I then began to steal; and ever since have been living chiefly by begging and stealing. I have not been out of prison a fortnight together, for three*

* " Juvenile Delinquency, its Causes and Cure, by a Country Magistrate." Blackwood and Sons, Edinburgh and London.

years. When out I cannot get employment. I have tried every place, but there is no one to speak for me. All the clothes that I have I got from the prison for overwork, but sometimes I am obliged to pawn them. I have two sisters; but one of them has been banished, and the other will do nothing for me. I have also a brother, but he has been banished. *I have led a miserable life, but I cannot do better.* I should be glad to go to sea, or anywhere that I could get a living.'"

Shall these things be in a Christian country, without any devoting themselves heart and soul, to rouse society to the duty and necessity of striking at the root of an evil which leads to such fearful waste of the life and the powers of our fellow-beings? Shall we still turn a deaf ear to the injunction, "they that are strong, *ought* to bear with them that are weak?" And will society still remain blind to the fact, so often forced upon its notice, if it would but see it, that it is the most costly and pernicious thing to the public, to leave a poor boy to lead such a life?

This class have a direct and *acknowledged* claim on society. The two last, the one in towns, the other in the country, have not legally, only morally. Let us close this chapter, by learning from the same "County Magistrate," one who has not only seen the condition of those perishing children with a sorrowing eye, but laboured to remove it, the history of one such, *as he has known it*. It needs no comment.

"Born in a cold garret or damp cellar, alike remarkable for the careful exclusion of light and air, his early days receive scantily of a mother's fostering care. In a few short weeks he is carried out into the streets with some slender filthy covering of rags, exposed to the cold and damp blast of our shifting temperature, that his shrill cry of agony may the better wring the pittance from the passer-by—a cry, it has been more than once established, made the more agonizing by the application of human agency. At night, when the absence of warmth and comfort, so essential to its normal state, compels its cry of complaint, quietness is sometimes secured by administering the same foul draught which is preying on the vitals of both body and mind of the wretched parents. Thus are combined in one unhappy union the most powerful ingredients which can poison the cup of human enjoyment, and engendering the seeds of moral and physical debility in this child of misfortune. So soon as the little urchin can lisp the cry of 'puir wean,' or its tiny limbs carry its stunted body, it is thrown out of its dirty den into the street to beset the doors of the more blessed, or interrupt the passengers on the busy thoroughfares, with importunate appeals for charity, in a tone of whining from which he never afterwards can completely divest himself. If he returns to his cellarage without the expected amount of prey, a sound beating, interspersed with curses, may be his welcome. He never hears of a God except as a name of imprecation. He seldom has heard mention made of heaven, but often of its opposite, as the place to which every outbreak of parental ire summarily consigns him. A Bible he never saw in the house; and, though it were put into his hands, he could not spell its simplest texts. The Sabbath he knows only as a day when the shops are shut, and all business arrested, except that of the whisky shop. The church bells are rung with solemn peal, and he observes a portion of people better dressed than on other days; but in his sphere it is a day noted only as one of greater idleness and sensuality than other days. He never was taught to pray, but, by example, his instruction in curses has been most abundant. He never was taught the commandments of his God, but by precept and practice was indoctrinated in their contrarieties. A Redeemer's love was never discoursed to him, and the solemnity of a judgment-seat was never disclosed. For continual absence from church and school his parents have ever the ready excuse of want of suitable clothing,—an apology which does not prevent regular attendance on the exhibitions of Jack Sheppard, and other such displays of youthful blackguardism. Perchance some kind Samaritan seeks to remove the real or fancied obstacle, by supplying suitable, sometimes superior, apparel, which is found unfit for plying the avocation of begging, but comes opportunely for the supply of a parent's sinful cravings; and speedily the well-intentioned gift adorns the stall of the old-clothesman, and the little boy revels in his hereditary rags. Some zealous Sabbath-school teacher, fearless of filth and fever, plunges into the sink of infamy, and seizing the little immortal as a waif on the social stream, he bears him to his school. A few Sabbath nights he sits listless and restless, but the whole subject of instruction to him is in an unknown tongue: the lessons of an hour are counteracted by the precepts and practice of a week. Attendance becomes irksome and occasional, and all sorts of lying apologies are told for absence, and tasks unlearned. The misappropriation of some book—very probably the volume of life—the gift of the generous teacher, bars return; and he answers no longer to his name, though he may beset the door to disturb others in the enjoyment of that which he has been taught to despise. He falls back to his former haunts and habits, and 'no man careth for his soul.' What can be expected from such a childhood—from such a culture in the spring-day of life? Do men gather figs off thistles? As we sow we reap. There is truth as well as poetry in the saying, 'The boy is father of the man.' To expect that the boy we have described should become an honest and useful member of society is little else than to expect a miracle. The poor boy grows up a delinquent—a moral plague and pest to all around, but assuredly more sinned against than sinning.

"Let us proceed with our dismal biography. The boy discovers no great distinction between begging and stealing. The penny wrung from the hand—not as charity, but as the price of freedom from annoyance—seems to him no more unwillingly given than when secretly filched from the pocket. At the age of eight or nine he makes his first appearance in judicial life at the bar of the police court. He neither understands nor cares for the majesty of the law. The buttons and the batons of the policemen excite much more of his awe and admiration than the magistrate on the bench. He is not yet learned in judicial phraseology and procedure. To the question of Guilty or not? he lisps out, 'I dinna ken;' or the ready lie—his earliest precept—'I didna do it;' or, with the natural disposition to shift blame on others, the reply not unfrequently is—'It was him that did it,' pointing to some tatterdemalion, who on this occasion occupies the place of the witness,—the next time to take that of the prisoner. If the mother were present, might not the little boy in very truth exclaim, 'The woman did give me and I did eat?' The charge is found proved. The magistrate has no alternative. To dismiss him would be to set him loose on society, with an impression of indemnity from punishment, and an encouragement to neglect in parents. He is therefore sent to prison for a brief period—too brief to accomplish the least practical good—but long enough to break the spell of the prison-house, and strip it of its terrors. He has found there the comforts of genial heat, pure air, wholesome food, and cleanly clothing,—to all of which he was a stranger. . . . The brief term of his noviciate has run its course. He returns to society with the additional brand of prison infamy, barring him all chance of employment. He returns to his wonted haunts and habits with a keener appetite for vice. Being now under the immediate surveillance of the police, it is not long before he is again detected in crime, and again arraigned before the magistrate. This ordeal is repeated the due number of times. The required number of minor convictions is completed, and then our youth takes an important step in the ranks of criminal jurisprudence. He takes a degree in the art of stealing, a diploma in crime. He is transferred from the police-court to the jurisdiction of the sheriff, and is now favoured with the benefit of the great palladium of British liberty, trial by jury. The greatest scrupulosity is observed that retributive and penal justice be fairly administered to the diminutive prisoner, who never had justice done to him in its fairest form—*protective and remedial*. For his trial forty-five citizens are called from their various active duties, at great private inconvenience and public loss. Many a juror would pay the value of the stolen article ten times told, rather than sacrifice his time in attendance at the trial. From the greater number, fifteen are drawn by ballot, that the youthful beggar should enjoy the greatest security for impartiality, and the absence of prejudice amongst a class who never knew, and, it is much feared, never cared whether such a being was or was not in existence amongst them. The charge is frequently of the most trivial pecuniary value—a pair of old shoes, a loaf of bread, when under the strong temptation of hunger, or a few pence filched from the fob of the passenger or the till of the whisky shop, from which he has been in the long practice of fetching the poisoned ingredients for his parent's daily fare. The offence is raised into an aggravated form, by the reason of the previous convictions, for offences, it may be, even of less value, and because, in the eyes of the officials of the police, he is considered to be habit and repute a thief, at a period of life when habit of character is yet unformed, and repute can scarcely exist beyond the police themselves. . . . . The accused party is sometimes so juvenile, that not unfrequently he requires to be elevated at the bar, so that the jury may perceive that it is a fragment of humanity, on which they are gravely called on, by solemn but most unmeaning oath, ' the truth to say and no truth to conceal.' The proceedings are conducted with a solemnity and a parade of the formula of justice, the same as if the charge had been one of homicide, and the criminal one grown grey in crime. It is to break a fly on the wheel. Jupiter Tonans hurls his bolt at the moth. *The parents of the child would be the more fitting occupants of the bar, and the child the more suitable tenant of the school.* The ferula of the schoolmaster would be more influential of good than the mace of justice, and the Primer and Shorter Catechism better authorities than even Hume and Alison, whose metaphysical distinctions of crime are quoted with gravity against the boy who could not decipher the title-pages of their ponderous volumes on ' *Principles and*

Practice.' The trial, as might be expected, results in a conviction; and now a lengthened period of imprisonment ensues, which, had it occurred at the first, might indeed have been, with the Divine blessing, attended with beneficial results. Whilst under this more extended discipline of the prison, the conduct of the youth is faultless, and the progress in education encouraging; mental powers, hitherto dormant, are developed under cultivation; dispositions and affections break forth at the voice of kindness, and the tendencies to evil hide themselves at the firm and calm voice of censure. All these moral appliances come too late: the habits are formed and indurated: the bow is only bent, not broken. The monotonous months roll on their wearied course, and the day of liberty approaches, marked often with a degree of restlessness, on the part of the prisoner, ominous that no permanent good has been accomplished. The prison gate is thrown open, and with it the flood-gate of temptation. The youthful spirits are elated at the fresh air of heaven, and the accustomed sights of well-known and frequented scenes. No provision is made for the refuge of the liberated prisoner, or to secure him honest employment. Not unfrequently old companions in guilt reckon the day of release, and watch the prison gate to hail the relieved prisoner, and to welcome him, often by a display of dissipation and riot, where all good resolutions are ridiculed, and mockery made of all serious and solemn impressions. At this point our modern system of prison discipline and criminal reformation halts, and leaves unfinished the begun good. The wonder is that any are able to escape the entanglements that beset them on release, and not that so many return to criminal pursuits. In a state of society where honest men, with characters untainted, can scarcely find bread by labour, it is not to be expected that those whose characters are bankrupt can find employment. It may be he has been taught a useful trade in prison, and showed superior skill in its prosecution; but out of prison, no opportunity is afforded him of applying that industry in an honest way. If he asks charity, he is told to go and work. If he asks work, he is told there is none for such as he. He begins to think that society and he have a quarrel. He finds himself shunned as a moral leper. He stalks about in idleness, shunning the daylight,—owl-like, he courts the night. He soon affords another illustration of the truth of the lines in the infant hymn, 'that Satan finds some mischief still for idle hands to do.' A spirit of recklessness, discontent, and revenge takes possession of his heart. It is this class in large towns, who are ready, on any opportune occasion, to make an outbreak on the peace of society, so that they may obtain bread or booty in the confusion. They can sink no lower, and entertain some hope of an undescribed and indefinite advantage in change.

"The criminal, the outline of whose mournful history we thus have attempted to sketch, now commits a more aggravated offence. Formerly it was an offence committed individually, and marked for cunning rather than audacity; now it is done in concert with others of equal age, and advance in crime, and frequently with some of the other sex,—the best helps of man in a virtuous course—the heaviest and surest drag in the downward course of profligacy. The offence, too, is no longer the simple act of theft, but the bolder one of housebreaking, or street robbery. A trial now follows at the justiciary; and the lad of sixteen, having already run the curriculum of the criminal courts, receives the sentence of transportation from a land which has little of attraction for him, and removal from which is the first happy event of his sad career."

"This is no fanciful sketch," adds Sheriff Barclay, "but what every one conversant with the administration of criminal justice cannot fail to recognise as true and of common occurrence."

CHAPTER II.

A SINGLE CAPTIVE.

We have hitherto been considering juvenile delinquents as forming a large class;—although this has been subdivided for the sake of convenience, we have still regarded them as constituting masses of individuals, though typified by single instances, and we have thus derived some general idea of the features which mark the class in its varied aspects. Yet we cannot reform whole classes as such; we may indeed adopt such general plans as, wisely formed and executed, may produce a very perceptible effect on the whole, by removing causes of evil, and applying remedial measures. The work of reformation is an individual work; for every one must bear his own moral burden, and by his own works shall each one stand or fall. The soul of each one must be acted on singly, and for its own sake. We shall, therefore, in this chapter endeavour to gain an insight into the actual condition of individuals of the class, and shall take various "single captives," who, from the solitude of their cells, shall tell their own mournful tales.

A SINGLE CAPTIVE. 51

The first is one of the gang of transported pickpockets in Preston Gaol; he was not one of the most daring, and there does not appear to be any culpable neglect on the part of his parents; his is a case which is probably a very common one. William Thompson says,

"At the age of 14, I was sent to the factory. At length I went strolling about the railway, instead of looking for work, watching the trains come in, very often getting three or four jobs in a day, receiving from three pence to six pence for each parcel. I very soon spent it, then returned home, and told my mother I had been looking for work all day. I went on in this way for a time, notwithstanding all that was said to me; work I would not, though I had the offer of several places. If my mother said any thing to me I would run away from home, and not show my face for a week. Then I had lodgings to pay, and clothing and food to find, how I was to do it I did not know, my mind was not given to work. I met a companion of mine, he showed me some money, I asked him where he got it? He said he had picked a lady's pocket in St. Anne's Square, *I thought it very clever of him*, so we went and got something to eat, paid our lodgings, and went to bed, and I got into bad company from that time. Thus we went on for a long time, one thing led to another, at length *the police knew me quite well from seeing me always among bad characters*. At last, I and another were apprehended in St. Anne's Square, on suspicion of pocket-picking, and *sent to Salford prison for a month*."

Is it not evident that a boy in the condition here described by himself, is not likely to be reformed by a month's confinement? Whether it would not have been a blessing to himself and to society, had he then been withdrawn from his career of vice, the subsequent history will show.

"I was again taken up, and sentenced to two months' in Salford; when my time was up, and I was restored to liberty again, I soon forgot all my good resolutions I had formed during my imprisonment. I was soon taken again for the same offence, and got two months; when the time expired, my mother came to meet me at the gate, and tried to get me to go to work, *but I would not go.* I again took to my former wicked life, *and went on worse than before.* I went to Stockport fair, where I got £4; then I took all the fairs and races within ten miles round Manchester, getting £3 or £4 at every place, sometimes more, till I came to Rochdale, then I was sent to Salford for fourteen days. I was not long out, when I was taken in Market Street, and sent back for three months. I was taken again, and got one month; when I came out I led just the same life for about six months, when I was taken again in Shud Hill, and sent back for three months more. When I came out, the fever was very bad in Manchester, and I was confined to my bed; I was soon removed to the fever ward, and the fourth week I was sent home in a very weak state. A many of my companions had gone off at this time with the fever. They were not missed, *plenty rising up as fast as they died.* I was not long at my old game before I was taken up and sentenced to one month's imprisonment; when I came out I went to Leeds fair, and stayed a week with some friends; I then went to Ripon hirings, and got £25; I then came to Manchester, and soon spent it all." Mr. Clay computes that at the age of 20, when this narrative was written, this young man had mulcted the public during five years of as much as £1800!

What a fruitless conflict has the law, with all its ponderous machinery, its active and vigilant agents, its denouncing bench of magistrates, here waged against a boy! He defies it all, and by his acts challenges it to do its worst,—it cannot change *his will*, which, with the elasticity of youth, rises more strong and resolute after each encounter, which reveals to him its powers. At first he was only idle and disobedient; then led away by a cleverness which promised to relieve him from the fruits of that disobedience; then he is taught, by a month's confinement only, that the once dreaded gaol is not so much to be feared; he was "soon taken up again," and during a two months' seclusion he appears to have formed some "good resolutions," which passed away like the morning dew, and he soon had the same punishment again. He does not now appear to have even a temporary remorse, for his mother met him at the gate, entreating him to go to work; but even in those first moments of new liberty he would not yield to parental love, and "went on worse than before." He plunges into a bolder career, and undertakes regular plundering expeditions, alternating his time between the gaol and the emjoyment of unlawful booty. Heaven then sends him a warning in a dangerous malady, but his heart is too hardened to listen to the voices of his numerous companions, who, swept off by the same fever, thus spoke to him from the grave. He continued the same fearful "game" unchecked! And this is the life of a youth who has not reached the term fixed by the law for the commencement of manhood! What is his maturer life to be, when its commencement has been so ripened in crime? This young man is one of thousands! Shall Christians not try if they have not a force more persuasive, more powerful to subdue them than the law?

We pass now to one who appears to have had no early restraining parental influence, and who still earlier plunged boldly into crime, leading on, by his example and encouragement, the other members of his family, and then one after another of his companions. The following is the narrative of Richard Clarke, at the age of about 18, sentenced to transportation:

"I was born in Stockport. I went to a day school, but did not learn to read. When I was 12, I went as a 'teir' lad to a print-works. I stopped there about twelve months, and then went to a worsted factory. I remained there six months, at 3*s.* 6*d.* a week. I then went to a cotton factory, at 5*s.* 6*d.* a week; I worked there about six months. *I began to thieve when I was* 10. I began at Salford fair. I saw a lad that I knew pick another's pocket. Half-an-hour afterwards, I felt a lad's pocket, and thought he had money, but when I got it, it was only a spectacle-glass. I then tried two or three more lads' pockets, and got some half-pence. I carried on this way for six months. Then I began picking women's pockets, but I could not do it well; they found me out, and would hit me; then I would run away and laugh. When I was about 14, my brother John, aged 16, myself, O'Gar, and another boy, ran away from home. The largest sum I had got at this time from one pocket was £23. I had given over picking poor peoples' pockets,—ladies, gentlemen, and farmers. We went to Bolton and Blackburn. I was a week away. I got altogether about 18*s.*; none of the others got anything; *they dared not try, and I kept them.* Then we returned to Manchester. I, my brother, and O'Gar stayed together; I went to Stockport fair; there I picked two or three pockets. I was trying a person's pocket, and got taken up with O'Gar. We each got fourteen days in Knutsford. When I came out my mother met me; I went home, and was good for two or three weeks, but did not go to work, *and have never been at work since.* Then I began going about in Manchester, sometimes alone, sometimes with *companions, and lived by picking pockets.*"

Such was the effect of his first imprisonment! He had now taken out his degree in crime, and thus continues:

"After I came from Knutsford I got among better-dressed thieves, and would often get as much as £8 or £9. One week with another I got about £3 10s. This went on for twelve months. . . I went to all the fairs I could hear of, into Yorkshire, Lincoln, &c. I was about six weeks away, and sent money home to my mother in post-office orders, about £1 a week, and the other boys did the same to their mothers. In that six weeks I got to my own share between £35 and £40. I returned to Manchester and stayed six weeks, continuing the same course of life. My regular practice, during this six weeks, was to go down Market Street and St. Ann's Square, and I got *about* 30s. *a day for my own share*. When Saturday was wet, and we could get nothing, *I used to go to church on Sunday, and pick pockets in the church as they were coming out*. I was then apprehended, and got three months for 'attempting.' On my liberation, I carried on the same way. *I did not care about imprisonment* in the New Bailey, for one of the officers, who is now left, used to bring me in tobacco, pies, and rum. . . I remained in and about Manchester for six months, growing *bolder and more skilful in thieving*. My associates used to come to our house, and give my mother money. *My gains were about £9 or £10 a week; all went in keeping my mother and in the public-house*. At this time I was dressed like a gentleman's son, with a cap and a tassel, and a round jacket, and a white turned-down collar. At this time I was about 15. I left Manchester for Wakefield and Leeds for a week, and got about the usual rate. I never run a chance of throwing myself away, *i.e.*, taking more than I wanted, and going unnecessary risks. When I got back to Manchester I went to Staleybridge wake, and got a few pounds; was taken up, and got twenty-one days at the New Bailey. I could have got away from the police after I got my sentence, but *I thought I would rather go into the Bailey, as several of my companions were there; the officers still got me tobacco and snuff.*"

Would this youth, dressed as a gentleman's son, who spent his £8 or £9 on his own indulgence, have thought it a reward for iniquity, a "premium for crime," had he, instead of a few weeks or months in the New Bailey, or elsewhere, been sentenced to some years in a Reformatory School, where his fine clothes would have been changed for fustian, his luxurious living for plain coarse food, and his life of idleness and nefarious skill for one of hard but honest toil? Yet he seems to have a misgiving that the path of life he was pursuing was not one of unmixed "pleasantness." He continues:

"At this time my little brother Edward, turned out—*I used to beat him for following me, and did all I could to prevent him getting into my own bad ways.*" This little brother, however, followed the example rather than the precepts given him, nor was he deterred by the frequent imprisonments nor the final sentence of transportation passed on his brother and sister, for when he came to see them in prison previously to their departure, Richard states to Mr. Clay, "My little brother told me this morning that last Saturday night he got £15 in sovereigns, at the Railway Station, and that yesterday he got £5 in Manchester."

After two more imprisonments, however, Richard says,—

"I became more careful about my money; I got a good lot of clothes, so that when I was taken up I could pawn them to pay a counsellor. I was out about six months. I was more cautious in Manchester, and travelled round Yorkshire at the fairs and markets. I came home again to Manchester, and again got three months' summary. After my liberation, I was only out eight days, and got three months more. After my discharge from that, I was only out four days, and got one month. When I got out this time, I swore I never would go into that prison again; the turnkey who had brought me things had left. I never have been in since. I determined I would practise no more in Manchester, for I feared transportation, and began to *travel*."

It surely is unnecessary for our present object to follow this hardened young pickpocket through more of these details of his plunderings. By "visiting" a variety of towns he of course increases his experience of prisons. "In Gloucester prison," he says, "you may play at cards and dominoes, and run and jump, and carry on any kind of game." Again, "I got my three months in North Leech prison. It is a 'silent prison,' but you have every opportunity to talk." He found Wombwell's wild beast show afford an excellent opportunity for picking pockets. "Some of the keepers," he says, "used to help us; when any person came in that seemed to have money, I told the keeper, and he would then go round and show the animals, and when the people were crowding together, I could pick their pockets. When I got this £12 from a woman, I gave the keeper £1 as near as I can recollect; I have gone into Wombwell's about sixty times, and been assisted by the keeper every time." One of his associates "lived with a woman," "Then," he says, "because he had a woman I must have a woman, and I found one that I had known before, aged about 17; we then went again to Worcester for a week, and got about £7 among us; we were not looking much for money then, *for we had enough*." He was at length finally arrested at Preston after this long career, when only 18, and sentenced to transportation; when looking back on the course of his life in his solitary cell, this is the result of his reflections,— " I have often thought, since I came here, that if any one could see what they must go through, when they begin a course of life like mine, they would never begin; I judge not only by myself, but what my sister and many others have said. I have a little sister about 10 years old, and God knows what will become of her! She can do all the work of the house, and is very clean." If this young man had been stopped in his course at its very commencement, and detained until he showed himself able to lead a life of honest industry, how many might have still trodden the right path, whom his example and co-operation were the direct means of leading astray. His elder brother, John, who, says Richard, began thieving after I did;—the unfortunate woman with whom he lives, and on whose skill, from his own timid disposition, he depends for a maintenance;— the sister, Ellen, of whom more will be said hereafter;—at least two who were transported with him, and the youngest brother, Edward, then at large. This last appears to have excelled even his teachers in skill and audacity; Richard says of him, " Edward *would* have it. He would see a woman pull out a purse and would rub his hands, and say, 'That's mine!' He can open a purse with one hand when it is in his pocket," so as to withdraw a portion of the contents, before sharing them with his companions. His sister also says, "My brother Edward was very daring. He could pick a woman's pocket as she was running along the street. If he had seen a thing that he fancied, he would say, 'That's mine,' and watch his opportunity till he got it."

Such are youths who are allowed to be at large, leading a life of crime and corrupting others! What to them is the check of a short imprisonment?

Our next narrative will introduce us more fully into the domestic history of one doomed almost in infancy to be a convict. It was taken down by the Schoolmaster of the Preston House of Correction, at the dictation of W. M., aged 11 years, and, at the time, serving an imprisonment of eighteen months for stealing money from a shop drawer. The boy had been previously committed twice for theft.

"I was born in Lancaster, and when we came to Preston I was very young; my father kept a jerry-shop in Heatly-street, till my mother died, about three years ago; my father was drunk every night, *very near;* my mother died through father beating her. She used to *sauce* him for going to other beer-houses to drink, when we had plenty of our own; and then he punched her up and down the house, and she was crying with him punching her, and when he was *agate*, she many a time shouted 'murder!' She did not die all at once; she was badly two or three weeks. We were getting our breakfast one Monday morning when father fetched us upstairs, mother was dying; my father was crying, and *Hanny* (the youngest child) was laughing; father tried to make it give over; (there was four children, James, William, John, and Hannah.) It was not long before father got wed again, it might be two, three, four, or five months, the woman's name was *Aggy S.*, she had a child when they were wed; father give o'er drinking a bit, but soon began again, and when he got his wage he came home drunk at twelve o'clock at night. He was a porter at the Railway Station, and was paid on a Friday night. One night he came home very drunk, and James and I were in bed; he made us get up, and said he would take us to the canal and drown us; he asked my stepmother for our shoes, but she said, ' If you are going to drown them, you might as well leave the shoes for Johnny.' He threw me in the canal *a good way*, but a boatman jumped in with his clothes on, and got me out, or I should have been drowned; then the boatman took out his knife, and said to father, ' If you don't let them alone, I will stick you;' there was two policemen on the bridge with their lamps, but they did not come to us; we ran away and got home before father; and when the policemen came to our house and wanted to know what father was doing on the bridge with the two children at two o'clock in the morning, which was not a proper hour; father threatened to punch them, and did push them out, and locked the door; he was as drunk as he could be, and had been knocked off his work. He drinks yet, but not so oft as he did; stepmother never got drunk. I have been to three schools—I first went to Trinity Day and Sunday School for six months, Croft Street Day and Sunday for three months, and Bow Lane a short time. When I was near nine years old, I went to the factory for three weeks. Johnny and me ran away once, when stepmother was talking to some folk, and we was afraid of going home again for fear of being licked. We had no caps, and we stole two Scotch caps, and got a month each for it, and that was the way we got into prison at first. My stepmother often locked us up in the house; and one day she tied Johnny to the bed and locked him up, but he got a table and the cradle, and got through the skylight, and a boy helped him down at the bottom of the yard.

A SINGLE CAPTIVE. 61

The second time I was in prison was with Francis and Peter Forrester—these lads took me to a shop and lifted me up to the window, and showed me the money-drawer with the keys in it; we then went to the back to see who was in the kitchen, and we came again to the front, when I went in and fetched £2 11s. from the drawer. I got six months, Francis eight months' imprisonment, and Peter seven years' transportation. About a fortnight after Francis came out, I met him in Bridge Street, I had been for coals, he had just stole twopence and was going to hide his clogs, to go to another shop in Walker Street; he did not like to go in himself, so he asked me, and I went in and brought out a cup with 8½d, that is what I am now in for, and Francis got seven years' transportation."

The extreme simplicity of this appalling narration is in itself one of its most painful features, for it brings before our view a mere child, so accustomed to the most cruel treatment, the most brutal conduct, that the development of these horrid details excites no particular emotion in his mind. Accustomed as many of us may be to witness the cold-blooded cruelty and the selfish apathy caused by drinking, such a night-scene as that here described, surpasses any that we have ever heard of; the father making his two little boys get out of bed, to come with him to be murdered; his wife standing by, and instead of a word of expostulation at so unnatural a purpose, desiring with a cool selfishness, which manifests a full realization of his intentions, that he would leave the shoes; the unresisting obedience of the poor boys to their unnatural parent, their going with him to death, (what, indeed, was life to them?) the fiendlike man leading his own children to the brink of the canal, and, not even then relenting, throwing the eldest in with violence, as if he were drowning a dog; all this may seem incredible to some, too revolting to human nature to be true. But investigations have been made by a reliable official respecting the truth of these statements, and the result most fully corroborated the poor child's narrative, which has also been confirmed by the evidence of the police force. The facts thus ascertained are as follow:

"His father's second marriage was to a woman with whom he had been connected in an illicit manner some time previously; they had moved from street to street, and in both, his wife and himself had rendered themselves infamous by their brutal and inhuman conduct toward the three boys. The little girl had, happily for the infant—been adopted by a maternal aunt. The canal atrocity was generally known in the streets mentioned, more especially Albion-street, where a woman had gone into the house the morning following the attempt to drown the lads, and had seen the 'children's clothes soaking wet on the floor, not having even been wrung!' Another woman stated, that her son had assisted one of the boys to descend from the roof after escaping through the skylight; the poor child was naked, and nearly starved, 'he eat more than a grown person' of the food given to him; and it was stated by a 'next-door neighbour,' that the woman 'almost *clammed* the children to death.' She was in the habit of swearing at, and beating them; the father, by his drunken and brutal habits, setting the example. The man and woman lived unhappily together, frequently separating, in which state they were at the time these inquiries were made; the woman living in a cellar in Bridge Street, alone. It was stated by several, that the street was full of people at the time M. was accused of throwing the children into the water; and so unpopular had he become, on account of his brutal conduct, that he narrowly escaped being roughly handled when removing his goods from Croft Street. The neighbours had assembled to publicly mark their detestation of his conduct."

This narrative, astounding as it is, furnishes, it is to be feared, only a solitary instance of the too common domestic condition from which much juvenile crime springs. What is to become of the poor boy after completing his eighteen months of solitude in the Preston gaol, where his mind has been subjected to none but the best religious influences, but where he has not been prepared by trial to cope with temptation, where a large portion of his childhood has been passed in a most unnatural condition, one devised to subdue the strong nature of a man, not to train and strengthen the powers and character of a child. The excellent Chaplain, who watches with fatherly anxiety over those who have been the objects of his care, gives the following sad particulars of the subsequent course of these poor boys:

"William, the elder boy, after completing his eighteen months' imprisonment, and learning the trade of a tailor, was placed by us with a respectable master in the trade, with whom the boy worked some weeks, coming voluntarily to our prison chapel on the Sunday mornings, neatly dressed, and, to all appearances, doing well; not living with his father, but with his master. This master, however, who, I fear, was chiefly interested in the boy on account of his usefulness in his trade, suddenly dismissed him a few days ago, for having, I am told, shown some sulkiness of temper; and before I could interfere in the poor child's behalf, he had lost his situation and gone to his father, with whom he is at present. In the mean time William's younger brother, John, now aged 10, had been committed for seven days, charged with the vagrant proceeding of 'sleeping out.' John, who is a fine and very intelligent boy, had been previously committed *three* times under the Juvenile Felons' Act. The story told to me by the unfortunate child on this last occasion was to the effect that his father and stepmother were quarrelling, and she said she would not have the children; that she came to the factory where the child was earning 1s. 8d. weekly, and got him turned away from it; that she afterwards beat him and turned him out of the house. 'I had been,' he says, ' two or three days without meat except what people have given me; I was turned out of doors on Thursday, that night I slept in a pig-cote; in a stable on Friday night; and in a carriage on Saturday night;' from which he was taken by the police on Sunday morning. The poor little fellow's commitment was only for seven days. Unfortunately he was discharged when I was from home, and though I have made all inquiries after him, they have been unsuccessful."

In March, 1852, these two boys were committed for felony; John, the younger, was sentenced to six months' imprisonment; William, the elder, to seven years' transportation.

" Truly," adds Mr. Clay, " while we endeavour to rescue such pitiable young objects from their parents' cruelty and bad example, *something must be done to make the parents themselves sensibly—if not painfully and penally—alive o the conviction that society ought not to—and will not—submit to the consequences of their conduct;* or rather, putting consequences out of the question, will no longer suffer such conduct to escape its due reward."

But society will continue to endure such shameful violation of the laws of nature and abuse of that parental responsibility whose privileges are so carefully protected by the English law, until some undertake the cause of the oppressed children, who will never lay it down, while life lasts, until society is awakened to its duties. Is there now no Clarkson, no Wilberforce, no Granville Sharpe to protect the children against the moral perversity and the cruelty of parents, the culpable neglect of society?

We turn to another more detailed, but not less instructive history, the narrative of X., aged about 20, then under sentence of transportation.*

"When I was a child of about eighteen months' old, my mother got married to a man who had been under the same circumstances as I am now in, but with having bad health he got his liberty after serving three years and a half. It seems that for some time after my mother had got married, her husband went on tolerably well as a moral man, but after a time he began to frequent the alehouse; till this time he seems to have had middling good health, and *to be in easy circumstances as a labouring man;* but this soon began to fail, for he began to get into debt, but still loved pleasure and drink. The first kind of wickedness which I learned to commit, was carrying things of small value out of our own house; you may perhaps ask me how this originated in me, which, no doubt, was in this way. My stepfather used to ramble in the fields on the Sabbath day, and if we came across any place where there were apples, turnips, or anything of that description, he would not mind taking a few, *although he often told me it was wrong to do the same.* I also learnt to curse and swear, for both father and mother were swearers, especially the latter; if she was offended by any one of us, the first word would be a curse, and perhaps a blow, with a demand why we had done so and so; we even heard my little brothers curse before they reached the age of five years; this all originated from the bad example of my parents. When I was about the age of eight years, my father and mother worked in the factory, and left me to take care of the house and four children; when I had arrived at the age of 10,

[* Abridged from the original MS., but otherwise unaltered, except occasionally in spelling and grammar.]

after being left to do as I chose for two years, I was ready for anything, and from this age may be dated my course of wickedness.

"About the age of six I was sent to a National School, where I continued to go, or rather should have gone, for the space of two years; but *four-fifths of the time I ran away*, for which perhaps my father might beat me, but never told me the value of education, or how to obey my parents, and I never knew either father or mother to go to a place of worship, except to bury one of their children, of whom they have buried three. Very seldom did my parents request me to go to the Sabbath School, and never went to such a place themselves. Having a good deal of spare time, and all the Sabbath to myself, I formed company with some lads of about my own age, by whom I was very well liked, for my father having taken me with him in the fields to places where were plenty of nuts and other wild fruit, I could of course show these boys where we could get plenty of such like things. But we did not stop here; from rambling in the fields we commenced robbing gardens, *which we did for a long time in the most crafty manner, without being in any way found out.* My conscience was so hard by this time that it never smote me; but my advice now is, not to know sin in any way, and by God's blessing resting upon your own endeavours, you will never practise it, *for the best preservative from sin is not to know it.*

"At the age of about 13, I commenced learning to work in the factory with my stepfather, who used me more like a brute beast than a child to whom he had promised to give support, protection, example, and encouragement. The factory was a thing for which I had no great liking, and my father did not explain its utility to me; steam-loom weaving was not a thing in which I took any liking, which no doubt made me very careless; my father had a term to check this carelessness in me, which he termed 'a pair of spectacles,' which consisted in a blow with some unlawful weapon, or a kick, which he said made me see better.

"By and bye my father was thrown out of work, and so remained for a long time. I played me for the space of two

A SINGLE CAPTIVE. 67

years; during this time I learned and made more progress in wickedness than ever I had before. I began to stop out late at night with bad company, committing all sorts of outrage, such as robbing gardens, playing tricks with gunpowder upon people while they sat in their quiet habitations, opening their doors, and throwing an old mop up the house all daubed with soil, and some such like thing. I also learned to swear in the most horrid manner, to fight and quarrel with my fellow-creatures, and if any one offended me the most brutal oath would come out of my mouth, (which, no doubt, originated in my parents.) At last, many of my companions, who were better disposed, would not have anything to do with me or say to me; in short, I was that debased, I, and more of my companions with me, could not even let the brute creatures alone; we had used to get cats, and other such animals, to torture them, setting them to fight, tying their tails together, and throwing them over a clothes line, to tear each other to pieces. Thus was my time spent from 13 to 15 years of age. . . I had now made such vast progress in that which was bad, that there was nothing but what I was ready for and equal to; I commenced making marauding expeditions in the night—sometimes not seeing a bed for weeks together, but ready for plunder night and day; robbing gardens, selling the fruit, taking the tools that might be in them, and selling them to the pawnbrokers and others who would buy them. I did not carry on these games long before I was, in a certain measure, stopped, for me and two more one night went to sleep in a boiler-house belonging to a factory; but we did not sleep the night out there, for about eleven o'clock at night the master and a police-officer came and took us all three prisoners, for which two of us got one month, and the other, being an old offender, got three months; this was the first time I ever saw a prison, either inside or out."

Such is the picture this youth draws of himself, in his, as yet, unconverted state, when looking back from his solitary cell on, what he truly terms, these " dark ages" of his life. The English law justly holds those to be innocent who have not been *proved* to be guilty; but, in the moral regard of a Christian people, should the legal proof of the violation of one of God's commandments outweigh the moral certainty of the violation of many, and a knowledge that a course of conduct is being pursued, which denotes a soul in open rebellion with its Maker? In other words,—ought a Christian people, who are bound together as members of one community, and who ought to remember that they are children of the same Father, and heirs of the same inheritance, —ought such to see their brethren overtaken in such heinous faults, and not reprove them in the spirit of meekness, using every method that Christian wisdom can dictate, to draw them by the cords of love into the ways of virtue? But leaving this view of the subject,—granting that we are not " our brothers' keepers," and that society is not called on in any way to interfere with the conduct of its members, until it has a legal sanction for doing so, what should, in justice to the child, to the parents, to the community at large, be the course pursued in such a case as that before us, which is one of thousands? Justice to the child requires, that as he must suffer for a condition to which he has been brought through a long course of evil training, society having tacitly permitted the sins which his own conscience did not condemn him for, he should so suffer as to enable him, *through a long course of good training, to give him the power, which he has not now, of be-*

coming a useful member of society. Justice to the parent requires that he should suffer from his criminal neglect of his child, by losing that guardianship of him which he has abused, while the duty of maintaining him, imposed by nature, still remains. Justice to society requires, that the remedy to the existing evil should be applied in the most effectual way possible. We shall, in the course of this history, see what remedies society does apply in such cases, and what is the effect of them. The boy's narrative thus continues:

"The first shock which struck me was the mass of bars and impenetrable walls; it seemed to me to wear more the aspect of death, than a place of correction; this I felt at first, but it made no abiding impression, and the reason it did so is, perhaps, as follows:—We mingled together, and my companions, seeing that I was much cast down, would now and then comfort me—if I may use the phrase—by telling me to cheer up, and that it would be better in a day or two. I tried to do so, and succeeded very well in stifling the still, small voice of God. While here I made as much progress for further imprisonment as possibly could be, by hearing men, of all ages, tell of their grand exploits, how they got their money by robbing, and that they knew of plenty of places that could be easily plundered. All these, and many other things equally as bad, I saw and heard; before I left it I got pretty hard, for I got once or twice in punishment. The time drew nigh when I was to be discharged, but some misconduct on the Saturday kept me from leaving the prison on the Tuesday morning, and I was kept in the black hole till about half-past three in the afternoon. I was about fifteen miles from home, without knowing a single yard of the way; however, I got to —— that night, though I did not go home till the next morning. My father told me to get work, and mind and not get into prison any more; my mother told me I was not the only one that had been in prison. I believe that this forms the whole of the reproof that I got from my parents, whereas, I firmly believe, that had my parents set the thing in its true colours before my eyes, I should never have seen the inside of a prison again. I did as I was directed, got work, and there remained till the ensuing spring, when I again broke out in my mad career. As soon as summer came, I commenced my old games with tenfold fury, stealing all that I could lay my hands on, robbing gardens in the most shameful manner, selling the fruit for a mere nothing, cursing and swearing, calling God's vengeance down on my head and the heads of my companions in the most brutal manner, a profound Sabbath breaker, hating and hated of the better of my former associates. I did not continue long before I was taken up for stealing apples, for which I got three months in prison, and a most horrid three months it was to me, for I commenced my old rigs of disobedience, until I assaulted the governor and one of the officers, for which I was taken before the magistrate and ordered to be whipped; this took no effect on me, for I had now got so hard that I laughed at it, although I should at one time have trembled to have thought of it. I kept growing harder, thinking nothing of what would become of body or soul; no sermons made any impression on me, nor advices from the minister or schoolmaster, but rather laughed at all who tried to do me any good; the four dozen lashes took not the slightest effect, but rather hardened my impenetrable heart, and ripened me for the fate that awaited me. The time came that I was to be released, with this promise from the governor for my bad conduct, that if ever I came for trial he would have me transported."

The youth went home, got into work, but was thrown out of it by his master's breaking; his parents refused to maintain him; he went marauding expeditions, and fell in with poachers; was taken up, but let off on condition of turning evidence against the others; he proved treacherous in this, and went to an aunt requesting to live with her, but he soon ran away from her. "It now," he continues, "gives me great pain, when I think of the blessed religious instruction which my aunt would have given me, for she was a Christian woman, with as kind a heart as possible; the law of kindness was in her lips, but the law of deceit, treachery, and hypocrisy was in my heart, even against this kind benefactor." He returned home; his mother deceived him, and would not help him; he became very destitute. "I went about the street," he says, "in the most ragged and filthy state, and in want of bread, but I did not obtain it from the hands of my mother. I was compelled either to steal or starve, and it would seem that my parents, at this time, were so hard that they did not care which I did. This lasted for about four weeks, when I was taken up for this poaching job—was tried, found guilty, and sent to prison for two months." This period he passed as before, occasionally doing better, but only "from dread of punishment." He got into disgrace just before he left, when the governor "renewed his promise" to have him transported, should he ever come for trial. "At the expiration of my time I left the prison, and went immediately home, and a most miserable home I found it. My father and mother had been engaged in the most furious quarrel with the two men with whom I had been poaching, saying that it was entirely through them that I was in prison." They assaulted the men furiously, and received a summons for it. "I had now made such rapid strides in the downward road to destruction, that I actually rejoiced to see my poor parents in trouble. I began my old games again, stealing all that came in my way, until I was committed for trial, and sent again to —— prison. The governor seemed now to rejoice to find that he should have the opportunity of sending so vile a wretch out of the country, for I was not fit to remain there; after a fortnight I was tried, found guilty, and sentenced to seven years' transportation."

We will now leave this unfortunate youth, who has run his full career of vice and reached the goal of daring and hardened crimes, before entering manhood. The narrative, written in solitude, with the vividness with which a newly-awakened conscience brings his former sins to remembrance, is interspersed in the original with expressions of deep penitence; it will portray the experience of hundreds, or rather thousands. And what did society do for him, what does it do for all such, to bring them into the right path? In a future part of this work we shall observe the effect of the new treatment which he is to undergo, having at length become a " child of the State."

There are some who doubt whether an innocent heart is ever to be found, even in those who have but lately come from their Maker's hands; whether in the young child there can ever be found any thing holy and good. Such narratives as the preceding would well nigh make us despair of human nature, did we not also contemplate it as it may be seen even in the very midst of vice and degradation. Such is the subject of the following narrative, and it will be refreshing to the spirit to turn for a few moments from childhood in its degradation, to the aspect it presents in the " Record by a Teacher of a departed Scholar in a Ragged School."

" If I would give a picture of a pure and childlike spirit, one of those of whom the Saviour says that ' of such is the kingdom of heaven,' it would be my good and gentle scholar, whom, in the early promise of life's beautiful springtide, God's angel bore away to open into a more lovely flower in His everlasting garden.

" Thomas B. is the only person of whom I never heard any ill; every one spoke well of him; he gained the love of rich and poor, young and old; those who saw him casually were struck with his sweet unassuming expression of countenance; while those who knew him more, and gradually felt, if they could not understand, the power of his winning gentleness and purity of soul, had awakened in them an unwonted kindliness towards a poor simple Irish boy. But probably no one loved him so much as I did, except his own immediate family, for no one knew him so well: yet they did not comprehend the beauty of his spirit, for, though kindred in blood, they were not so in soul, and, as his mother said, 'did not half know how good he was' till he was passing away.

"I first saw Tom in June, 1847, at the Ragged School; he was then about 14 years of age. I was teaching a class of rough, wild boys; he was brought in by his cousin, one of the lowest, dirtiest, most vicious-looking, in the school. Even on that first evening I was struck with something remarkably refined and gentle in him, united with a childlike simplicity and gaiety of manner and appearance; the boys told me that his father had lost £100 in the potatoe disease; this I did not credit at the time, but afterwards found that it was probably true; for the family had been little farmers, and on the failure of their crops, they had been obliged to part with their stock to pay their rent; having at length been forced to quit the farm, they had come to Bristol, having relatives there, but these were living miserably among the lowest Irish, and so Tom's family now lived. As he attended regularly, I was surprised not to see him come when I took the other scholars to the Museum; he did not appear on the following class night, and on inquiring the reason, I was told by poor Patrick, who some months after was called 'home,' that Tom was then following his sister to the grave, that the whole family were in the most overpowering grief, the eldest brother especially being uncontrolable in his sorrow, beating his head against the wall, and refusing to be comforted. I had not yet made personal acquaintance with any of my scholars or their families, except Patrick, whose sickness had demanded my care, but I felt a strong prompting to try to pour some balm into the wounded heart: and meeting Tom when returning home, I asked him to accompany me. The poor boy was sobbing in all the agony of the first deep sorrow of a loving child; he could only repeat, 'She *was* a good sister to me!' I spoke to him of the heavenly home, and told him he must strive so to live that he may hope to meet her there. 'Do you not think, Tom, it would grieve her now if she thought you were doing wrong?' 'O yes,' he replied, 'I am sure it would; she always bate me when I did wrong; she bate me as good as my mother; she *was* a good sister to me.' Finding that he was totally unacquainted with the hopes of the Gospel, I read to him, when we reached my house, the Raising of Lazarus. It was deeply affecting to me to bring the Saviour thus for the first time to the heart of a mourner; he was soothed, and carried the Testament away with him. Little did I imagine, when I consoled that poor boy for the loss of his sister, how deep a hold that act of kindness would have on him, and how, by giving me a strong influence over him to a degree quite unknown to myself, it would impart a guiding and strengthening influence to my counsels, which no other could have; little did I know that the consolations I then offered him would support his own dying bed, for when, nearly two years after, I stood by him as he was passing to the unseen world, and asked him if he remembered what I said to him after his sister's death, he replied with animation, 'I remember every word as if it were this morning;' little did I anticipate that I should ere long apply to myself the words of Christian support and counsel which I then addressed to him, for I feel that his pure, loving, childlike spirit, transplanted to the Father's mansion, ere it was blighted by sin or sorrow, will have a soothing and purifying influence on me, and I hope help to fit me for them.

"On returning home after a few months' absence, I did not find Tom at school. I learnt that the whole family had been ill of fever, it was believed owing to the violence of their grief; —they were then just dismissed from the hospital, without any resources, unable to procure work at once, and hardly strong enough to do it. I sent for Tom, pleased that my former notice of him had not led him to encroach on me; his mother brought him to my house; she was so different from her son in deportment and manner, that I wondered how he had been nurtured under her influence. So I found all the rest of the family, who had at once sunk from their former condition to the level of their relations in Bristol, and now, having been obliged to part

A SINGLE CAPTIVE.

with all their clothes, were completely destitute. I gave them some help, and, endeavoured to get Tom a place of work. His open and pleasing countenance attracted many to him, and a respectable surgeon, engaged this poor ragged Irish boy, to be in his own house. When recommending him, I wrote that 'I had known him but for a short time, yet that I should be much disappointed if he did not find him perfectly truthful and honest.' This was a lad from a Ragged School in one of the worst localities, living in the midst of scenes of vice, the cousin of one of the worst boys in the school, and that I could so write of him, was a striking proof of the transparent purity of his character; to this another teacher, a labouring man who lived near, bore his characteristic testimony by saying, 'There is not a *bit of blackguardliness* about Tom.' I told him what I had written, and that he must not fall short;—I saw that he was determined not to disappoint me;—and his mistress told me after his death, that not a single fault had been found with him, even by the other servants, during the whole time he was there. When he came to show himself to us in the new clothes provided for him, the sweetness and goodness of his looks, and the refinement of his appearance, elicited the remark from a lady, 'Any mother might be proud of such a son.' Yet there never appeared in him the slightest consciousness of any superiority, or of being an object of interest in others; and the kindness he received excited no vanity in him, only a happy loving gratitude. He continued to attend the evening school, gaining the love of his teachers by his docility and application; without any remarkable talent, he had great quickness of perception and readiness of apprehension, and I seldom taught him anything which he did not seem fully to understand and remember. Though ready to show any acts of kindness in his power to his school-fellows, and winning their love by the sweetness of his disposition, which even they could appreciate, he did not associate with them, and his native purity seemed to shield him from any contamination from them; I was often struck with the gentleness with which he suffered his rude cousin to lean familiarly upon him, though he greatly disliked the coarseness of his manners, and suffered much from his insolent rudeness. I promised my class a temperance medal at Christmas, if any had kept without drinking a month. There were many candidates, but Tom was the only one whom the unanimous voice of the class pronounced worthy; I wished him to take the pledge, but he said it was not necessary; I saw he felt that his promise to me was sufficient; when he was dying, eighteen months after, I asked him if he remembered his medal; he replied quite simply, 'I have always kept my promise.' I told him I was sure of it though I had never reminded him of it. After his death, his mother and brother said that they had often pressed him to drink, but unavailingly; even at his father's funeral he had steadily refused, without assigning a reason, 'for,' she said, ' he was always so secret;' even when ill, though the medical man ordered him porter, and she urged him to take it, he would not.

"In the summer of 1848 his second brother returned to Ireland in a deep decline; the family went into the country to get work, and Tom was taken from his place. They returned in the autumn with their small means exhausted, for the father had been dangerously ill. Tom came to school very poorly clad, but beautifully neat and clean;—he looked as good and gentle as ever, but thinner and taller, and I felt a misgiving that the seeds of decline were in him. Troubles thickened round them;—Tom could get no work; the father was taken ill again, and at Christmas died in the infirmary. He was at school that evening, and one of the boys told me in their usual heartless tone—for they do not comprehend the solemn mystery of death—'Tom's father died this morning.' I replied with indignation, ' How can you speak so; do you not see how he is feeling it?' He was sitting pale as a marble statue, but calm and firm; after school I took him aside, and spoke to him words of Christian comfort; he wept tears of a calm and deep sorrow, which showed how his soul had been refined and elevated since his first great grief; he little knew how soon he was himself to go. Soon after, he received the news of his brother's death; these sorrows and great exposure to the weather brought on a violent inflammation of the lungs.

" As soon as it was known that he was ill, many friends came around him; his mother and brother were quite surprised at the attention shown him, thinking him friendless, and supposing that they were indebted to me for all the aid which had been given him;—they were indebted for it to the love with which he inspired even casual acquaintances. One gentleman, who had been but for a short time his teacher, and was unused to visit the sick and afflicted, told me he was grateful to God for having led him first to one whose sick-bed it was a pleasure to visit;—he often sat by him for a long time, affectionately holding his hand, and administering to his wants; he brought with him a physician who attended him gratuitously with the greatest kindness; indeed the attentions paid him were so numerous and frequent that jealousy was excited among the low neighbours, and complaints were made to the priests, that the protestants were trying to convert him. Tom suffered much, but bore patiently and courageously all the painful remedies that were applied;—indeed no one who saw his countenance so serene and bright, especially when lighted up by one of his loving smiles, could have imagined that he was so ill. Everything about him was neat and orderly though poor; his pure spirit could endure nothing but what was pure; —how was the scene changed when that spirit had fled! He was so contented and thankful for everything, that it was long before I discovered that he was lying on straw, he had stopped his mother when she was going to tell me of it; and though I repeatedly begged of him to tell me if he wanted anything, it was only a week before the end that I discovered, when arranging his pillow, that that too was only of straw, so anxious was he to avoid troubling any one. When his first attack had somewhat subsided, he thought he was getting well, but I saw the fatal drops of consumptive perspiration on his forehead. His mother too clearly perceived that he was marked for death, and was unrestrained in her grief;—the loss of her daughter, her older son, her husband, were nothing to this, for she had placed all her hopes in Tom; but she was selfish and violent in her sorrow, and he could not bear to have her near him; I generally found him alone, but he said he was quite happy, and still looked forward gladly to life, taking a vivid interest in all that concerned his friends and the school, and rejoicing in the love and kindness of all who came to see him. But one night the complaint took an unexpected and fatal turn, and it was believed that he could live only a day or two;—his teacher, Mr. —, now thought it right to tell him in express terms how near he was to his end; then for a time his spirit sank, and a tear started to his eye; the solemn news was quite unlooked for by him, though his mother had so continually bemoaned to him his approaching death; so full was his innocent spirit of life. Mr. — was very unhappy at his great ignorance of the promises of the gospel, 'yet,' he said, 'he is so pure in heart, so childlike.' I added, 'We need not fear for him;—Jesus has said, of such is the kingdom of heaven.' I was always very careful not to interfere with his views as a Catholic, and he assured me that I never did;—while abstaining from bringing before him much which I should otherwise have desired to do, it was my aim to breathe into his soul a confidence in his Heavenly Father's love, and an assurance that He orders all for us in wisdom and mercy; that every suffering he endured was to purify and elevate his spirit, and prepare it for the heavenly mansions. These views I dwelt on when I saw him on the following day; his soul was cast down, he was suffering and sorrowful even unto death. He said that he had had a happy life, (a beautiful proof of the brightness and contentment of his spirit in the midst of privations and sorrows,) that he would gladly have remained on earth, if such had been the will of God, but to that he was resigned. I left him more cheerful. He lived a fortnight longer;—there was no one near him with whom he could have spiritual communion, and his mother's frequent loud lamentations were of a kind to harrow up his feelings, yet never did she or I ever hear a word of repining, or even a sound of impatience from him; it was a happiness to me that my daily visit to him soothed and cheered him, and poured balm into his spirit. 'Peace I leave with you,' &c., was the text he most delighted to hear from me, for he had seen it in his prayer-book, and he liked to find that we had holy thoughts in common. He regretted that he was not better acquainted with the Scriptures, and with hymns, which would now have been a comfort to him. 'There is a happy land' was the only one familiar to him;—the 11th and 20th of John were the only chapters that he knew, and now he was too weak to read. I told him that the recollection of him would give an additional earnestness to my teachings of the others; this pleased him; he wished to be remembered. I delighted to perform for him various little offices which he could not bear his mother to render him on account of her roughness;—he told her that I tended him as if he had been my brother, and said 'the lady touched him like silk.' His readiness in apprehending spiritual truths was remarkable; passages which I read to him, but feared were above his comprehension, he evidently enjoyed, and if he did not fully understand them, still received their spiritual meaning. His powers continued to the very last. Two days before he died, when I entered his room, his countenance was expressive of wearing pain, but when I laid a beautiful heartsease before him, it was wonderful what a transformation came over him, and what radiant delight was in his smile as he contemplated with wondering admiration the beauty of the flower. Never did his spirit seem stronger or brighter than on that day; he looked too full of life to die. I reminded him that it was now a fortnight since he had received the summons, and expressed the hope, in which he fully accorded, that he was better prepared by his sufferings to leave this world, and happier in the prospect of another; I spoke to him of the joys prepared for those that love the Lord, and said, 'I think you love him.' He replied gently but firmly, 'I *hope* I do.' The day before he died, I found him panting for breath and in great pain, yet still he responded to my whisper, 'Heaven is your home;—your Father's love is still with you;' beautifully did he open his eyes on me when he heard me weeping, and begged me not to trouble for him, though he knew I grieved much for him. Early on the morning when he died, his cousin came to see him; he had been striving lately to improve, evidently touched by Tom's spirit, for he had taken a warm interest in his welfare; when his cousin had read a little to him, he shared with him a cordial that was by him, telling him that this was the last time they should taste anything together, and with his dying breath assured him how pleasant and easy was the path of virtue, if he once firmly resolved to walk in it. Soon after he breathed his last; nearly his last words were, 'Lord Jesus, have mercy upon me.' He left the most peaceful happy smile on his half-parted lips;—a wonderful beauty remained on the deserted covering of his blessed spirit till the grave closed over it.

"Every thing in my departed scholar's character was in such perfect keeping, and seemed so natural to him, that while he was with us, we did not perceive how remarkable it was. Brought up in the midst of falsehood and vulgarity, we expected him to be truthful and refined, and felt that he could not be otherwise. Almost from an infant he had shown that delicacy of feeling which was so striking in his last illness; he would associate with none but the children of their landlord, and was the peculiar charge of his eldest sister, a superior young woman. He never had told a falsehood ' since he knew that it was wrong to do so;' and was grieved when those around him did so. Tom was deficient in natural energy, habitually submissive to control, and satisfied with his condition; yet he had a moral courage, a determination to do what seemed to him right, and a quiet self-respect and independence which are rarely found in connection with a gentle and amiable character. 'My darling child was so courageous,' said his mother, 'he often went to his work when he was really ill.' When with those among whom his station in life had thrown him, he seemed a being of another sphere. The Heavenly Father has removed him to his true home, and the remembrance of his pure and loving spirit has still an influence on all who knew him. I shall ever be thankful that I had the privilege of helping to lead him heavenward, and in the blessed mansions of the Father may I meet him, as one of the beloved of the Saviour,—a child of God."

CHAPTER III.

THE GIRLS.

WE have now contemplated Juvenile Delinquents, both in classes and singly, and have felt more painfully the condition of childhood when neglected and perverted from observing the purity and beauty in which it may exist, even when surrounded by misery and vice. But we have hitherto considered boys only ; the condition of delinquent girls requires a not less close and earnest attention.

It is unnecessary, in this place, to enlarge on the influence which woman has on society in general, whether for good or for evil; but it is needful, in reference to our present subject, distinctly to bear in mind that there are certain duties, that there is a certain sphere appointed for the female sex, in all grades of society, which cannot be neglected or perverted in the highest or in the lowest without the greatest injury. To woman, in all her varied relations, is peculiarly confided the early watchful care of the young beings who are to constitute the next generation ; it is she who is to call forth and foster the first opening germs of the spiritual nature ; she must pour into the young heart a love which should always remain a deep and pure spring of holy affection within it; while, as the energies and passions of the boy display themselves with an impetuosity which, as yet, is beyond the power of self-control, and with difficulty yields to stern authority, she should retain a hold over him, made stronger even by her very weakness. In mature life duties not less important are consigned to that sex, to which the Great Author of Nature has given, with less vigorous mental and physical powers, greater susceptibility both of body and of mind, greater delicacy and refinement of feeling. To her the sanctity of the home is committed; she is to awaken and cherish the tenderer and purer feelings in those whose daily pursuits would otherwise harden their very nature, and chain their souls to the sway of the world; and as the Saviour first revealed himself in an undying form to a woman, and confided to her the first message of his approaching glorification, so to woman are the blessed messages of the Gospel still intrusted, whether to the young child at his mother's knee,—in the sacred intercourses of the family circle,—in the abodes of misery and vice,—at the dying bed.

If it is the appointment of the Heavenly Father of all, that woman should have such a relation to society as the helpmate of man, and if she is adapted by Him to fulfil such duties, fearful is her condition when she departs from it, and most injurious to all around her; for God's laws can never be broken with impunity. Earnest should be our endeavours to save the young girl, while yet it is time, from entering a career in which she may work yet greater evil than the delinquent boy.

In the present chapter it is proposed to show that while girls placed under favourable circumstances are less prone to evil than boys, yet that, in the degraded classes we are considering, they sink even lower than children of the other sex, and that their very natures appear more completely perverted; that the present system adopted towards Juvenile Delinquents is even more certain to prove their ruin than that of boys; yet that a wise and kind system adopted towards them will prove them to be equally reclaimable.

Though the author's own personal experience might suffice to prove all these points, yet it will be more satisfactory to bring forward the testimony of others differently circumstanced, and who view society under varied aspects.

Mr. Thompson, of Aberdeen, thus speaks of the children in the Industrial Schools in which he takes so active a part. [*Vide* " Social Evils, their Causes and their Cure;" by A. Thompson, Esq., of Banchory.] " A poor half-starved outcast girl, trained up in ignorance and filth and sin, is even a more painful and a more degrading sight than a boy of the same description. She seems to have fallen, or to have been forced, into a state farther below her right place in the world than the boy; and yet, owing to her more plastic nature, it is easier to raise her up again."

Mr. Wichern, the benevolent founder of the Rauhe Haus, near Hamburg, thus speaks of the girls in his little colony, in his report for 1835:

"The most important feature of this autumn has been the reception of the girls: thirteen of them, from 6 to 16 years old, I have gradually received from Dec. 1. *Their destitute and vagabond state is, at least, equal to that of the boys, and in some cases greater; the labour of rescuing them, decidedly more difficult.* The time is too short to furnish matter for this year's report; we have, however, as yet, no cause to repent admitting them. Our household arrangements perfectly ensure separation between the sexes; my own sister superintends them, in an entirely detached house. The girls, like the boys, *live a practical family life*, all ages mixing together, without any of the formality of a school—and in their case, also, only elementary education is given. Four of the elder are employed in house-work, and we hope to qualify them efficiently for service. Amongst them, as amongst the boys, *steady, well-regulated labour serves as a safety-valve for their untamed energies.* Besides house-work and cooking, the weekly washing for the establishment, and the daily peeling of nearly a sack of potatoes by the younger ones, these girls have made nearly all their bed linen, much of their wearing apparel, and have knitted a great number of stockings."

Of the difficulties experienced with the girls, he thus speaks:

"We find that though a wild boy, conscious of his own strength, may resist for a time, he soon yields to constraint, and probably, before long, acknowledges thankfully the benefits bestowed on him in the form of compulsion; or he obeys from fear of a power which he feels to be superior; while the brutalized girl says decidedly, 'I will not,' and abides by it; or furiously gnashes her teeth, clenches her fist, and stamps with her foot, in vain attempts to give vent to her rage."

The Bishop of Tasmania gave a similar opinion of the greater degradation of female than male convicts in his evidence before the Lords. ["Reformatory Schools," p. 316.]

The master and mistress of a Ragged School, in a very low part of Bristol, have invariably found it more difficult to retain a hold over the girls in the most degraded families, or even to bring them under school discipline, than the boys; it is far more difficult to awaken their minds, or to give them a pleasure in learning, and the voluntary teachers who give occasional aid in the school make the same complaint; they have not unfrequently given up in despair the attempt to teach the girls, while the same individuals have been able to make considerable impression on the boys.

Let us, then, admit it to be a fact that young girls when low and degraded are worse than boys in similar circumstances. Why is this so? Why, from the very nature of things, must it be so?

The answer may be briefly this, that in the case of the girls there is a greater departure from what ought to be their education and training, even than in that of the boys. In order to perceive this, let us reflect what is the training of girls in a well-ordered family in the middle and the labouring classes of society. The little girl early serves her apprenticeship to future maternal duties, by bestowing motherly cares on her doll, and in a lower class becomes a little nurse of a younger child, even while she would seem to require fostering care herself; her affections and young powers are thus called forth; she soon shares the mother's household duties; even at 10 or 11 years of age she has acquired a habit of care and forethought which will enable her to take, if need be, the mother's place, and do what nothing but love could have taught her; in the mean time, an education has been given to her adapted to her future circumstances in society; she has, perhaps, been stimulated to progress by her brothers, whose attention to study has been more undivided, and mingling in well-ordered society of her own class, with a modest reserve, and yet with the freedom natural to purity and unconsciousness of evil, she is prepared to fill the station to which God may call her. But observe the girls of the pariah caste, or rather of those families where there is no fear or love of God, no regard to human law, no self-respect, no pleasures but those of animal gratification, no perception of anything pure or beautiful. There is no loving tenderness called out in the little girl, for she receives none; the next unhappy babe that enters the world after her, cannot call from her fondling caresses which she has never known; it is probably carried in the arms of a drunken or mendicant mother, as she has been, to draw its first impressions of life from misery and vice, until locked up at home with one or two older ones to exist as best it may; perhaps, happily for it, to meet with a premature death from the fire, or the scalding water, from which its young nurses could not protect it. But still the girl is kept at home to be the drudge, not the helpmate, of the mother, and is thus more exposed to the close contamination of the scenes which pass there; feminine delicacy there is none, nor anything to call out the higher parts of her nature; she cannot in general be spared to go to school; when she can obtain permission to do so, she is listless and indolent, for her powers are unused to any intellectual exercise. If sufficiently young, skilful teaching may incite in her a desire of knowledge, but otherwise the feelings of personal vanity, which exist most strongly in the most degraded, are the only ones which seem to call forth any real and lively interest in her; her intercourse with the other sex has given her no self-respect, and inspired her with none but the lowest feelings; she is prepared even in girlhood to fall headlong into an abyss, the dangers of which she cannot know till she experiences its horrors—the depths of which she cannot comprehend till she is plunged too deep to be extricated from it.

The boys in the same families have been equally neglected, but the greater vigour of their natures has carried them into the open air, and led them to quicken their faculties by active exercise, by observation of the objects around them, and by the self-reliance caused by the very neglect which has driven them at so early an age to depend on their own resources to obtain a living; hence, though equally unprincipled with the girls, and more prone to overt and daring mischief and crime, they have far more which can be worked on for good, and their powers having been awakened and strengthened even more than is usual in the higher classes of society, it is far more possible than in the case of the girls to excite to progress in a right direction.

A few extracts from the records of a Ragged School Teacher will give some idea of the very low degree in which the minds of these girls are called out, even on the commonest objects, and how little prepared they are to derive any pleasure or instruction from reading, if possessed of the mechanical power of doing so.

"Feb. 1849. A large class of girls, who were more orderly than before, and seemed more desirous of learning. Most of them were able to read in the Old Testament Irish Lessons, and therefore must have had some schooling. The Creation.—No one of the class had ever seen the sun rise, and one did not know what the rising of the sun meant. In connection with 'herb bearing seed,' I asked what seed we eat as vegetables? they answered, 'Carrots, turnips, parsnips, cabbages,' &c., and only ——, who attends the morning-school, said, 'Peas and beans.' There is much more difficulty in interesting these girls in their lessons than the boys;—these require only to be restrained, and show an eagerness to acquire knowledge, while the girls manifest an indolent listlessness from which it is very difficult to rouse them. When the master gives a general lesson to the school, the boys are generally attentive, and evidently taking in ideas, but the girls are bold, and keep noticing the boys even without encouragement from them. When I question them on the following week respecting the subject of the lesson, they can tell nothing about it, while the boys answer by acclamation. Some of these girls are very decently dressed, and evidently higher in social position than most of the boys, but the roving habits of the latter have quickened their powers of observation, and developed their powers; the girls have not had their faculties awakened; they are consequently lower in their taste and feelings, and there is less to work on. The younger girls are more alive to instruction than the older ones."

Yet persevering effort will tell even on such girls as these.

"March 28. A general lesson on the Map of Europe; I was able to fix their attention pretty well; the younger ones seem quite interested and eager to learn, but some of the great girls are perfectly careless; two or three, very decently dressed, manifest no desire for improvement, and can hardly read at all.

"Nov. 1852. The nature of our evening Girls' School is now greatly changed from what it was three years or more ago. The girls attending it are equally ignorant, equally poor, perhaps poorer; but since we have established in it a spirit of order and obedience, we have found that the thoroughly low bad girls who used to come will not attend; they prefer to be in the streets, and though I have occasionally had promises of attendance from some of them, they never come. In fact, we have scarcely ever girls from the same families whence wild tattered boys attend, and often show great delight in receiving instruction. The girls who form our evening-school, are principally such as have been prevented by the poverty of their parents from receiving other instruction, and who are at work or employed in their families during the day. Yet even with those who evidently come from a desire to learn, I find the same difficulty, arising from the complete sluggishness of their intellectual powers, and the same inferiority to the boys in mental activity. Their complete ignorance even of the most common Scripture knowledge is painful to witness, as well as their difficulty in fixing their attention on even an interesting object so as to gain any idea from it. It has been a great aim with me to awaken their minds more than to give mere mechanical instruction; and it has often been most pleasing, when I have succeeded in doing this, to observe the surprise and delight with which they seem first to have discovered that they had the power of thinking. They all seem grateful for instruction, and conduct themselves so well in school that I can hardly recognise them as the same girls whom I have seen at other times wild and disorderly in the streets."

Now the deficiency in intellectual power and activity in the girls as compared with the boys, here complained of, is not universally true, as all who have had an opportunity of comparing the youth of the two sexes under *equally favourable circumstances* will readily admit. The powers of the two are of different kinds, and probably will not in general admit of an equally high development in after life in the female as in the male sex; but a greater precocity is usually exhibited by girls than by boys, and certainly not less pleasure in the exercise of their intellect. The different kind of education usually given to boys and girls in most cases prevents a fair comparison, but we have the testimony of experienced persons who, at different periods, have conducted the education of boys and of girls, that the latter exhibited even greater quickness and power than the former in the acquisition of the classical languages, and other branches of knowledge requiring clearness of reasoning and sound exercise of judgment; we know that in two neighbouring British Schools, one for boys, the other for girls, possessing similar advantages, the government inspector found the proficiency of the pupil teachers, and of the children in general in the Girls' School, in no way inferior to that of the boys.

If then the degradation of the girls of the perishing and dangerous classes is even greater than that of the boys, and if on their early training the wellbeing of the next generation so greatly depends, should not especial efforts be made for their rescue? And yet they are by far the most neglected; for them but very secondary efforts are made in the establishment of Industrial Schools, and for the convicted among them there is no Government Juvenile School or Prison,—no Philanthropic Farm School;—no public Asylum, abroad or at home, has been instituted, to train up and reform the poor little girls who have broken the laws of their country.

As we have taken "a single captive" to learn how a boy thief becomes a hardened adult criminal, so we may learn more from the history of a single girl, and one not originally among the most degraded, than from any general statements.

The following details, dictated to the chaplain of the Preston gaol, the Rev. J. Clay, will throw a ghastly light on the lives of young women living in our very midst, and will show how effectual might have been the help offered by a Christian hand in an early stage of this fearful career. The narrator is a young woman, lying, with several of her accomplices, under sentence of transportation; their several histories, given independently to Mr. Clay, fully bear out the truthfulness of this story, which to persons unacquainted with such a phase of human existence would seem almost incredible.

"I was born at Stockport, my father was a pensioner, and had 1s. a day; my father and mother were both sober and industrious, *but my mother would have done anything to have got us meat*. My father was more shy, he was a shoemaker. I went for nearly three years to a Roman Catholic School, at threepence a week. I went to the factory at 10 years old, and worked there till I was 12. Then I went to service at Mosley, at a boarding-school. I stayed there until I was 14. I then left on account of the small wages. I came home, and was sent by my father to learn to be a lad's cap-maker. I was learning for three months, and then I came home again."

Hitherto we observe nothing either in the circumstances of the family, or the training of the child, which would lead us to anticipate any but a life of honest industry; an effort has been made by the parents to keep her at school, and she has been there trained to useful labour; the parents are not addicted to vicious habits, and are secure from actual starvation; there is only a little intimation that the mother is somewhat over anxious for the bread that perisheth.

"When I came home, I saw that my brother Richard was dressed very fine, besides having a gold ring and a watch. My brother was not then living at home regularly, because he could not stand my father's reproaches. I used to say to my father, 'How well Richard's dressed!' And my father would say, 'But who thinks anything of it? he's a prig.' My mother was more unhappy about it than my father, and often followed him about the town, begging him to come home. When I was just 15, my mother gave me three-pence to go to Knoll Mill Fair, and I met my brother there. He told me what to do, and I stood before him so that nobody could see his hand, while he picked a woman's pocket of 7s. 6d. and a purse. He gave me a shilling, and then told me to go home. I went into a show, and picked a young woman's pocket of 1s. 6d. *I trembled very much when I did it;* I met the young woman again in a short time, and she was crying. I heard her say the money was her mother's. *I cried too, and would have given her the money back*, but was afraid of being took up. I dared not take the money home, so I took it to a stay shop, and paid it in advance towards a pair of stays. I remained at home three months *without doing any thing more*. At the end of that time my little brother Edward was taken up for picking pockets, and got three months. He had been taken up three times before, and had only been out three days. During 12 months he had only been at liberty four days."

The family was thus already known to the public as a criminal one. Had Christian effort been directed to it, ere this, and even now had a watchful eye been kept on this girl to lead her right and to infuse into her a principle of duty while her conscience was yet tender, what might not have been the result. The co-operation of the parents would have been readily enlisted before this period, for they had reproached their sons, though they had not firmly restrained them. But soon Ellen's family affection itself leads her across the barrier,—she has the prison brand upon her; she is no longer visited by qualms of conscience, and launches fearlessly into the career of vice, giving us only occasionally such glimpses of better feeling, as make us doubly mourn over her, and lament that a hand was not stretched out to save her.

"One of the witnesses against him was one of his own companions, and after he had been the means of convicting him, I leathered him just outside the court. I was taken up for the assault on this witness, and remanded in the New Bailey a week. I was then bailed out by two navvies. [These two men were perfect strangers; this kind of security is very common.] My mother met me in the street, and we were treated to some rum by a companion of my brother Richard's, James O'B., who had £100 which he had stolen from a woman. My brother was then in Gloucestershire picking pockets. O'B. gave me money to complete the purchase of my stays. I had been at a fair with another young woman only for a day, and we got £3 between us. When I got home again, my mother had a letter from Richard, saying that he was put back for trial at Gloucester for pocket-picking, and wanted money to pay for a counsellor. I went by the train to Oughton, and at the station picked a woman's pocket of 15s. which paid for my place to Kidderminster. I went in a waggon from Kidderminster to Worcester, with five or six other females, and got 15s. more from them. I stopped all night at Worcester. I went in an omnibus to the Gloucester station next morning, and picked a lady's pocket in the omnibus of £1 2s. I got into Gloucester on Friday night; saw my brother next morning; told him that I would try to get some money for a counsel; and went to the market, but it is a very poor market, and I only got 10s. 9d. I could not get enough money to fee my brother a counsel, and he received three months, having been recommended by the jury to mercy on account of his being so young. I then went to Derby, and then to Sheffield, where I saw O'N., whom I had previously known in Manchester through my brother. I went to Rotherham Statute Fair and got about £4. I saw O'N. again, who said, I think you have done better than any of us! for a great many pickpockets were there. I then went to Bam Statute Fair, but got nothing, for it rained, and no people came. I returned to Sheffield, and

THE GIRLS. 95

then went to Hull. I went to all those places by myself, having heard O'N. and his companions say they were going. It was the fair, and I got between £6 and £7. I seldom kept my money, for other travellers in the lodging-houses used to say they were hard up, and borrowed it from me. O'N. wanted me to live with him without being married, *but I would not.* My eldest brother John, was then in Hull, serving a month for picking pockets. I waited till he came out, and then he leathered me for coming away from home. I ran away from him and went to Leeds, there I met O'N. again, and the askings were put up for us to be married. I filled up the three weeks by going to Sheffield and York, and got about £10 or £11 at both places together. We were married at the Old Church. Up to this time, I could only pick outside pockets, but O'N. taught me how to raise outside dresses, and to pick inside pockets. I was married on the Thursday, and on the Saturday I got 10s. in the market. On Monday my brother Edward came to Leeds. We all went out, and Edward picked a pocket of 13s., but he had been watched, and we were all took up, *and we got three months.*"

Such is the commencement of her married life! Let us now observe what effect this imprisonment of three months had on her.

"After our liberation we went to Hull, and found Prince Albert was going to lay the foundation stone of Grimsby Docks. At Hull I got 17s. We went to Grimsby, and Edward and I got 30s. each. From Hull we went to Newark, where we got £7; then to Redford £4; then to Sheffield, where I was took up for 30s. I had just taken from a woman. *This brought me six weeks,* and O'N. (my husband) two months in Wakefield. I travelled after I came out, until O'N. came out, and got in the fortnight about £15. Then we went to Selby, and got £4 in the market. Then to Hull, and got £5 at the station. Then to Manchester, when I and my husband went to live with my father. While I lived at Manchester, I went out with O'N. almost every day by the trains six or seven miles out of

Manchester, sometimes second, sometimes first class, having very good clothes. The largest sum I ever got was £22, going from Manchester to Stockport. *O'N. did nothing but 'shade me off.' He was a great drunkard, and I had to pay from 20s. to 35s. every week to the beer-shop for him. We carried on this way for about six months, making on the average about* £10 *a week.* We lived at my father's all this time. He used to fret and cry, and tell us we should get into disgrace, but we took no heed. He was too good-natured with us. We then heard that Preston Market was very throng on a Saturday, and for 13 weeks we came over, O'N., Richard, and I—every Saturday. O'N. and I went together, and Richard and O'G. At night we shared all equally. The largest sum I ever got at Preston was £17, and the smallest about £3. I used to call £4 and £5 nothing. It was owing to the wet day we went into the shop, few people being in the market, when the offence took place for which we are transported. *Although I was three years at school I never learnt to read.* Once when I was at Preston Station, I got some money in a purse (9s.), I took the purse, a red silk one, and put it in the water-closet on the Manchester side of the station. It was put behind the pipe, over the seat. (This place was searched, and the article found.) This was about two months ago. When I got a purse in a crowd, I used to take the money and put the purse into some man's pocket. I've done this 18 or 19 times. It was the best way of getting rid of the purse. J. O'N. lived with another young man in a furnished cellar. They dressed very well, and each kept a woman. They used to have beefsteaks and beer regular to breakfast. I used to go out on Monday and get £2 and £3, *which would satisfy me for two days*, and then I would go again on Wednesday or Thursday, and again on Saturday, and generally got in the week about £20. I was never satisfied with less. O'G. did not do much; he used to be clammed. My brother Edward was very daring. He could pick a woman's pocket as she was running along the street. If he had seen a thing that he fancied, he would say, 'that's mine,' and watch his opportunity till he got it. John had no heart (energy) for thieving. He lived on a woman who kept him.

K. and M'G. were 'guns,'—that is, they taught younger thieves, and screened them when they were practising. K. kept a 'picking-up' woman, that is, one who commits robberies in the street, K. coming up at the right moment to screen or rescue her."

Such is the history of this unfortunate young woman, as recorded by herself, and such the associates to whom she is bound by the closest ties. The husband, her partner in crime, says of her, " Ellen was very clever, and after we were married I did not *do* so much, except to assist Ellen. *I have no fault to find with her.*" We shall shortly see what a home she had: parents not as yet vicious, bringing up their children at school, and sending them early to work; *but thoroughly unprincipled, and self-indulgent, as well as easy towards their children's misdoing.* Her remaining at school, and then in a place of work, does not indicate any thing radically bad in her, and her remorse when she saw the suffering caused by her first misdeed, shows a conscience not as yet seared. But when she had once launched in the career of vice, when she had once the prison brand, and was received on her discharge from the Bridewell with drunken festivities, what could arrest her in her course? Did any imprisonments, whether longer or shorter, check her in the slightest degree? Could she have been stopped by any proceeding but entire separation from her companions in iniquity, and a lengthened detention where she would be subjected to new and healthy influences, and detained for a length of time under reformatory discipline? Having at last felt the happiness of a virtuous course, she would be prepared to begin life anew, as a useful member of society. Some will be sceptical that such would ever be the case. It is indeed possible that it may not be so; but have we not abundant instances of success, which should not only encourage us, but render it *imperative on us as Christians* to make the trial? Others will object to the expense of maintaining an able-bodied girl some two or three years in an asylum. They forget that the public will have to maintain her at any rate; that if she is in a Reformatory School, where she will help to maintain herself by her own work, the expense will probably be from £12 to £15 per annum, and that at the end of a few years she will be a productive labourer in society; but that as she has been living, she has taxed the public for a luxurious maintenance for herself and her husband, some £500 per annum, to finish her career in this country by transportation, a very costly procedure, and one not very certain in its results. The excellent Chaplain thus speaks of her:

"Ellen C. indeed possessed a natural disposition, which, had she been blessed with Christian parents, might have contributed to their and her own credit and happiness. Her narrative throughout betrays a wish to palliate their conduct, and at her interviews with them, since her conviction, she appeared quite forgetful of herself, and only solicitous to assuage their anxiety about her, and to warn her brother Edward from his dangerous course. This determined and skilful girl-thief of 17, who at the latter part of her short run of crime, was not satisfied with less than a weekly booty of £10 or £20, 'trembled very much,' when she made her first successful essay upon the pocket of a young woman, from whom she purloined 18*d*. 'I met,' she says, ' the young woman again in a short time, and she was crying; I heard her say that the money was her mother's. *I cried too*, and would have given her the money back, but I was afraid of being took up.' What an affecting contrast between this girl's character and fate, as they are and as they might have been! And how sad to think that our backward civilization *possesses, as yet, no means for saving from moral destruction, thousands who, like this poor child, possess natural qualities which, by God's blessing, would amply repay the labour of cultivation!"*

The unfortunate young woman whose narrative we have been considering, was not trained to dishonesty by her parents, though indirectly encouraged in it. But the instances are unfortunately very numerous in which little girls are taught to steal by their mothers, before they can have any idea of the sinfulness of the practice. An example of this will be given in the next chapter. Mr. Clay in his twenty-seventh Report, unveils to us what he truly terms the "terrible system which, in effecting its nefarious purposes, uses without compunction or scruple, these poor infants, sacrificing them, body and soul, to mammon in his most hideous form." He first mentions a case which fell under the notice of Mr. T. Wright, of Manchester. While pursuing his benevolent labours among the outcast and friendless in the New Bailey, he came in contact with a little girl who was apprehended for a robbery from the person of a lady, under circumstances which showed *great skill and long practice* in the child, and at the same time, that she was an instrument, an apprentice pickpocket, "working" for concealed employers.

"'This little girl,' says Mr. Wright, 'whilst an inmate of the Salford Gaol, related that *she had been brought from Dublin by two women on purpose to pick pockets*. They dressed the poor child in the character of a little maid, and thus attired, she followed a lady into a silversmith's shop, and succeeded in extracting from her pocket a purse which contained twenty sovereigns! She afterwards followed a lady into the Fishmarket, and again succeeded in extracting this second lady's purse, with which she was making off when the lady discovered her loss. The fishmonger said, no one had been near her but her little maid. She declared she had no little maid with her. The child was overtaken, and placed in charge of a police officer. When searched, she had upon her person the two purses; of the contents of the second I was not informed. She was tried at the following Sessions, and sentenced to six months' imprisonment. I apprized her father a little before her liberation. He came over, and I have not since heard of her. Some time back much crime of this description was committed here by *children, most of whom came from Ireland.*'"

What will a six months' imprisonment do in reforming a child so trained and inured to vice? This is not a solitary instance; from the information given by some of the gang of pickpockets to Mr. Clay, there appears to be an organized system in which young boys and girls bear an important part, for their stature renders them more adapted to reach the outside pockets of ladies which present ready facilities. The master thief, who has become too tall for practice in that line, takes in pupils, by whose gains he is maintained "in style."

THE GIRLS. 101

" These girls," says one, " are natives of Dublin. . . . .
When they came to Manchester, they were quite plain in their
dress, and no person on earth would suspect them. I believe
there is nowhere their equal in being expert at ladies' dress
pockets. When they first came to Manchester they got immense of money in shops and omnibuses. . . . . When
an omnibus leaves, they get into it, and being dressed like any
gentleman's girls, with one of these French baskets in their hands,
they get close beside a lady, and contrive to place their shawl
or mantle over the lady's dress pocket, which shades their
hand. . . . When these two girls and their mothers and
myself was getting a glass of liquor, they told me they was
often sending £20 to their fathers and brothers in Dublin."

What these poor children are to become when
they have served their apprenticeship, is learnt from
the account of female pickpockets, given by one
of the gang to Mr. Clay. It presents a picture of
hardened vice in woman from which we would fain
turn without more than a cursory glance of horror.
But if we would provide a cure we must know as
fully as possible the real nature of the complaint.

". The women now *travelling* look so maidenlified and comely
in their person, that no human being would suspect their
being pickpockets. Their attire is generally of the best, but it
is not so with all. Some of the female *wires* are dressed in the
first style. There are three of them attending the shops
where the most ladies go; one woman acts as servant, while the
wire acts mistress. When they go into one of these shops, as
any other lady might do, they are on the watch to see when
purses are pulled out, and the mistress gets close to the lady
who has shown the purse, wires her of it, and then contrives to
give it to the 'servant,' who goes away, while the mistress
remains in the shop, and if she is clever gets another purse
before leaving it. There are now in Manchester three of the
cleverest lady-wires travelling: one from Birmingham, one

from Leeds, and one from Liverpool. The oldest of these three is about 24, and the youngest about 16. This youngest keeps a young man, who is dressed like any gentleman, with his gold watch, and curb chain attached to it; and she dressed so that any magistrate that saw her would say she never could be anything of the sort, only her speech instantly condemns her. Last summer at Birkenhead and Chester Railway Stations one or two of these lady-like wires attended regularly. They frequent also private sales in town and country. To see them with books in their hands, like other ladies, and giving now and then a bid for an article,—but they never came away with anything *bought* at the sale. They look into the newspapers for intelligence about sales, and also about concerts, which they attend, never going inside, but watching as the people come out. I knew one woman and her man who got more money than any three women travelling. They had their own horse and gig, riding from fair to fair. Not long after coming out of Wakefield, where she had done twelve months, both she and her man got transported, about three years ago at Derby. She stood nearly five feet ten inches high, and her man the same. There is now in Manchester and Liverpool about fifty or sixty of these women wires, one day dressed up in their best, another day quite plain, to escape any information that may have been given." The same informant gave Mr. Clay a list of 103 males, and 44 females whom he *had personally known* since 1838, and who have undergone transportation!

Would a Christian esteem any effort too great to rescue young girls from such a life of crime, before they have become hardened in it? Would society reasonably complain of the cost of any schools of prevention or cure, which should save it from such a tax levied by the dishonest on the honest, and finally from the cost of transportation?

But at present the law renders unavailing the efforts of the benevolent to rescue these poor children

THE GIRLS.

after they have incurred the penalty of the law, by supporting the authority of the parent even when it is exerted only to plunge a child deeper into crime. This subject was referred to in "Ref. Sch." p. 252, and the evidence of Mr. Rushton before the Lords' Committee cited as an illustration. The following extract from the journal of the Chaplain of the Liverpool Gaol will forcibly bear on the subject in reference to female children:

"Jan. 9, 1845.—A day or two ago, a girl 14 years of age, here for the *seventh* time, and who was yesterday discharged after three months' summary conviction, expressed to me a desire to be placed in the workhouse or elsewhere in safety, in order that she might be removed out of the way of bad companions, and be protected from ill treatment and bad example at home. She reports both her parents to be very much addicted to drunkenness, and as being in the frequent habit, when in a state of intoxication, of fighting in a violent and disgraceful manner. Her mother encourages her to commit thefts, generally drinks the proceeds, and has several times deprived her of articles of clothing to be pledged for the same purposes; she professes to make no concealment as to where she disposed of her plunder; to a person, who, if the child is to be believed, seems to carry on a systematic trade with young thieves, having regular prices for the various articles. In order to obtain the parents' acquiescence in any arrangements I might be able to make for the child's welfare, I called at the residence, and have seldom seen a more wretched picture of misery; not many shillings' worth of furniture in the house; no bedding, but a little loose straw in the corner of the room, covered with an old rug, and everything seemed to corroborate the child's statement. I was recognised by a little boy who had been three months in the prison, and when I made known my errand, the mother expressed a willingness to concur in anything I might recommend, and I afterwards called upon Mr. —

at the parish office, who promised to endeavour to provide for the child. Yesterday morning, however, the mother called at the gate, and insisted upon taking the child home, notwithstanding all remonstrances; being half intoxicated at the time, the governor refused to give up the child to any one but the father, who was sent for; he too had been drinking, but appeared capable of taking care of the girl, who was accordingly given up."

A similar instance is found in the public records of another town. In the *Newcastle Chronicle*, Aug. 9, 1852, the following passage occurs in an article on Juvenile Criminals, signed Daniel Liddell.

"Every town produces instances of carelessness and cruelty on the part of parents. A month or two ago, a girl, 12 years of age, belonging to this town, became an inmate of a gaol in a different part of the country, and the ladies who visit the gaol considering her to be destitute, and one who might be reclaimed, made arrangements for her advantage upon her release from confinement. The mother, shortly after this, visited her daughter, for whom she seemed previously to care nothing, and obtained money from the ladies to bring her back to this place. It was reported that she remained for some time in that place, and was seen drunk in the streets, and the Chaplain of the gaol applied to me for information as to her character and habits. I visited her and found that she was in receipt of parish relief, and also obtained something considerable from the bounty of the charitable who gave without proper inquiry. I recommended that the mother should not be allowed to hold intercourse with her child if it could possibly be prevented. The law does not permit the benevolent to take the charge of neglected children against the consent of the worthless parents, but this law should be evaded."

We shall now proceed to inquire whether the present system of treatment of juvenile offenders is more or less injurious to the girls than to the boys, prejudicial and inefficacious as we have shown it to be to children in general.

The following is extracted from the Report of the Liverpool Borough Gaol, in 1846:

> "Two general facts observed in the prosecution of the inquiry into the condition of the families of the prisoners, may be thought deserving of notice. *First*,—that whilst it was found that several boys who had been in prison, had obtained, and were following honest employments, *there appeared no instance of a girl who had commenced a criminal course having become reformed.*
>
> "*Second.*—That the girls in the first instance, before they had become thoroughly identified with the criminal classes, had generally been addicted to drink; whilst among the boys there were only one or two instances of that propensity before or subsequent to the commencement of their criminal courses."

We shall shortly see how little effect is produced on the woman, as well as the girl, by imprisonment, when once that deadly habit has been formed.

"Very many," says Dr. Harty, physician to the prisons in Dublin, to the Lords' Committee in 1847, "*especially females, have been confined more than* 100 *times,* and yet some magistrates will give them five, seven, or ten days at the utmost; they come in wearied, and go out refreshed to their work."

A still more conclusive proof of the injurious effect produced by imprisonment on females, is afforded by the following table, derived from the "Thirteenth Report of the General Board of Directors of the Prisons in Scotland."

PREVIOUS IMPRISONMENT of PRISONERS in the Prisons of Scotland, from July 1, 1850, to June 30, 1851.

	Once before.		Twice.		Three times.		Four times.		Five times.	
	M.	F.	M.	F.	M.	F.	M.	F.	M.	F.
Edinburgh Prisons....	506	495	254	290	153	181	102	124	56	86
Glasgow Prisons	384	281	192	171	116	131	95	95	70	63
Total of all the Prisons in Scotland	2,040	1,289	946	716	519	495	367	341	226	256

	Six times and under Ten.		Ten times & under Twenty.		Twenty times & under Fifty.		Fifty times and upwards	
	M.	F.	M.	F.	M.	F.	M.	F.
Edinburgh Prisons.................	119	256	71	266	27	191	8	15
Glasgow Prisons	98	93	27	44	4	22	..	..
Total of all the Prisons in Scotland..	387	571	164	526	40	353	8	15

It thus appears that while the total number of persons committed to the prisons of Scotland during that period, was 13,562 males, and 8,288 females, the number of previous commitments of the females nearly equalled that of the males; and that the number of women who became thoroughly hardened after repeated imprisonments, was more than four times that of men. This painful fact respecting the recommitment of female prisoners was adverted to in " Reformatory Schools," p. 315; and it was also there shown from a paper handed to the Lords' Committee, in 1847, that the tendency of girls to crime increases with their age, under the existing system, more rapidly even than that of the boys.

The following more recent data, derived from the Report above quoted, corroborates the same fact.

Ages of Criminal Prisoners confined in Prisons in Scotland from July 1, 1850, to June 30, 1851.

	Under 16.		16 and under 18.		18 and under 21.		21 and under 50.		50 and above.		Total.	
	M.	F.	M.	F.	M.	F.	M.	F.	M.	F.	M.	F.
Edinburgh Prison	234	171	239	244	436	529	1,601	1,818	177	150	2,687	2,912
Glasgow Prison....	243	106	191	135	431	274	1,301	966	107	114	2,273	1,595
Total of Prisons in Scotland........	1,309	496	929	573	2,128	1,252	8,397	5,392	799	575	13,562	8,288

Punishments of Prisoners.

	Under 16.		Total.	
	M.	F.	M.	F.
Edinburgh Prison	62	24	202	130
Glasgow Prison	182	32	688	252
Total of Prisons in Scotland	272	114	1,688	556

We here see that girls under 16, convicted of crime, are little more than one-third of the number of boys, while the proportion of female convicts gradually increases with age, until the whole number amounts to five-eighths that of males. Another result, important to our present subject, is derivable from the same Table. The number of girls under 16 subjected to punishment was nearly half that of boys, rather a high proportion, but the whole number of females punished was little more than one-third, showing that while girls are more refractory under imprisonment than boys, a habit of passive obedience is afterwards induced, which however does not in any way lead to reformation. A single instance from the records of the Bristol police *(vide Bristol Mercury)* illustrates this, and the effect of imprisonment on girls. In the *Mercury* of Feb. 14, 1852, we find the following paragraph:

"Monday.—An old offender, named Caroline Davis, was brought up, charged with being disorderly on Tower Hill. *The prisoner was only liberated from gaol on Saturday last.* She expressed contrition for her present offence, and promised amendment for the future. *The magistrates said that for once they would take her word, and discharged her.*"

We know not how long she kept her promise, but find her charged with a similar offence on Aug. 7th, when she was fined 5s. or 10 days' imprisonment. Nevertheless on the 14th of the same month we find

"Caroline Davis, a poor unfortunate girl, *who spends seven-eighths* of her time in Bridewell, was again sent back to her quarters for a month, for assaulting P. C. 26. On hearing her sentence she became exceedingly violent, and was obliged to be removed on a stretcher."

Of how little avail this was, the next notice will show.

"Sept. 17.—Caroline Davis, a poor unfortunate creature, who spends her time between the station-house and the Bridewell, was committed to the latter place for one week for her old offence of being drunk and disorderly. *Whilst the prisoner is in gaol she behaves in a most exemplary manner;* but no sooner is she liberated than she again takes to the bottle, gets drunk, and annoys the public with her filthy and disgusting language." Again in

October she was brought up, and remanded, " being in an unfit state to be brought before the bench." In the following month having been brought again before the magistrates for similar offences, they consign her to a medical man, to have her sanity investigated. This poor young woman has been 61 times in Bridewell; she began her criminal career at 13, and has been known to attempt suicide.

What a mockery of justice is this, for a bench of magistrates to be constantly inflicting a punishment which is thus publicly stated to produce no impression! What means would have been too costly to have rescued this poor creature from such utter degradation before she was yet so hardened; to have placed her early under a firm, but kind reformatory discipline which surely might have had its effect in childhood, since even now she yields to its influence? What would have been the benefit to society of being saved from hearing her low and debasing language; of beholding the revolting spectacle of a woman transformed into a brute?

This is by no means a solitary case, but a very common one, as all governors and chaplains of gaols in large towns can testify. The following is the opinion of the Rev. D. Baxter, Chaplain of the East Prison, Aberdeen:

" To send a little girl of 9, 10, or 12 years of age to prison for ten, thirty, or even sixty days, is of no avail, and, in the nature of things, can never promote the reformation of the offender, a statement illustrated and confirmed by sad experience. By and bye, they become the victims of prostitution, and considering the parentage, the habits, the degrading associations and pursuits of female prisoners, it is scarcely matter of surprise to find them unable, however willing, while in prison they profess themselves to be, to abandon their sinful course. For, however painful and humiliating the observation, it is too true, that *when once young girls have been seduced and degraded, they are more difficult to rescue than boys.* Once in prison, many of them are continually going and coming. Indeed, to them the prison is a kind of necessary and wholesome retreat, in which, during ten, twenty, or thirty days, they get themselves physically purified, and their enfeebled powers renovated, and then return like the dog to his vomit, or the sow that was washed to her wallowing in the mire."

The Chaplain then mentions a number of instances of young women who had been not only in that prison, but for a long period in the strict seclusion of the Perth Prison, who returned 15, 16, even 28, and 29 times. He speaks of most of them as having been "early victims of prostitution," and expresses his conviction that if at the commencement of their career they had been placed for a long period "under judicious religious, moral, and industrial training," and afterwards cared for, they might have become chaste, useful, and respectable members of society. "Thus," he concludes, "what an amount of evil, inflicted on the several communities to which they belong, would have been prevented. And while it would be both imprudent and cruel in the highest degree to relinquish or diminish our efforts for the reclamation of these unfortunate girls, it would be much more effective, and attended with less expense, to endeavour to prevent persons falling into this fearful gulf of misery, than, after they have fallen to try to lift them out of it."

THE GIRLS.

There is indeed so strong an opinion prevailing of the uselessness and injury to girls of imprisonment, both as entailing certain loss of character, and completely hardening the girl, that crime is often left unpunished, from an unwillingness in the sufferer to prosecute. The following is an instance:

"Y. Z. is a girl of 14. Her parents are poor working people maintaining a good character, and having brought up all their children to attend their parish Sunday School regularly. They have had a good character from their teachers, and no suspicion of dishonesty has rested on the family. This girl got work in March, 1852, with a copper-plate printer; her mother supposed her still at work, until a few weeks ago, when she made excuses time after time for not bringing home her wages. On inquiry it appeared that she had left her place, though coming home at the usual times to her meals, as if at work. She had also been associating with two boys and a girl, of very low character, though all at work, and had been spending her Sundays with them unless forcibly kept at home by her parents. Last week her former master, the engraver, having discovered losses, came to the house to inquire whether she had seen any one lurking on his premises, he had no suspicion of her. On investigation it was proved that 'a marine store' dealer had been buying plates of her which she had been bringing home from time to time, having been allowed free access to the premises after she had ceased to work there. These plates she sold for $1\frac{1}{4}d.$ each, and being the property of various gentlemen, and the work on them being valuable, it will cost from 18s. to 27s. to replace each of them. None can be recovered, *all having been melted.* The distress of the parents and family on this discovery cannot be described. What is the master to do? He feels certain that to prosecute the girl will be her ruin; he knows that it will also be the ruin of an honest labouring family, who will be at once sunk in the eyes of society and lose their own self-respect by a public prosecution;—besides, such a step would involve him in great expense, without replacing his loss. He went to the father and told him that he did not want to prosecute her, but to try to get her placed in security from further evil. But some of his customers are very angry at a loss which may prove injurious to themselves, and threaten him with consequences if he does not prosecute. The girl had run away on the first alarm, and is returned to her home frightened, penniless, and seemingly penitent. Is the father to give her up to an unwilling prosecutor? Would any institution receive a girl, even if not prosecuted, under such circumstances? I confess that I advised the father last night to send her off by the first train this morning to a relation at a distance, with a full disclosure of the circumstances, and contributed towards the expense. Did I do wrong in helping to frustrate 'the ends of justice' and thus rescuing a whole family from certain ruin, as well as a girl from certain infamy? And yet there ought to be *security* that she will not again thus injure society, and will have an opportunity for reformation. The parents can neither *feel* or *give* that security if she is at home."

Such is the testimony of the girl's teacher. Had there been a Reformatory School to which she could have been committed, her crime would not have gone unpunished, nor would she have been thrown again on society in the hardened state in which she too probably still was. In this case it appears that the girl's parents held a respectable character, but had been unable to keep her from evil. The following touching letter from an aged woman to the Gaol Schoolmistress at Liverpool respecting her granddaughter, is another striking instance of the absolute necessity of such institutions as we are advocating, as the only means of rescuing a young creature from a certain life of crime.

" Madam,—I feel obliged to you for interesting yourself about such a bad girl. She told you part of the truth; she ran away on Easter Monday, pawned some of her clothes, went to —— and staid about a fortnight." Then follow details of her going to various shops and purchasing various articles in her grandmother's name;—this was discovered; she was taken at the advice of a friend to the "lock-up," but released on her promising to do so no more. " She was very humble and wept: I took her home; it was Friday, and on the Monday she went off again, and was met by a friend of mine with two large bundles. . . . She has robbed us of pounds in money; silver did not do when she could get gold; dresses have been missing, but we could not tell where they went. Is there any place for such? She is not fit to be near a house. My dear daughter died May, 1843, leaving five children, and begged we would take the two girls, the two boys were out apprenticed; Mr. —— died two years after her; he was an attorney. It would have broken my dear daughter's heart if she had been living. Can you instruct me what to do in this case? My husband knows nothing about such things; he is in his 74th year, and I myself have not been well this four years. Will you excuse me for writing to you in this way; you see I have been writing to you as if you were an old friend, and if you ever come to ——, please give me a call; summer will be here soon, and it is a pleasant sail. What is the custom when they are discharged out of gaol? Would you have the goodness to write me and tell me? I should like to know if she is sorry for what she has done, and if she is humble, and how she conducts herself. I shall write to her grandpapa, but *he cares little except for drink, and he has £200 a-year in money coming in. The aunt is independent also.* If I am obliged to have that girl, she will soon teach my other granddaughter; she is a very nice girl; she might be nothing akin to Mary Ellen.

" I am yours with respect, &c."

Surely in such a case as this, the natural guardian of the child should have been compelled to furnish the cost of her support, and those around her should have been protected from her injurious influence and conduct, by her being placed in a Reformatory School.

But, it will be urged by some that if girls do become so degraded in character, after they have once fallen into vice, they cannot be reclaimed.

Their condition is not hopeless, even when they have fallen into deeper sins against God's laws than simple theft. The following is from the Master's records of a Ragged School, at Ipswich:

"A. E. M., aged 14 years. Her father and mother lived in adultery till the last three months, when her mother died. Her father told her he did not want her at home. She went to service, got acquainted with bad companions; carried on a system of private prostitution; robbed her master, and was sent to the Borough Gaol, where I found her. This girl, after remaining in the Institution three months, was restored to her father, a reformed character, who received her kindly, and said she should not want for anything so long as she did what was right. She has since obtained a situation, and is doing well. She has often taken tea with us since she left; this is a privilege, and she thinks it a very great one too. We always promise the inmates when they leave, if they do well, they shall come and take tea with us, as a friend; but if they do wrong, not to come nigh us—and by so doing we judge of their conduct.

"Ann M., aged 18 years. Mother died when she was only five days old. Never knew her father; she was brought up by her grandmother, who died when she was 12 years old, when she was left without friends or home; from this time she has been living on her prostitution. During the last six years she has sometimes slept in lodging-houses, at other times in stables, pig-sties, sand-holes. When recommended to the Institution from the Ragged School, she was one heap of rags and disease. But through the attention there received, she was restored to health, and having *redeemed her character, she left the Institution for service*, March 15th, 1852."

The Chaplain of the Aberdeen Gaol gives the

following encouraging statement respecting the results, on delinquent females, of other treatment than that of prison discipline :

"Satisfactory reports have been received respecting the females sent to the Institutions in Edinburgh. Several of them are in the House of Refuge in this city. One of them especially, E. M., who was liberated in January, after undergoing an imprisonment of sixty days, for the first time, is giving the highest satisfaction. She is well educated; had been in excellent situations as ladies' maid, but had the misfortune to become the victim of intemperance. If she abstains from drink there is no fear of her. In former reports I have noticed particularly the case of a young woman, who had been sixteen times in prison, and liberated in May, 1850, as a remarkable instance of female reformation. When, after much intercourse with her, I felt and expressed a hope of her being under salutary impressions of divine truth; my predecessor in office kindly warned me not to be too sanguine in my expectations, as, in his opinion, she would be in prison again in a fortnight, or the course of six weeks at most, and I confess that I felt no small anxiety concerning her. A. D., however, has now been almost two years out of prison; and still she may relapse. If she do, I shall be very sorry for it. But in the meantime, I have to state that I have again received from her another letter, of date the 29th of March, from the place of her nativity, thirty miles distant from Aberdeen, 'with thanks and best wishes for my welfare,' accompanied with a packet, and pre-paid, the contents of which greatly astonished and gratified me—'three hundred excellent tracts;' requesting me 'to distribute them among the poor prisoners.' Is it too much to hope that this young female, noted as one of the most malicious and untameable of her kind, is now sitting at the feet of Jesus, 'clothed and in her right mind?'"

What should be the principles and plans adopted in schools intended for the reformation of delinquent children, will be considered in a future chapter. If a variation from the general system were needed in the case of the girls, it would be to make especial efforts to introduce them as completely as possible to what, in a well-ordered family, would be common domestic duties, to awaken in them healthy affections, and to call out their intellectual powers. Under such judicious training, experience shows that when once the girl's will is controlled and engaged to work with her instructor, progress is even more rapid than with the boys, and that even in a Free Day or Ragged School, if the girls can be detained under good management, they much more quickly than the boys exhibit a change of demeanour. But it is too often forgotten that low tastes and desires cannot be rooted out except by the introduction of more agreeable ones; that the intellectual powers cannot be cultivated in those who have no sense of duty, unless the doing so is made pleasant; that corrupt affections cannot be expelled except by the awakening of pure ones; that if it is necessary in the case of the boys to employ the healing influence of nature and of attractive labour as means of reformation, it is still more needful with the girls. And it is from this forgetfulness that the conductors of Penitentiaries for erring females have so often to lament failures; such institutions are too much like gaols, where the unfortunate young women are confined within walls, forced to occupations which present no attractions to them, secluded from intercourse with those who might lure them back to the ways of virtue, or, at any rate, make them feel that they are cared for by those who love virtue. It is from such forgetfulness that in an admirably managed Workhouse School, where the boys, employed in agricultural labour, were happy, active, and intelligent, the girls were listless and dull; they were confined to mere household work, without the pleasing variety and nameless charms which lighten the duties of a true family, and had had little to call them out, or to give them the needful stimulus. But let schools be provided for delinquent girls, with as much care to adapt them to the female character, and to supply what has been hitherto neglected, as has been done for the boys, and a great blessing will be conferred on society.

The importance of this subject requires that a volume, rather than a chapter, should be devoted to it; but space forbids a further considerations of it here. May the women of England, who feel the blessing of the early nurture they have received, look with an eye of the tenderest compassion on these outcast little ones, and each one do what in her lies for their rescue!

CHAPTER IV.

THE PARENTS.

We have hitherto been considering the young, both boys and girls; we have seen them in a condition in which we could hardly recognise any remaining trace of that winning loveliness, that confiding obedience, that innocent gaiety, which are the charms of childhood; we have beheld them prematurely old in vice when scarcely beyond infancy, and have shuddered if we contrasted them with our own young children, bright with life's opening joys, budding with beautiful promise, the tender care of their parents. We have had glimpses of the fathers and of the mothers of these wretched young creatures, and have felt that the life they were leading was inevitable, if the authors of their being were so corrupt to the very core. The actual condition of the *parents* of those children who form the criminal class, it is now our purpose to investigate.

It would be very unjust to bring a general and sweeping accusation against all those parents whose children exhibit vicious propensities injurious to society. We have already stated that such tendencies are confined to no class, and it is but too well known that many pious parents have had unworthy children; but when these criminal dispositions are early manifested in families in the higher ranks of society, or of such as are living in obedience to the laws of God and man, regard to public opinion, if not the higher motive of parental duty, leads to a restraint and discipline of the child which prevent him from being exposed to the interference of society for its own protection. In the classes we are now considering, even well-intentioned parents are frequently so entirely ignorant of the right way of training ill-disposed children, and are besides so deficient in moral power and self-control, or in the means of exercising due restraint, that they are absolutely unable to correct in their children what they nevertheless deeply lament. The condition of these parents is generally the consequence of early deficient education; and here the aid of the Christian friend will be most gratefully accepted, and the parent will gladly make any possible sacrifice to enable his child to be placed where that will be done for him which he is unable to do.

It is not of such parents as these that we shall at present speak, but of those who are, either directly by their participation in the crime, or indirectly by their vicious characters, the cause of their children's delinquency. For some description of the character and condition of these we must again listen to voices from the prison.

Those who are known as "professional thieves" in towns, are in many ways very different from those who infest the rural districts. The following statement respecting them was made to Mr. Clay by a man of very superior education and talents, then lying under sentence of 10 years' transportation. Mr. Clay thus speaks of the narrator:

"E. R. seems to have observed minutely, almost philosophically, the character and circumstances he has chosen to deal with; and,—drunkard, gambler, and housebreaker, as he has been,—to offer, in his way, the example of a character in which much intelligence and resolution are united to the smallest amount of moral sense. The man has read, and remembers his reading. His handwriting is superior, and his spelling almost faultless. I have had it in my power to test the truth of some of his statements, and have reason to believe that his relation is trustworthy throughout, though embracing but a small part of the whole truth."

E. R. thus speaks:

"Respecting men of my stamp, (*i. e.* professional thieves,) who have received any education, . . I am enabled not only to form an opinion, but to guarantee the truth of what observations I may be induced to make, grounded on personal, practical experience. I cannot say that I am acquainted with more than twelve or fifteen persons who have received an education that might be classed as respectable; and I am certain that is nearly all, as I am intimately acquainted with the class, both in the metropolis and in the provinces. Most of these men attribute their dereliction from the path of rectitude to intemperance; some to vanity; others to gaming, and some few say, women are the cause. *I only knew one instance of actual distress.*" He details this case, and mentions another, as a contrast, the son of a timber-merchant, "who had received a superior education, and I cannot assign any reason for his adoption of that course of life which ultimately banished him from his native land. He was a profligate drunkard, and has said to me, '*I dare not be sober; I should go mad.*'" He belonged to the first class mentioned by E. R., "well organized housebreakers; not those who commit burglaries at random, or use violence, but a class who systematically arrange their proceedings, and by means of well-contrived instruments effect their purpose. These men never take any thing but money, plate, jewellery, or something very valuable. Another class are those who have received a tolerable education, as far as reading, writing, and arithmethic. Men who *have been carefully brought up by respectable parents, and who have been apprenticed to some trade.* These are more numerous than the former class, but, like them, are averse to speaking about their earlier life; never acknowledging their birthplace, name, friends, &c.; their motive being to screen their relations from shame and disgrace. These men form the most active members of any gang requiring mechanical ingenuity; and are very seldom what is termed out of luck; as they do not squander their money in thoughtlessness, gambling, or flash clothes, like those I shall now mention, (a third class,) who are the very dregs of society, and are about eighty per cent. of all professional thieves. This class consists of the refuse of London, Manchester, Birmingham, &c., with a very small number from the agricultural districts. Five-eighths of these are the lower description of Irish, though principally born in England. *The whole of this class, with few exceptions, have been nurtured in crime from their cradle. Dirty, filthy, ragged, hungered, and neglected by their parents, they commence a petty career of pilfering;* and from instruction imparted by others, in gaols, and places of common resort. Those who have escaped the hulks, have become cunning and practised thieves; especially such as have followed picking pockets, as their mode of living; and these are eight out of every ten."

Such is the testimony of one who speaks from personal knowledge respecting a large class of persons, who, having had from their own parents a training to vice, are leaving a similar legacy to their children. If the information here given is correct, four-fifths of those who form the convict class have been so nurtured in degradation and vice, that unless when young snatched from such an education to evil, they must inevitably fall into it. It does not necessarily follow that the parents are convicted criminals or ostensibly paupers, but it is evident that they are so completely deficient in moral training, and devoid of any means of gaining an honest livelihood, that the children must inevitably fall into vice or pauperism, two conditions not far removed from each other. Such a class of persons has existed from time immemorial, and no means hitherto adopted have proved efficacious in checking their increase, or diminishing their injurious influence. With them society has been carrying on an unsuccessful warfare some three hundred years at least, for in the Citizens' Memorial to Edward VI. it is stated that "it is evident to all men that beggary and thieving do abound;" and the First Ordinances of Bridewell describe them in 1557, as persons "who never yield themselves to any good exercise, but continually travail in idleness, training such youth as come to his or their custody to the same wickedness of life." Against such persons the most severe legislative measures have been passed in vain; neither threats nor inducements have availed to induce them to change this mode of life. They are not peculiar to our own country; Manzoni, in his celebrated work, "I Promessi Sposi," most graphically portrays these "vagabonds" who, from the different circumstances of the two countries, were not those addicted to "beggary," an occupation monopolized by a different class, or to "thieving," too quiet a calling, but were bravos, a word sufficiently indicating their mode of life. It was not for want of vigorous measures that these Italian vagabonds were not repressed; most severe edicts were issued against them in consequence of the "intolerable misery" which they caused; the galleys were threatened to the refractory, and officials had "the most strangely ample and indefinite power of executing the order;" yet they "lived as they had lived before, their customs wholly unchanged." All were defined to be "bravos and vagabonds, who, whether foreigners or natives, have no occupation, or having it do not employ themselves in it," attaching themselves to some cavalier "to render them aid and service," professedly, one would suppose, a very lawful calling; and for the reputation alone of being a bravo, on the testimony of two witnesses, they were to be sent to the galleys for three years. Yet these people continued to flourish with a "rigogliosa vitalità," an obstinate vitality, and "murder, homicide, robbery, and crimes of every kind," were on the increase notwithstanding the most vigorous resolutions of the most determined governors, "wholly to exterminate a plant so pernicious."

The "vagabonds" in our own country do not wear about them any outward and visible sign, striking to the common observer, which like the "ciuffo" and the armed bearing of the Italian sufficiently indicate his mode of life; but on that very account they are perhaps more insidiously dangerous, differing only in the manner of the evil they do to society, not in the degree. Nor has our legislature taken any more effectual mode of restraining or of extirpating them than was adopted by the rulers of Italy. " Rogues and vagabonds," still baffle the most vigilant and energetic magistrates, who can only award them as a punishment a period of repose and cleansing in a gaol, to go forth renovated and refreshed for their lawless work. These are the PARENTS of a new race, and every generation, *if the evil is not arrested*, must become more hardened and experienced in vice than the former one. We shall better comprehend how little hope there is for the children of such persons, when we have a clearer insight into their condition.

In our own day the "vagabonds" assume the name of "travellers," and cloak their real purposes under the pretence of carrying on some low trade, in the exercise of which they wander about the country without any settled home. The particulars of their habits and mode of life obtained by Mr. Clay from the members of the gang above alluded to, as being under his care, and also from E. R., convey most vividly the true nature of the class.

"The gipseys, romaneys, half-breeds, and travellers," says Mr. Clay, " so far as my informants are personally cognizant of the facts, roam chiefly over the counties of Oxford, Berks,

Surrey, Sussex, Hants, Kent, Dorset, Devon, Cornwall, Wilts, Somerset, Hereford, and some of the adjoining Welsh counties. In Dorset, says one, they are almost as common as labourers. Their occupations, sometimes real, more frequently pretended, are hawking, tinkering, knife-grinding; basket, mat, clothes-peg, and broom-making; umbrella mending; fiddling and fortune telling. They live in ' camps.' Some have house-waggons and carts; sometimes they lie in outbuildings. A few of them, especially those who come nearer the true gipsey, deal in horses. The real means of support of the great majority of them are derived from imposture, trespass, theft; robbery from fields and from barns; stealing fowls, sheep, and horses, to say nothing of housebreaking and burglary. Their impostures are generally practised upon ignorant and silly domestics, who, besides being cajoled out of their own property, become unconsciously or willingly, instrumental to their effecting more serious robberies from their masters and mistresses. They entice young men and women too, to go off with them; and often get them transported. Two of these very convicts, H. and G., had themselves been ' 'ticed off.' H. lived with them for a considerable time, learning their manners, and acquiring their habits. . . . . He speaks of what is no doubt generally suspected, if not generally known, namely that these thief-vagrants move through the country, carrying rushes, and pretending to be chairmenders, though they have never mended a chair in all their lives, or on pretence of hawking small articles at the farmhouses, carefully noting what may be pilfered, and returning at night to profit by the observation; sheepstealing is very common among them. . . . . ' If there were not so many gipseys, travellers, and fortune-tellers,' says H., ' there would not be so many robberies. They get the servants, both men and women, to rob their masters. They do not frighten them to do it, but entice them. They are very selfish and greedy. They have tried to make me get my father's potatoes; and they often wanted me to tell them where my sister lived; and at last I told them. She lived where there was only two or three ladies, and it was to be done on the Tuesday night after this job we was taken up for. Many of them are guilty of assaults when they are in company; but single they are cowards. In companies they will carry sticks with lead or iron in the end. They are barbarous! very barbarous!!'" .... All Mr. Clay's informants refer to the dirty and filthy habits of this race. H., on whom these things made a more vivid impression from having been brought up respectably, states that when he first went among them he was in so filthy a condition that he actually changed clothes with a scarecrow which he saw in a field. Their appetites are equally disgusting, providing themselves with animal food by craftily causing the death of sheep, pigs, &c., and begging them from the unsuspecting farmer. A taste for snails as an article of food is probably derived from their Transylvanian relatives. "Though these remarks apply in general to travellers, half-breeds, and pure gipseys, yet," says Mr. Clay, "when a distinction has been made between them, the assertion is alike in all the narratives, that '*half-breeds*' and travellers are much more profligate and dangerous than the true gipseys."

This assertion is suggestive of serious reflections. The gipseys themselves are thus described by the shrewd and intelligent convict, E. R., who, during his vagrant life, had frequent connection with them.

"Gipseys, romaneys, didycoys, 'our people,' as they call themselves, are certainly a distinct class, both in manners and customs, and notwithstanding the favourable light in which they have been placed by Bulwer, James, Ainsworth and others, I must assert that all trace of their manly bearing, their disinterested generosity, &c., has disappeared; and in justice I must also add, so has every trace of bloodthirsty vengefulness. I have heard several gipsey songs, and one called the 'Gipseys' Tent,' in which a very glowing picture of the poor romaney's life is given. If the author had passed one night with me in one of those tents upon the Forest of Dean, at a 'didycoy's switching,' (gipsey wedding,) he would have seen enough to cure him of his gipsey romance, and also to induce him to buy up all unsold copies of his song. Many of these people profess to be Roman Catholics. I am, however, convinced that very

THE PARENTS.

few possess the slightest knowledge of the doctrines of Christianity. I never knew but one gipsey that could read, and he was a returned convict, and had been taught whilst a prisoner. I have been assured by them that they were formerly ruled by kings of their own race, and I have seen two persons who claimed that distinction." He here mentions several families of gipseys, in one of which the women were nearly all of them married legally to young men unconnected with the gipseys, until admitted into the tribe by marriage. "There are many reports," he continues, "respecting the gipseys' indifference to the quality of their food. I am aware that they eat animals that have been drowned, smothered, strangled, &c." He then mentions the manner in which animals are destroyed, and their bodies obtained from the farmer, and adds, "I once saw a young horse killed at a steeple-chase, and after it was skinned, I saw a party of gipseys cut up the carcase and remove it to their carts, ostensibly for their dogs, but I knew to the contrary. I do not for a moment doubt but that I have often eaten horse beef among them. . . . . Both genuine romaneys and the mixed breed are the most selfish, brutish, ignorant, and grossly sensual people I ever met with. They are overbearing, tyrannical, and cruel, when opportunities offer, and on the other hand, when in adversity, they are fawning, cringing, deceitful, and mean. In persons of the lowest grade of society, there are some redeeming qualities; but the gipsey is destitute of all. I have seen them compel their women to kneel to them and kiss their feet!"

No wonder is it that from such a race, and their "more dangerous and profligate" allies, rise men who, at an early age, are prepared for every crime. The seven desperate Uckfield burglars, mentioned by Mr. Clay, were all between the ages of 18 and 34; and one of them, aged only 25, in his detailed statement, enumerates 24 cases of burglary he had committed, besides one case of sacrilege. All of these men, with the exception of one, who had never known any other existence than that of a gipsey or traveller, declare, with more or less earnestness, after their consciences have been somewhat enlightened by their solitary confinement, "*that it would be a good thing for the country if all 'camping' was done away with.* It would be a good thing to the poor people, as well as to the gentlefolks and farmers." Whether the "putting down camping" would eradicate the evil is more than questionable, even if it *could* be done. The attempt would be useless while they would have such compensating resources as E. R. describes, from his own personal knowledge, to exist in Herefordshire. This is a very criminal county, which will not be wondered at after the perusal of the following:

"I have had many opportunities of observing the state of Hereford, having travelled throughout the county in 1844 and 1845 with a bazaar, and also on other business. I believe that the majority of criminals are vagrants and tramps, who infest the country in the summer and autumn, under pretence of hop-picking, cider-making, &c. I have passed scores of them on the same day between Leominster and Weobly. Their mode of existing is this: following each other in twos and threes, from village to village, and farm to farm—they obtain some food, and are never refused cider. Thus they travel through the country, sleeping in outhouses and barns. *The labour test keeps them from the casual ward of the Unions*, and in the winter they flock in droves to Merthyr Tydvil, Blenavon, Dowlais, and other iron works in the adjoining county of Monmouth, and in South Wales, where they beg or steal in the day time, and sleep at night in the cabins and about the furnaces. In Herefordshire, low cider houses, where beer is also sold, abound. In the city much better order is maintained; vagrants are apprehended, or sent out of the liberties; *but several gentlemen in various parts of the county, hold out, as it were, a premium to vagrants, by allowing every one who calls for it, bread, cheese, and cider.* Amongst these are . . . . This I have ascertained from parties who have frequented these places, and with whom I have conversed while journeying from town to town. In fact, I was at Sir —— ——'s about a horse we had purchased from his steward; and that gentleman (the steward) told my partner that he has known upwards of 100 tramps to call for the relief in one day. We saw then about a dozen waiting. These are the parties who form the bulk of criminals in Herefordshire, and will continue *to do so under the present system.* . . I saw one morning at a place called Pembridge, upwards of 20 men, women and children turn out of a barn where they had spent the night, and pass on to their different stations of begging and plunder: not even following the example of the brutes, by giving themselves a good shake."

It is probable that even the existence of such a class of persons is unknown to the larger portion of the community, still less the extreme degradation of their mode of life, and the utter hopelessness of attempting to diminish their numbers, or to improve their condition, by any external appliances or treatment, whether coercive or eleemosynary. The only means of rescuing the children from an education which, probably in each generation, will leave a more permanent impression in adult age, *will be by compulsorily subjecting them to a religious, moral, and industrial training.* The advantage and efficacy of such a course is strikingly shown in the Aberdeen experiment, some account of which was given in "Reformatory Schools," Chapter iv., and which is described in detail in Mr. Thompson's "Social Evils, their Causes and Cure."

Another aspect of vagabondism is more familiar to us, and though perhaps less revolting to the inexperienced observer, is not less productive of juvenile crime. This is exhibited in cities among a class who, like those in the country, generally have some professed calling, though this, by no means, supports the family. A domestic missionary in Bristol, the Rev. J. Shearman, describes, in his report, individuals of this class as, " in general, born in vagabondism, trained in vagabondism, and, in after life, becoming the parents of a vagabond family. Very commonly at the end of life they die either paupers or convicts. I have," he continues, " observed the life of this order sufficiently to warrant me in saying that the following is too true a sketch."

"Parentage commences early in life, often clandestinely. An infant is born; the bed upon the floor, and made up of straw gathered from many places, with cloths of several forms and colours. I have seen a mother with a black eye before her child was a month old. In due time the child learns to talk, and takes lessons in swearing and obscene phraseology. I have heard of the unmarried father placing his child between his knees, and amusing himself by teaching its little tongue to swear at its own unmarried mother—every effort of the little thing being laughingly applauded! The child is a pauper, sixpence a week and a loaf being its allowance. The child gets big enough to go to school. It has conceived the idea that it is a place where confinement and whipping are practised. It refuses to go. The father says, 'it shan't go then!' In some cases the father does consign it to the Ragged School,

THE PARENTS.

but when he has done so, he generally troubles himself no further about it. The child runs about the streets in rags, its head unacquainted with combing, its skin seldom washed, and its 'young idea' about right and wrong very vague. The child (boy or girl) arrives at the age when parish pay ceases. It must, therefore, try to get 'summat.' The character and living of both parent and child are barriers to its employment for respectable work. If a boy, he is sent forth with hearthstone, matches, or a 'cadging' bag. If with the last, he is expected to investigate and 'overhaul' every heap of cinders or rubbish that seems likely to yield anything, from an old shoe-string to a sixpence, or a silver-spoon. If the child is a female, and not wanted to stay with the younger ones, she ventures into the world with matches, or pins, or blacking, or firewood. Growing upwards to adult age, the boy or girl becomes more and more irregular, unmanageable and profane. The boy-man smokes and drinks. From being the pet he has become the terror of his parents. Will not work regularly. Defies his father, and sometimes beats his mother to make her find him 'bacco' money. The grown-up girl sells wood, or gets work at a factory, or seeks the way of infamy—often with the mother's knowledge. The eldest son gets a female companion, and proclaims her to be 'his wife;' very shortly after he gives her to understand that she must not only maintain herself, but him in addition. In some cases the 'wife' reverses the idea. The grown-up daughter gives an addition to the household. Passing an entry in E. Street, I was shocked by an outburst of screeching abuse. I entered the house from which the noise came, and found two women, one on each side the fire, and each with an infant at the breast. A group of children were in the apartment. The noise arose from a quarrel between the two women on the one side, and a boy about 13 on the other. Each side was heartily abusing the other. Several boys were outside looking in through the open window, and seemingly enjoying the scene that was being acted within. The disturbance died away as I entered. I found *one of the women to be his mother, the other his sister*. I knew not which of the trio exceeded in coarseness of epithets.

The mother suckling an infant, her own last born child,—the daughter similarly engaged, opposite to her, yet, as declared by herself, unmarried, and a boy not more than 13 years old, *son of one woman and brother to the other*, abusing them both, while their language to him was of the coarsest kind, and a group of boys enjoying the scene, and by language and gesture encouraging their young hero in his daring. The younger parents often hang upon the elder ones, until the latter are driven to pauperism; one of them, the grandfather, working in the parish 'oakum shop.' They at last die off. The next generation bring up their children as they themselves were brought up, and afterwards pass away to a pauper's grave, if not to one that is still more ignominious. Thus each generation is a circle of vagabondism and pauperism; each circle is linked with the past and subsequent ones, and chains are made that entrammel and retard the commonwealth. If the community is to progress in virtue and wisdom and godliness, these chains must be removed. The melting power of Christian love and faith must be brought down upon them, and wisely and perseveringly applied, 'here a little, and there a little,' until they are in a state for forming 'vessels unto honour' to the glory of God."

Who can read this most true report of an eye-witness, without perceiving that legally-convicted juvenile delinquents form but a small part of the whole number who really merit the appellation? Who can say that it would be an unjust interference with "the liberty of the subject," to *compel* such children as are already a plague, a nuisance, and a burden to society, and preparing to be yet more dangerous to it, to attend an Industrial School? Who does not see that it would be the highest economy in the Guardians of the Poor, instead of giving "sixpence and a loaf" weekly to a pauper child, to

THE PARENTS.

transfer the money to a place where it can be taught to work as well as to eat? And who can doubt that parents ought to be made in some way to feel the responsibility to God and to man, when they have brought into the world those who must become members of society at no distant period?

Now it is evident that vices of almost every kind may be looked for in such a condition of existence as we have here described; yet one stands forth so pre-eminently as the fertile cause of almost every other, that it requires especial notice—the vice of intemperance. Most truly says the well known philanthropist, Alexander Thompson, of Banchory, " There need be no hesitation in denouncing intemperance as the monster evil of our day—*the great producer of crime and misery.*" Truly says Mr. Clay, in his report for 1849, " If the offences to which habitual drinking has ultimately led could be ascertained, I believe we should find that four-fifths of the recorded offences have sprung from it." And such must necessarily be the effect, for intemperance deadens and destroys all good affections and holy aspirations; it gives the animal nature unbridled sway over the spiritual, and thus places man, God's noblest work, below the level of the brutes, to which the Creator has given instinct as a certain guide.

The united testimonies of judges, chaplains of gaols, and of prisoners themselves, the "Voices from Prisons and Penitentiaries," the appeals of missionaries to the poor, all these have sufficiently supported the oft-repeated declarations of the professed advocates of the Temperance Reformation to this effect. But those who have never come into personal communication with the families of drunkards, who have not watched the debasing effects of this one bad habit on the whole character of the parents, descending from them to their unfortunate children, who have not themselves almost hopelessly toiled for their rescue, while the great enemy was still powerfully at work, such can have but a feeble conception of the evils visited on the children by the intemperance of parents. "How often have I wished," says Dr. Tuckerman, of Boston, U. S., in a Report of his Ministry to the Poor, "that I could bring those who have a strong general interest in the well-being of society, and whose opinions exert a most important influence where I have no power, into the families of poor and intemperate parents. There let them see in what wretched rooms these unhappy beings are sometimes lodged; rooms as cold as wide chinks and broken windows can make them; the poor, broken, and scanty furniture; and the bed, not unfrequently lying upon the floor, and without a bedstead, and, it may be, consisting only of straw and shavings. There let them see to what deep degradation our nature may be brought through abandonment to the sin in which these parents are living. Will it be said that parents in this condition are beyond the reach even of hope? I think otherwise; for no one is to be considered, or

THE PARENTS.

treated, as beyond hope while God shall spare him. But I am not now pleading for those parents. I would direct attention *to their children*. Here are boys and girls with bodies that are seldom washed, and which are covered at best with filthy and tattered garments. These children probably go to no school, and they learn nothing but from the example of those with whom they associate. They are unaccustomed to any regularity in their meals, and they look for their food perhaps almost as much from home, as at home. They are now, it may be, caressed with the extravagance of intoxicated affection, and now beaten with the extravagance of intoxicated anger. *They are every day deceived by their parents, and they every day, in their turn, deceive them.* At one hour they are kept at work to procure fuel, or perform some other service; and in the next are allowed to go where they will, and to do what they will. They every day hear profaneness, and see intemperance, and witness parental contests; and are daily the companions of those who live amidst the same scenes, and are forming under the same influences. They are allowed also not only to drain the cup which an intemperate father or mother has not quite emptied, but their portion of it is sometimes given to them. If they are advised or encouraged by these guardians of their morals, it is to be more wary, more cunning, more artful. Not unfrequently also do these children fall into the service of the lowest of the profligate. They are ready for any guilty service within their power, by which they may earn anything; *and they have not an association with wrong, but the fear of detection and of punishment.* What then is to be expected from these children? Is it surprising that very early they become greatly depraved?"

The results on children brought up in such homes as are here described by an eye-witness, may be confidently predicated; yet a few facts from the same trustworthy source may strengthen conviction.

Mr. Wells, the Superintendent and Chaplain of the Boston House of Reformation, thus writes:

"I cannot call to mind one boy I have had with me over 15 years of age,—and I have had 30 such,—*who had not, to more or less excess, been accustomed to drink ardent spirits;* and five-sixths of these may fairly be considered to have been intemperate. Of those between 12 and 15 years of age, I think that three-fourths would have allowed themselves in the same indulgence whenever they had an opportunity to do it; and that two-thirds of those were in the way to confirmed intemperance! I have myself seen boys under 15 in our Boston House of Correction and common gaol. These lads were sent there for various offences; but a *considerable number of them were sent specifically for intemperance;* and it is a matter of notoriety, that far the largest number of them, whatever were the offences of which they were convicted, were accustomed to drink ardent spirits whenever they could obtain them. I have known lads in that prison *who were decidedly drunkards before they were* 12 *years old, and who have again* and again been there for intemperance before they were 15 years old."

Surely while our own gaol statistics give us such clear evidence respecting the inebriated habits of the parents of our young delinquents, we must consider the children rather objects of compassion than of indignation, rather as the subjects of wise reformatory treatment than of avenging justice, for it will be evident to all who have given it any practical attention, that the drunkard's child is placed in a position, both physically and morally, in which it is almost impossible that he should, without aid, grow up to any but a life of vice and disease. Surely, too, the efforts of all Christian men and Christian women are called for to check this evil, which is, at the same time, a symptom of spiritual degradation and the fruitful cause of crime. It is the testimony of Mr. Clay, after an experience of thirty years among the convicted, that "prominent among the first effects of the moral disease of the country," (the origin of which he has before stated to be "lack of knowledge of all that is truly useful and good for man,") " which at the same time are secondary causes, we see 'sensual, devilish' INTEMPERANCE; the moral Upas tree with its roots deeply bedded in the soil of ignorance, and its branches loaded with deadly fruit,—outcast children, wives driven to suicide, savage violence, robbery, rape and murder." [Report for 1851, p. 61.] Nor is the testimony of the prisoners themselves less forcible, as contained in a petition presented in the preceding year to the House of Lords. It stated that the "petitioners have had painful experience of the miseries, bodily and spiritual, produced by beer-houses, and are fully assured that those places constitute the greatest obstacles to the social, moral, and religious progress of the labouring classes. *They are alike injurious to old and young. By frequenting them, parents bring their families to disgrace and ruin, and children are familiarized with vice and crime.* They combine whatever is demoralizing in the ale-house, pawn-shop, fence-shop, gaming-house, and brothel. Your petitioners have all been drawn, by frequenting beer-houses, into offences and crimes, of which they might otherwise have remained innocent. We speak from our own direct and better knowledge, when we declare that beer-houses lead to sabbath-breaking, blasphemy, fraud, robbery, stabbings, manslaughters, and murders!" Whether or not we can join in the prayer of these 247 male prisoners that the government should " take such measures as will lead to the entire suppression of the beer-house curse," all who have any real interest in the reformation of juvenile delinquents must perceive that a most important step in this, would be to make every possible effort to draw the parents away from their soul-destroying habit of drinking, and by the infusion of religious principle, with the secondary aid of comfortable houses, and the means of wholesome and rational amusement, rendering the beer-shop less an object of attraction than the home.

A valuable comment on the foregoing remarks is afforded by the following tables, derived from the " Fifteenth Report of the Inspectors of Prisons of Great Britain." It appears from it that of the 192 juvenile prisoners in the Bath Gaol in 1848-9, only one-sixth were entirely without parental care; the remainder therefore had parents who were unable to restrain them from being injurious to society. Of the 625 adult prisoners, only one twenty-sixth were known to have been comparatively respectable, while above a third were notoriously vicious; only one-fourth themselves attributed their offence to poverty, while about a third acknowledged that vices akin to drunkenness were the direct cause of their present punishment. What is the actual condition of the children of these convicts? What are their future prospects?

TABLES drawn up from the Chaplain's Books of the Bath Gaol, referring to the year Sept. 30th, 1848, to Sept. 30th, 1849.

AGES OF PRISONERS.

9 years.		10 years.		11 years.		12 years.		13 years.		14 years.	
M.	F.	M.	F.	M.	F.	M.	F.	M.	F.	M.	F.
4	..	2	..	4	..	9	1	15	2	21	3
4		2		4		10		17		24	

15 years.		16 years.		17 years.		18 years.		Above 18.		Total.	
M.	F.	M.	F.	M.	F.	M.	F.	M.	F.	M.	F.
17	2	24	5	23	4	52	4	311	122	482	143
19		29		27		56		433		625	

Of the 192 juvenile prisoners there were—33 orphans; 17 having only a father living; 43 only a mother living; 93 total number of fatherless or motherless children, or orphans.

Previous Character of Prisoners in 1848-9.

Reputed thieves............	114	Comparatively respectable	24
Vagrants	27	Unknown	379
Profligates	16		
Drunk and disorderly ...	83	Total	625

To what cause the Prisoners attribute the Offence they commit.

Bad company	122	Passion	7
Drunkenness...............	128	Other causes	163
Profligacy	40		
Poverty	165	Total	625

To what Christian Denomination the Prisoners consider themselves to belong.

Church of England	251	None at all..................	261
Romish Church............	85		
Other denominations ...	28	Total	625

Whether in Work or not when the Offence was committed.

In work, 126.   Out of work, 499.   Total, 625.

How often the Prisoners have attended a Place of Worship during the six months previous to committal.

Attended occasionally, 295.   Not at all, 330.   Total, 625.

Prisoners' Condition in Life.

Destitute, and living on the accidents of life............	300
Poor, but occasionally employed	245
Poor, but regularly employed at 12s. per week	64
Mechanics, who are receiving from 12s. to 40s. per week	14
Tradesmen or farmers' class................................	2
Above the former	0
Total	625

A still more remarkable proof that poverty is not the great incitement to crime is afforded by the last report of the Rev. G. H. Hamilton, Chaplain of the Durham County Gaol. He states that "815 able-bodied men, out of 1,364," (the number who had been in the Gaol during the year 1851,) "were in full employment and good wages when they became criminals." From a Table in the same Report it appears that this employment was of a kind which showed that these men belonged not to the low and degraded, but to the industrial classes—a large proportion of them having good trades, and *an average of five, during the last five years, being even classed as professional men and schoolmasters!* The 644 married and widowed prisoners had 975 children under 16 years of age. What is to become of these with one parent at least in prison; in 110 cases the only parent? Those can best comprehend who have seen the miserable condition of such children, morally and physically; those only can realize who have themselves witnessed it, the wretched state in which they are, perhaps with no one to care for them, for it is not to be expected that the Guardians of the Poor should seek out those whom the law has made orphans; nor can any one know, until it has been thus proved, how important to her children are the cares of even a convicted mother.

We have hitherto been speaking of classes; let us now verify the description by considering a few individual cases. Mr. Clay, in his 27th Report, gives us some important particulars respecting the parents of the young transports, whose narrative has been already given:

"An Irish soldier," he says, "named Clark, on his discharge from the army, with a pension of a shilling per day, settled first at Stockport, and then at Manchester with his family, consisting of his wife, three boys and two girls. The father worked occasionally at his trade as a shoemaker, and could have earned a comfortable living by it. The two elder boys and the elder girl obtained employment at the factories; the girl, however, after a little time, exchanged this occupation for domestic service, in which she continues a year or two. The parents, as is too frequently the case, *bestowed no moral or religious care upon the children, who, in consequence, soon picked up bad companions; and beginning with petty thefts at such places as Knoll Mill fair, gradually entered upon a course of systematic crime.* The second son, Richard, led the way, and all the rest of the children (the youngest girl excepted, who, at the period of the narrative, 1850, was only 12,) followed in quick succession. At first the parents remonstrated, 'scolded, and gave good advice;' *but never hesitated to accept all that was offered to them of their children's ill-gotten gains.* In a short time the father became 'a great drunkard;' whilst the mother, it is evident, *encouraged and assisted practices which provided means for enabling her and her husband to live in idleness and luxury.* The man does not appear to have quitted Manchester, but the woman took a more active part in the proceedings of her children; frequently making long journeys to meet one or other of them on discharge from prison, and occasionally making herself useful in passing stolen bank notes."

Richard Clark, the second son, in the narrative already given, speaks of the encouragement given him by his parents:

"All this time," he says, "my father and mother knew how I was going on: they both would scold, and give us good advice; and my father was cruel to my mother, saying that it was her fault we were so bad: but it was *his fault, he would not work nor exert himself*. Although they gave me this advice they would take share of the money that I got; my father would not do it at first, but latterly he took it as much as my

THE PARENTS. 143

mother. He became a great drunkard. Since we began to thieve he would drink as much as we gave him." Afterwards the mother became an active accomplice. " She attempted to pass one of the stolen notes through my sister Ellen at a shop. My mother was taken up, and also my father, and afterwards myself. We were remanded three days, and obtained a lawyer's assistance, and were all discharged. My mother did me out of the note, for she got it back and denied it to me. My mother paid the lawyer out of the note, and I got £4 15s. for the one I kept, from a fence (public-house). . . . . If my father would have gone to work I think we should have given over. I have often tried to *make* my father work, by giving him no money."

To the conduct of these parents, first in conniving at the guilt of their children, and then in actively participating in it, what evils can be directly traced! What loss to society, what moral degradation to their own children, and to those drawn in by their example! Had the first of their offending sons been at once placed for a length of time under reformatory discipline, and *had the father, who was actually receiving public money for his support, been made to feel the responsibility under which he lay both to society and to God, for the moral control of his offspring;* how many fewer sufferers would there have been! The parents of the other members of the gang of pickpockets already spoken of, appear equally to have neglected the moral training of their children. Ellen's husband, John O'N., lost his own father at eight years of age, before which time he had learnt to read and write. He then went to a factory till he was 14, when, according to the statement of his wife and her brother Richard, *he was driven from home by a stepfather, who, Ellen affirmed, had caused another son to be transported.* He afterwards ran away to Liverpool with two other boys, and plunged into a life of crime. Thomas O'G., aged 18, says in his confession:

"I was born at Sligo. I believe I was four years old when I came over with my mother to Manchester, my father being dead. My mother married again about nine years ago. *My stepfather behaved very ill to me.* He was never satisfied with the wages I got. If I was out of work he would begin grumbling, and *at last would turn me out of doors. He has done this three or four times.* I went to a Catholic school, but learnt most of my learning in prison. It was the C.'s that led me off. They had given me money before I began to steal myself. I had been living at C.'s about three weeks, my *stepfather* having turned me out. Old C., at first, seemed against Richard and Ellen's bad conduct, *but would take the money they gave him.* Mrs. C. encouraged them more. C., the father, would not work. I continued to work off and on. *When I was at work I never stole.* But when I was out of work *my stepfather would not let me have anything to eat, and that drove me to thieving again.* The C.'s got above me, and I went with other lads."

Here there is no want of the means of support, nor apparently any vicious tendencies in the boy himself, led him to crime, but the cruel and illegal conduct of him on whom devolved the duty of a parent. The father of another of the gang, James O'B., is thus spoken of by one of the accomplices:

"This young 'Slaver's' father encourages *his children in badness.* I heard him say with his own lips, that James was one of the best lads travelling; he said to me, 'Johnny, *I wish you would take my young one a wiring* (pocket-picking) *up the*

THE PARENTS. 145

country; for the lads he is with will do him no good. He keeps telling me that he will soon beat James at 'buzzing,' for if he was bigger he could wire a man of his poke."

In the preceding cases it does not appear that the parents themselves trained their children to theft, though they were the indirect instigators of it, and participators in its forbidden fruits.

The following is an instance of the manner in which these unfortunate children are actually instructed in vice by their parents: The facts are derived from the depositions taken at the examination of the prisoners, a mother and her little girl!

"I was in ——— St., Liverpool," says the principal witness, "at about half-past seven o'clock in the evening of Wednesday, the 19th Nov. last. I was induced to watch the prisoners closely in consequence of hearing the elder prisoner ask the younger to go and see if some flannel was loose which was at a shop door. The little girl went across to that shop door. I saw her touch the flannel, and then come back to her mother, and I heard her say, 'no, mother, it's tied.' I was about two yards from the prisoners when I heard these words. I followed them about 100 yards, when I heard the elder prisoner, the mother, say to the little girl, her daughter, 'go and see if any of those victorines are loose,' pointing to a shop where I saw victorines hanging at the door. The younger prisoner, the little girl, went to the shop door, and I saw her pull the victorine now produced out from between the two strings they hung upon; she wrapped it under her shawl, and ran a few yards below the door of the shop; she then crossed to the opposite side of the street. The mother at this time had gone four or five doors above the shop on the same side of the street. The child looked about, and then saw her mother looking in at a shop window on the other side of the street, and she crossed over to her. The child was about giving the boa to her mother, when I went up to them and said to the mother, 'you ought to be ashamed of yourself, teaching your children to take things from people's shop doors.' The mother denied it, and began to storm at me. Constable —— came up; I told him what I had seen, and he took the prisoners down to the shop; the little girl carried the boa, which was shown and identified." About 18 yards of Coburg cloth were found at the woman's house; she made no defence; the little girl said, "*as I was coming past, the boa was lying at the shop door, and I picked it up.*"

This proved to be the third offence of the elder prisoner, and she was transported; the agony of both parent and child when the sentence was pronounced, —their despairing grief when they were removed from the dock, and then fell senseless on each other to the ground, deeply moved all present, even such as were little accustomed to be touched by the sorrow of a prisoner. When afterwards she was consigned to the Milbank penitentiary, her heart-rending sorrow at losing her child, and earnest entreaties in her behalf were most touching. The poor little girl had a short imprisonment awarded her. Why was she not transported? *She* had committed the crime; she had added perjury to theft, and was evidently a hardened thief. If the law *must be avenged*, why did not the actual perpetrator of the crime receive an equal punishment with the instigator? why did the one receive a sentence of *transportation for seven years*, and the other *imprisonment for fourteen days?* Such a disparity was a virtual acknowledgment that the little child was *not responsible, and therefore not guilty in the sight of God.* And yet, how is she treated? She is torn from the

THE PARENTS.

parent to whom nature has bound her by the tenderest ties of affection, and whose guilt she cannot comprehend,—she is familiarized with vice in a crowded gaol,—she has a prison brand affixed on her,—and is then thrown on the world; the law has done for her its BEST—and its WORST! Must these things be in our land?

Scarcely less affecting is the condition of the children of beggars, who are forced by their parents to what cannot appear to these ignorant little beings a crime, and are then numbered among "juvenile delinquents." A fact illustrative of this was related at a public meeting in Liverpool, by Wm. Rathbone, Esq., of that place; it is valuable not only as being one of common occurrence, but as recording some of the painful experience of the late lamented stipendiary magistrate:

Mr. Rathbone "happened to be on that day sitting on the bench with Mr. Rushton, and a child was put into the dock,—a child of whose beautiful appearance any parent might be proud. She was placed in the dock for begging about the streets. A policeman had traced her mother to one of those low lodging-houses, in which no fewer than fifty-one persons were found huddled together. He found her with five children whom she was totally unable to support. What did she do? She sent those children into the streets to beg,—*to be punished if they did not bring home to her the means of subsistence.* Mr. Rushton turned round to him and said, 'Good God, what shall I do with the child?' (She was a beautiful child, six or seven years of age, whom the officers had to raise up in the dock that she might be seen.) 'Shall I return her to her savage mother?' The woman was Irish. He said to her, 'Now will you go home? If you do, I'll send you.' She replied, 'No, sir, I will not go home!' 'What then am I to do for this child?' said Mr. Rushton. 'I have either to commit her to prison or to the tender mercies of her unfeeling and savage parent. What a dreadful calamity it is, that I have no place to send this child to. I believe I must commit her to gaol for twenty-one days, as the safest place for the child, and removing her from the protection of her mother.' *And the child was accordingly sent to gaol!*"

Such parents are very common in all large towns, living in idleness and even luxury on the gettings of their children, who, thus early exposed to the grasp of the law, are initiated almost in infancy in the " secrets of the prison house." How the professional beggars spend their ill-gotten wealth is shown by the following statement of facts, quoted from the *Times*, by Dr. Bell, in " Blackfriar's Wynd Analyzed," p. 30.

" Late on Saturday night the investigation was made. There were ascertained to be 278 professed beggars in the district. Of this number 10 were found at public-houses, drinking rum, gin, beer, &c. The other 260 were distributed among 26 lodging-houses. They were found to be busy cooking and eating beef-steaks, eggs and bacon, bread and butter, and drinking coffee; others were drinking beer and smoking. The next day, being Sunday morning,—and to this fact we would call particular attention,—between the hours of nine and eleven o'clock, another search took place Pretty nearly the same number of persons were present, who were engaged in preparing or partaking of an abundance of good food, of a similar character to that which formed their supper on the preceding night. Those among the men who had finished their meals, *were smoking and playing cards with boys and youths!*"

It is a very common idea that the parents of juvenile thieves are extremely poor, who have a difficulty in maintaining them honestly. The facts already cited will have proved that this is not always the case. But as it may be said that these are individual and selected cases, it will be advisable to refer to some other evidence of a more general nature.

The following is the testimony of the Chaplain of the General Prison at Perth:

"At this date (May 27th, 1852,) we have in custody 93 juveniles, of whom, according to their own statement, 65 were not driven to crime by actual destitution. As regards the character of their parents, 60 are said to be honest and industrious, while 16 are of an opposite description. As to their circumstances, 57 are reported to be good, and 19 bad; 17 of the boys are orphans."

These brief statistics furnish matter for important inferences. The boys sent to this, the general prison, for strict separate confinement, are not in general those charged with a trifling or a first offence. Only about one-sixth of these are orphans, that is without what ought to be parental care,—two-thirds of the parents are "said to be" honest and industrious, and therefore ought to have kept their children from vice,—nearly the same proportion are in good circumstances, and therefore are capable of maintaining their children.

A still more striking fact, in reference to the condition of the parents of juvenile delinquents, is derivable from the following extracts from the memoranda of the Chaplain of the Preston House of Correction, respecting the prisoners in that gaol, under 17 years of age, in the month of August, 1851:

"A., aged 16. First offence. 'I ran away from my work, and they kept saucing me at home for having done so. I then ran away from home, and got into bad company. Was now and then at a Sunday School, but can't read.' Weekly earnings of the family £2 8s. Parents are sober, but they never attend a place of worship."

"B., aged 12. Second offence. Has a drunken and profligate father, who could maintain his family, and earn 21s. weekly. The father has been three times in prison."

"C., aged 10. Third offence. Has a drunken and brutal father, who allowed the child to acquire bad habits without making any attempt to restrain him."

"D., aged 12. First offence. Both parents drunken. Three children at home. Earnings of the family 22s. The boy never went to any school."

"E., aged 16. First offence. Father dead four years. Mother in Manchester with five other children. Boy got into bad company, and ran away from Manchester. Has attended National and Sunday Schools five years. Mother appears blameless."

"F., aged 14. First offence. 'My parents live in Preston. Father is a weaver, and gets 12s. weekly, besides 7s. 6d. for collecting for a burial club. *He gets drunk every Tuesday night* after he comes from collecting. My eldest sister is a two-loom weaver, and earns 17s. 6d. net (!) My next sister is a two-loom weaver, and gets 9s. 6d. Another sister is a dress-maker, and gets 7s. or 8s. I got about 4s. or 5s.; but I was just going to be put on two-looms, and should have got 9s. 6d. I have a brother a shoemaker, who gets about 12s.' Total earnings of this family upwards of £3! The boy has been to a Sunday School five years, but can read very little."

"G., aged 14. First offence. 'Father's wages 30s., but he joined a turn-out. Father sometimes teetotal, but drinks *now*. Parents never go to a place of worship; some of the children go now and then.' This boy cannot read a letter, but evinces good feeling. The total earnings of the family when the father is at work, are £2 1s."

"H., aged 15. First offence. Parents have seven children.

Total earnings of the family £2 12s. 'Father drinks almost every Saturday night, and sometimes on Sunday. He never attends chapel, (Rom. Cath.) but mother and the rest of the family attend, and show me a good example.' Boy affected to tears, and being his first offence good hopes may be entertained of his permanent amendment."

" I., aged 14. First offence. Mother dead. Father a drunkard. Earnings of the family 23s. The boy quite ignorant, and never enters a place of worship."

" The above," says Mr. Clay, " constitute the whole of our Juvenile Offenders now in confinement; during the month we have discharged seven Irish children, aged from 9 to 16,—who had been sentenced to short imprisonments for begging; *and who, when at liberty, tramp about the country and maintain themselves by begging.*"

Such are the children who inhabited the Preston Gaol during the month when the record was made; *such the parents.* Of the nine whose brief history is given, not one child was driven into crime by want; all had sufficient, many plentiful homes; but their homes, except in one case, that of E., were the scenes of drunkenness and neglect of religion; in all cases one parent, in some both, being evidently by neglect and bad example the cause of the child's evil doing. Seven of the children had been convicted of felony, two of misdemeanour; but the seven others who were then discharged, had not been breaking directly any of God's laws; they had only been gaining a livelihood in a way which human law has made illegal; they had been punished for it in a way which never has checked, and never will check the evil; they were the children of beggars, to become by and bye the parents of a similar race.

But it will be said that many circumstances tend to make the inmates of this House of Correction an exception to the general rule, and that the full supply of work in a populous manufacturing district, together with the present cheapness of food, and the actual state of that portion of our population, will render such a return an unfair sample of the actual condition of our juvenile delinquents. Yet careful investigation into the real state of their families, in different towns, and under different circumstances, will most certainly elicit the fact, that it is not so much poverty which fills our prisons with young criminals, *as the vicious conduct and culpable neglect of parents*. During the year 1850, there were twenty-four boys in prison, some more than once, who had been more or less frequently attendants, but in most cases very irregular ones, at St. James's Back Ragged School in Bristol. The master of that school states, from his personal knowledge of the families of these boys, that only one of them—A, [*vide p. 22*,] was absolutely without a home. He had been in the Stapleton workhouse, had escaped, and the parish authorities, when applied to by the master to apprehend him as having absconded with the clothes, and to again give him a home, preferred ridding themselves of him altogether, refused to take any steps to capture him, and thus left him to a lawless life. Two other boys had been deserted by their parents, but had homes with other relatives; all the rest were living with their parents, who had nominal means of support, many of them trades, and all of them professing habits of honesty. The same master bears testimony that during five years' experience in this school, which is situated in one of the very worst parts of Bristol, and frequented by many in the lowest depths of poverty, as well as of vice, the most wretchedly poor in the school are not those who have been the subjects of police interference; and that those who have infused the worst moral influence in the school, as well as those who have been most frequently before the magistrate, *are boys whose parents could have well supported them, and who might have been gaining an honest livelihood, had they been trained " in the way they should go."*

Reference to an official document in another populous seaport town, fully corroborates this. In the year 1845, the Governor of the Liverpool Borough Gaol instituted an inquiry into the state of the families of the juvenile prisoners. There were in the gaol at that time, sixty-six—forty-eight families were visited, and this was the result of the inquiry:—

- 3 No parental care.
- 7 Homes plentiful and sufficient, *but parents, one or both, more or less given to drink.*
- 4 Fatherless: had decent but barely sufficient homes.
- 4 Homes barely sufficient, *owing to the drunkenness of parents.*
- 7 *Each parent of bad character.* Two girls lived with their mothers, who kept a brothel.
- 8 *Parents following occupations unfavourable to morality.*
- 15 Parents decent, homes comfortable.
- 5 Homes plentiful and sufficient.

Of these forty-eight then, three only were destitute of parental care, and, as such, ought to have been brought under parochial guardianship. In all the other cases, the children had homes which might have been comfortable *had there been a well-regulated life in the parents.* Twenty of these lads appeared to have decent homes. What the interior of these homes really was would not appear to the casual visitor. We have known a family in which the father boasted that he could earn a guinea a day, and certainly could obtain three guineas a week; there were times when his house might present the appearance of respectability and comfort—he himself being above the average of working men in his deportment; and yet, in general, there was starvation and misery in his home, and nothing but the most persevering Christian effort could have rescued his two boys from falling into the perishing or even the dangerous class. "In one of the cases visited," says the report of the Liverpool Gaol, "from the father's statement it appeared that the lad was wholly to blame; but when his wife came to fetch the lad from prison, it turned out that though he might be, as the father had said, of a thievish disposition, the father himself was a drunken, idle fellow, and had not given his wife a penny for nine weeks, though he had received nearly £2 a few days previous. She kept a mangle, and went out charring. I sent the wife and boy to the overseer, and the man is now serving a month's imprisonment for 'neglect of family.'"

THE PARENTS.

Of the 66 juvenile delinquents, the families of 18 were not visited. They were all outcasts on society.

- 2 Had bad homes and ran away.
- 1 Mother in service—lodged with a brickmaker.
- 1 Turned out by stepfather some years since.
- 2 *Orphans just out of the workhouse.* ⎫
- 3 Had parents, but only one lived at home. ⎪
- 2 Parents absconded, therefore no home. ⎬ *Known to live by thieving.*
- 1 Orphan and houseless. ⎪
- 2 Orphans from Chester, whither they were sent. ⎭
- 2 Parents and homes. [Query, did they exist?]
- 2 Strangers, both had parents, one at Manchester, the other at Glasgow.

Can it be denied that, in these eighteen cases of juvenile delinquency, either the parents or society are mainly chargeable with the guilt of these poor children, who themselves should be the objects of our warm pity, as well as of our reprehension and chastisement? And can a Christian citizen hesitate to acknowledge that such corrective training and religious principle should be given to these young offenders as may enable them to rise above the circumstances in which they have unhappily begun their career, punishment being, if possible, administered to the parent, as really the guilty party? No further evidence can be needed to establish the following positions.

First, that the great mass of juvenile delinquency is to be directly and mainly attributed to the low moral condition of the parents, and to their culpable neglect of the early training of their children, or their incapacity to direct it.

Secondly, that actual poverty is in comparatively few instances the direct cause of juvenile delinquency.

Thirdly, that since parents are invested both by divine and human law with certain rights and privileges over their children, they ought to be regarded as the guilty party when they neglect the duties entailed by their privileges, and held responsible for their conduct up to a certain age.

Fourthly, that society having a right to protect itself from the injury caused by parental neglect, should deprive parents, who are either unable or unwilling to control their children from falling into vicious habits, of their abused authority.

Fifthly, that parents thus deprived of the care of their children, are not thereby released from the duty imposed by nature of maintaining them, and that such maintenance should, as far as possible, be imposed upon them.

Should these positions be admitted, and the principles involved in them be fully carried out in the treatment of parents who have thrown their children upon society by their criminal neglect, there will no longer exist that premium on vice which is at present almost necessarily attendant on every effort to reclaim criminal children. The vicious parent who either directly instructs his child in crime, or culpably neglects his moral and religious training, at present suffers no penalty further than the withdrawal of him from his care during a few months' imprisonment, during which time he is relieved from the child's maintenance; he may then claim the custody of him on his release, defying, as we have seen, all attempts of magistrates, chaplains, or benevolent persons desirous of saving a young creature from ruin, to withdraw his offspring from his care. He continues his course of direct training of the child to vice, deriving profit from his unlawful gettings; the young delinquent, as he is called, is again detected, again puts the country to the expense of his trial and punishment, and a similar condition of things continues, the parent still feeling in possession of his rights over the child, however much he may neglect his duties to him. Surely in such cases the parent should be regarded in justice as the true criminal, and made to feel by a certain administration of law, that society will hold him responsible for the just exercise of rights which the law, human and divine, has intrusted to him. The principle that rights involve duties is distinctly acknowledged in reference to parents by the poor laws, as well as by the enactments respecting illegitimate children, and the neglect of these duties is punished. A father who leaves his children chargeable on the parish, is liable to imprisonment for such neglect, and not unfrequently receives it; and one who devolves on the unfortunate woman whom he has led astray the charge of his offspring's support, may be sought out in the remotest corner of the kingdom, and forced to pay not only the cost incurred for the child, but that of his own apprehension. The enforcement of these laws even at pecuniary loss, is felt to be the vindication of a principle most important to the well-being of society. And why is this responsibility of the parent limited to the physical wants of his child? Why is he compelled to provide it with the "bread that perisheth," to support his animal life, and yet permitted unchecked to starve his spiritual nature, to administer deadly poison to his soul? These are strange anomalies in our laws! The hand of justice arrests him if he leaves his child a burden on the workhouse, but allows him to go unmolested when he leaves him, a far heavier burden, in *the gaol*. This is certainly a strange " premium on crime !"

"The last duty of parents to their children," says Blackstone,* "is that of giving them an education suitable to their station in life, a duty pointed out by reason, and of far the greatest importance of any. For, as Puffendorf very well observes, it is not easy to imagine or allow that a parent has conferred any considerable benefit on the child by bringing him into the world, if he afterwards entirely neglects his culture and education, and suffers him to grow up like a mere beast, to lead a life useless to others, and shameful to himself. Yet the *municipal laws of most countries seem to be defective in this point, by not constraining the parent to bestow a proper*

* Blackstone's Commentaries, vol. i., p. 449, 15th edition. 1809.

education upon his children. Perhaps they thought it punishment enough to leave the parent who neglects the instruction of his family, to labour under those griefs and inconveniences which his family so uninstructed will be sure to bring upon him."

This punishment has not proved sufficient to check the growing evil; and the experienced are beginning to feel with the City Solicitor of London, in his evidence before the Lords' Committee, that to legislate for the purpose of preventing crime, we "must begin by increasing the civil responsibility of parents and parishes, in regard to the conduct of children." The importance of enforcing parental responsibility was attested by many other witnesses of weight, and the Lords stated in their Report, "The Committee also recommend the trial of a suggestion made by witnesses who have given much attention to this subject, that, wherever it is possible, *part of the cost attending the conviction and punishment of juvenile offenders should be legally chargeable upon their parents.*"

Let us hope, then, that the legislature will not long delay to give to magistrates the authority needful to enforce this responsibility, and to transfer it when abused to more trustworthy persons. The law will then have done all it can do; no legal enactments can change the heart and the life. This is the work of a Christian people, of every individual among them who is a true follower of that Great Master, who came " to seek and to save them that are lost." These parents are undoubtedly degraded and vicious;—we probably cannot repress a feeling of indignation against them when we look at their morally perishing children, and regard them as the authors, not only of their being, but of their vices. But when we consider their own early nurture, the influences under which they grew up, the condition in which they are now living, deep pity should move us for their own sake, as well as for that of their children, to strive by every means which in us lies to improve their condition, to awaken in them a feeling of self-respect, and a desire for the salvation of their immortal souls. By such means will they be led to feel a far higher responsibility towards the young beings whom God has given them, than any legal enactments can enforce; thus will they gratefully become fellow workers with those who are labouring for their children's good; and thus may we hope that the iniquities of the parents will no longer descend from one generation to another. When the barren land has been abundantly watered by the heavenly dew of Christian love, then, " instead of the thorn shall come up the fig tree, and instead of the briar shall come up the myrtle tree : and it shall be to the Lord for a name, for an everlasting sign that shall not be cut off."

CHAPTER V.

PRESENT TREATMENT.

In the foregoing chapters some faint idea has been given of the moral disease with which we are attempting to grapple. We have endeavoured in the youthful patients before us to point out the symptoms of their morbid condition, which in some is merely accidental, the effects of external circumstances which may be removed; in others of a long habit of vice, and a total absence of all regenerating principles; in others again, it has borne the stamp of a deep-rooted and hereditary malady. We have looked into the homes of these children, and beheld there not wretched poverty striving in vain to satisfy the children's cravings with a morsel of bread,—not ill-paid industry, begging only for liberty to work,— not fathers and mothers living in the fear of God, and striving, if they could bestow on their offspring no other gift, to give them such knowledge as would guide them here and hereafter; but we have seen, in some cases, homes where the weekly earnings of the families might supply them with every needful comfort, in most, a condition above actual poverty, but where vicious indulgence, the gratification of the lowest animal tastes, hardened the heart against all good and holy influences,—stifled the voice of conscience,—deadened all natural affections; we have encountered those who would not work, but who lived unblushingly in the face of society as " professed thieves," acknowledged vagabonds by calling, travellers on the highway that leadeth to destruction,—and these were the parents of children! We have beheld them rejecting or neglecting proffered means of educating the young beings whom they had brought into the world, and leaving them to grow up as wicked as themselves.

Here is the actual state of things. It is in vain for us to endeavour to close our eyes to the fearful and contagious nature of this disorder, or to attempt to evade the retribution which will result to us from its neglect, by shifting the blame upon others, and saying, " It is the fault of the parents, let them only be called to account; did we bring these children into the world,—did we make them what they are?" These parents were once children; how were they trained? What Christian, who knew what to them would be the consequences of their training to vice, led them in a better way with the strong hand of love? How did the State correct them when they became its children? What attempt was made to cure them of their mortal disease?

But what is the present treatment of the malady? Let us consider what we should think of an infirmary, a house of cure for the body, in which all the patients, whatever their diseases, were subjected to a similar treatment; in which a certain stern curative discipline, which had been found to be efficacious as a preparatory measure for a short period in a particular kind of stubborn disease, was employed for all?—in which this treatment was applied to the patient for a certain time fixed before his entering, by some arbitrary rule, quite irrespective of the effect it had upon him, or his actual condition; and in which, moreover, when the patients returned again and again—the disease evidently having gained a stronger hold of them after each course of treatment—the nurses, and even physicians, all acknowledging that they anticipated as much when the patients were first brought under their care, and that those who submitted the most submissively to the discipline, usually appeared the most untouched by it,—the same treatment was persevered in? Should we not at once unhesitatingly declare that it was adsolute infatuation to continue such a system? And if we fortunately did not live under a Russian despot, whose will was law, and who willed that his subjects should thus be cured, without giving them the option whether they wished to be healed; or under the deadening cloud of Austrian tyranny, which shut out the knowledge of what was better; or among the millions whom the "heaven-born" Emperor of China binds with an irrevocable oath to the wisdom of their ancestors;—if we lived in a free country, where the voice of the people could be heard, where the words of the newest wisdom could penetrate to the remotest corner, to the humblest hearth—should we rest till we had roused the people with one voice to demand that an institution should be removed, which was so unjust, so injurious? Such an infirmary would excite the reprobation of all, and its continued existence would be still more extraordinary—a greater anomaly—in an enlightened age, when not only principles of sound political economy, but of Christian philanthropy, were widely disseminated, should it be proved that the support of such an institution involved the nation in great expense, without answering the proposed end, and that more philosophical plans, which had been proved to be effective, were proposed for acceptance, and rejected.

Yet, the Gaol continues to be the only infirmary provided by the parental care of the State for the cure of her erring children's souls! To this, all her young criminals, more or less guilty, infected with soul-contaminating guilt, or just showing their first sin-spot, are indiscriminately consigned; all sharing the same treatment, for the time arbitrarily assigned, and coming back again and again, unreclaimed; while our police courts are infested with them, our prison cells swarm with them, our felons' docks are filled with them—and then they are withdrawn for a short time again from our sight, only to return more hardened. All this continues at enormous expense to the State, and while more economic, more truly effective plans are proposed for acceptance.

These are not vague rhetorical statements, nor is the parallel we have drawn a poetical metaphor. They are sad and serious facts, and every part of our parallel is based on deep-seated truth.

In our former work sufficient proof was given from the statements of gaol chaplains and other experienced persons, that the present system is most injurious and unjust as regards the child; further evidence would hardly convince one who was unmoved by it. We shall now proceed to show some of the effects of the system on society, and point out the error of the principle on which it is founded.

In the first place, the present treatment of juvenile delinquents is calculated to train up adult ones, and thus to entail a continued burden of vice and expenditure on the country.

This is strikingly shown in the following statement contained in a letter addressed by the Rev. J. Carter, Chaplain of the Liverpool Gaol, to the Mayor and Town Council, dated April 25, 1850:

"The number of boys now in custody is 115, of girls 39; of these a very large majority (I am afraid to say how large) have been brought into their present circumstances through parental neglect, or failure of parental influences, and it must be evident that neither effort of mine, nor any *penal* appliances, can ever counteract the consequences of these defects, aggravated as they are now by the contamination of evil association. *Hence, the expense of each succeeding imprisonment, be it greater or less, which fails of its object, is so much thrown away.* In support of this statement, suffer me to invite your attention to this fact, that of thirty boys and thirty girls, *not selected*, but taken in order from the respective registers of those in gaol in the month corresponding with the present one, in 1847, eleven only do not appear to have been re-committed, twelve have been transported since, twelve are now in gaol on re-commitments, and twenty-five have been re-committed, (several frequently,) and, with few exceptions, are known to be still living in criminal habits. Now, leaving out of account the cost of apprehension, and that of carrying out the sentence of transportation when awarded, the expense of prosecution and maintenance of these in gaol, on the nearest and fairest computation I can arrive at, may be stated to be £1,123. 16*s*. 9*d*. But it will not escape remark, that the expense of juvenile crime is not to be estimated solely by that incurred while they remain in that category. There are, at the moment I write, forty-three male and thirty-seven female *adults* in the gaol, who commenced their career of crime as *juveniles*, and only four of whom have yet exceeded the age of twenty-one years. The aggregate number of times which these have been in the custody of the police is 678, of their commitments to gaol, 539; and the cost of their several prosecutions and maintenance whilst herein has been, on the lowest computation, £1,877. 1*s*. 6*d*. Some are for trial, and possibly may be transported, thus entailing further heavy expense; but the rest, be it remembered, will, in the course of a few weeks, *be let loose upon society again*, to be maintained by the public, partly by plunder, and (if detected) partly out of the corporation purse. The amount of property *ascertained* to have been stolen by these is £255. 17*s*. 2*d*., inconsiderable perhaps in amount, but forming little or no criterion of the danger to which the public is exposed, or the extent of mischief such characters are capable of perpetrating. In many cases the criminal has been arrested when intending to commit crime, and before the completion of the felony. Now, gentlemen, these facts and figures are fairly ascertained and recorded, and I pledge myself to their accuracy. The instances cited are not selected to make out a case, but are taken honestly, as I am prepared to convince any one who will do me the favour to investigate, and are laid before you without embellishment or exaggeration, simply to show the tendency and effect of our system. Take any other period, and make the same inquiry, and the results, I will answer for it, will not be more encouraging,"

Subsequent observations made by the same Chaplain, some of which were laid before the Conference at Birmingham, led to the same results, which must be highly unsatisfactory to the mere political economist, and far more so to the Christian who beholds in each one of those 134 children, not only a future member of society, but an immortal soul!

We may, by reference to an individual case, gain some idea how such a cònsequence almost necessarily follows in these gaols which are not under the separate system.

The following anecdote was mentioned to Mr. Clay by E. R., the professed thief already referred to:

"I remember a boy named B., he had been a shop-boy to a mercer; he was tried in May 1849, and got six months. A letter carrier from the post-office was tried with him, for receiving, and, I think, was sentenced to nine months. This man's name was P. The boy worked with me, and was a native of the same country. *I knew several of his relatives who were respectable farmers.* This poor boy was an orphan; he was an intelligent boy of about 14. He told me, he was first induced to rob his employer through seeing others do so. Cash not being attainable, as each individual sale was checked and rechecked; goods were abstracted. He commenced with a handkerchief; then, gradually becoming habituated, he commenced a wholesale system of plunder; the man P., receiving and disposing of the property, and giving the unfortunate boy what he pleased. This lad expended his portion of the proceeds in concert rooms, shooting galleries, &c.; and by degrees began to drink. *He was a lad, who, having been well brought up, was thrust into the company of young, but in many instances practised thieves, by the very law that should have protected him from such contamination.* He became so hardened, that he explained to me the full particulars respecting the means for effecting the entrance into the shop and office of a former employer; describing very minutely the situation of the various doors, &c. He told me where the most valuable shawls were, and told me the private marks used to prize the goods; described where the cash-box was, and the best business days. This boy could speak the slang dialect, as well as any lad in the place, and had not some kind friends met him when he was liberated, I know well he would have been another victim added to the thousands utterly ruined. *I am convinced of this, having too bitterly experienced it, that communication in a prison has brought thousands to ruin; I speak not of boys only, but of men and women also."*

It will be said, that this cannot occur in many prisons, where care is taken to prevent any communication among the prisoners, and where admirable instruction is provided for the young convicts; surely by such discipline they must be greatly benefited.

The very name of a Prison School is an anomaly.—Education is not a mechanical instilling of certain elements of knowledge, or it may be of divine truths, which, thus formally conveyed into the mind, lose their precious influence. It is not the mere training and exercising the powers which the God of nature has given to the child, so that like well-formed and nicely-polished machinery, they may be ready for use. This, though a part, is but a small part of education, and the knowledge so given,—the powers so trained,—may be preparative for evil as well as for good; it is even more than probable that the knowledge and power thus placed in the hands of one whose heart is unconverted, will most surely be to him a means of greater evil. It is only when the child's *soul* is touched, when he yields *from the heart* a willing obedience, when he can freely try and exercise his growing powers, and apply the knowledge he is gaining to aid him in the performance of his daily duties, and to refresh and invigorate his mind with healthful, intellectual food, —that the work of education is really going on. And *can* this be done in a gaol, even by the kindest and most devoted teachers? The ponderous walls around him crush his soul, as well as confine his body; the healing influences of nature must not reach his young spirit, and the high barred window excludes all but some small portions of heaven's air and light; his heart is withered by the daily sight of the rod, which, even if unused, is emblematic of constant coercion, perhaps a memorial of past agonizing torture; to exercise his powers in any but the appointed routine, is an offence to be punished by increased severity; daily duties he has none, other than submission to the prison rules; the refreshment and invigoration of his mind is an evident impossibility for a child debarred from all that nature makes indispensable for childhood. Most true is the testimony of one of Her Majesty's Inspectors of Schools, respecting the inevitable effect which a system of coercion must produce.* "That school is ill managed in which the moving principle is terror of the rod. *The steady growth of an unhealthful moral condition in it, is not easily seen by the master in its relation to a false system of discipline; the Inspector recognises it, however, from the moment the threshold is passed. He sees it in the very faces of the children.* If sentiments of fear are habitual to their minds, it is not to be expected that a kindly and cheerful subordination should be depicted in their countenances, *but rather a sullen apathy, or the sinister expression of a silent, but resolute opposition of purpose.*" Such must necessarily be the aspect of a Prison School. Let us observe a single one. We cannot select one where the strict separate system is carried out; the visitor, if introduced into the school, vainly seeks for any thing which may deserve that appellation. He does not at first perceive any scholars, but only sees a number of little wooden cells or cubs, a raised seat or small pulpit opposite them, being occupied by the teacher, who alone can see all, and whom only the scholars can see. In vain does the visitor seek in the spacious room any thing which can realize his idea of a school. We will follow a

* "Extracts from the Reports of Her Majesty's Inspectors of Schools." Preface, p. 5. London: Longman, Brown, Green, and Longman.

PRESENT TREATMENT. 171

stranger to a prison-school conducted under circumstances as favourable as possible, in a prison where every effort is made for the moral improvement of the inmate.

" The benevolent chaplain of the Liverpool gaol, who takes the warmest interest in the condition of convicted children, permitted me to visit the schools in that establishment. I followed him, after passing through many barred gates, guarded by numerous powerful turnkeys, up a long, narrow, winding stone staircase, bounded by ponderous walls. It was a sickening approach to a school-room, the entrance to which should be pleasant and attractive. The door opened on a large gloomy room, neat and clean indeed, but unadorned by any maps or pictures to delight the youthful mind, and allure it to the pursuit of knowledge. About 45 girls were here of different ages, but principally under 15, for the elder ones were sent into the adult ward, where, at all moments when strict surveillance is relaxed, they may learn lessons of vice they will never forget, from experienced criminals. There were several children only about 12, some younger; the youngest prisoner was not there, she was gone down to the court to be tried with her mother; she was only 9. The girls were arranged in classes at their lessons, much as in an ordinary school, one mistress presiding, near whom a cane lay ostentatiously on the table. But if the air of the room, and the prison dress of the children had not indicated the nature of the place where I was, the looks of almost all the girls would have told most plainly that some heavy oppressive influence lay upon them; it dulled, though it could not conceal, the low and vicious look of many; it blighted and crushed what might have been, in a healthy atmosphere, bright and happy faces. The badge of a red collar on some young children, indicated that they had undergone the sentence of a second conviction; some in dresses with yellow facings, under conviction of felony, had to look forward to 18 months, or even two years, dragged on in this dreadful monotony. One of these, a pretty, innocent looking child I had seen here two years before ; she was enduring at least her sixth imprisonment, having been, as it were, educated in the gaol; she then hoped that this would be the last time; she soon however returned after her discharge; after that confinement the chaplain obtained her admission into an institution in another town; she did well there, and was sent into service; she thought her mistress severe, ran away, and was now here again. What will become of her on her discharge from this place into the trials of the world, her powers having been thus long cramped, but her will unsubdued, her heart untouched? Who will be long-suffering towards such poor creatures, and win them with love, such as that with which Christ loved us? Most of the girls whom I questioned looked forward to going to a *home* on their discharge, but those who knew what this home would be, desired that they should be severed entirely from influences which could be only degrading. Five poor children were in their own dress, they had not yet been tried, and were as yet unsubdued; one of them was locked in a cell to keep her under due restraint. The schoolmistress seemed one who, if any one could, would infuse some intellectual life into her unfortunate charge; she had entered on the work from an earnest desire to do some good to these poor children, but she felt a constant sense of disappointment weigh on her spirits. She endeavoured to guide them by the spirit of love, rather than of fear, and scarcely ever used the cane; she rejoiced to have won the affection of many, whose marks of tenderness she felt very touching, they were quite emulous of doing her any service, and delighted when she showed them marks of love. But she felt most painfully that massive walls and physical coercion could not give her that control over them which free moral influence only can give. Her utmost vigilance could not prevent their occasional communication with each other, and then what could be the subject of their conversation? Their lessons had excited no emulation, they were compulsory; play, and the thousand little interests that occupy the thoughts of healthy childhood, were of course banished far from a prison; their intercourse could only be of the details of their own vicious lives, the particulars of their trials, the incidents which supply prison gossip. So the dull routine of lessons and work must go on to the child, and she leaves the gaol; if more instructed, not more prepared to resist the evil in the world, most probably better acquainted with its crimes, and more ready to plunge into them. Such was the belief of this prison schoolmistress, founded on many years' experience. Many of the girls when they first come here cannot sew or knit; while they are learning these arts their interest is awakened and their conduct is good; but as soon as they are familiar with them they become careless and disobedient. This fact illustrates many important principles. It was now the dinner hour, a time usually given to social enjoyment, but the same heavy gloom hung over the scene where each, though in a large company, must be absorbed in her own solitary meal. There was nothing to break the painful monotony but the sobs of one little girl; just before she was taken up, her mother broke her leg; she longed to be with her and nurse her! I did not see the boys in school, for they were going through their prison exercise after dinner; but the room where were some thirty mothers with young babies, was a fearful sequel to the girls' school. I shuddered to see the gentle natures of women so degraded, and to think under what influences these poor infants were to be reared. Yet even here were proofs of the existence of some better nature, in the newly-awakened tenderness with which these wretched women were beguiling the prison hours by bestowing unwonted cares upon their young ones; one felt that a mission to them on their discharge might win some to the ways of virtue. Faith in human nature must never be lost, if we would be the means of awakening it to a new life. I rejoiced to find that one who had had so much cause for disappointment as the gaol schoolmistress had a strong conviction that the girls under her charge were just as susceptible of good influences as any others, and that if placed in circumstances where they would be for a sufficient length of time wisely controlled, judiciously trained, and kindly treated, they might all become useful members of society; but I fully agree with her in thinking that this can never be done in a GAOL."

Such is the opinion of those most qualified to form

a correct judgment. Capt. Williams, H. M. Inspector of Prisons, states in his evidence before the Lords' Committee in 1847: "At Wakefield, where I know that every care is taken of the boys, *and where the education given them is such as would qualify them for almost every situation attainable in their state of life*, the frequency of recommitments has not diminished, but I believe increased."

In the General Prison of Scotland at Perth the separate system is carried out with the utmost care, and the Board state in their last Report the conviction, that "the system is productive of highly beneficial effects, as well in a sanitary point of view, as in reference to the progress of the juvenile prisoners in the various branches of education." The governor observes, that "the state of order in the juvenile class throughout the year has been excellent." The surgeon remarks that, "It is impossible to see these boys in their wards, all employed in learning their several trades or tasks, or to hear them at their lessons given to them by their schoolmaster, or finally to witness them on parade, all clean and in good health, without being impressed with the notion, if not conviction, that they must benefit by all this regularity, care, and discipline." And yet, so far from reformation having been really effected, it is stated by the chaplain, the Rev. W. Brown, that "of 76 class boys, who were liberated between the 1st of July, 1850, and the 31st of December, 1851, a period of

18 months, and who were especially inquired after, it has been ascertained that 29 have entered into crime, 14 of whom are now undergoing sentence of transportation." This statement was made May 27th, 1852. It appears, then, that the result of all this excellent training is, that of these boys who appeared so orderly, more than one out of every three relapsed into crime, and in the cases of more than one out of every six this was of so serious a character that the highest secondary punishment had been awarded to it. The quality of this forced conformity to external decorum, is stated by Mr. Smith, the governor of Edinburgh Gaol, in his evidence before the Lords. "The behaviour in prison," he says, " of the worst characters is good generally:— the very shrewdness and intelligence which enables them to be very dangerous outside the prison, leads them to behave well inside the prison, to evade the prison punishments." So powerless to reform is the best prison school!

It has been already shown that, after a first imprisonment, terror of the punishment in the mind of a young culprit is gone, and that it therefore no longer operates as a deterrent. One convict in the Perth Prison is stated, in the last Report, to have spent five years out of seven in prison, being then there for the third time, and having commenced his career at the age of 14. The same frequency of recommitment is not usually found to be the case with adults, and a reason for this is assigned by the experienced

Chaplain of the Manchester Gaol. "The *disgrace* of a prison," he says, "though equally inflicted on both juveniles and adults, is not so keenly felt in the one case as in the other, and therefore a great part of the effect is lost upon the youthful offender. Boys are generally more comfortable in every respect" (*except the loss of their cherished liberty*) " in prison than out; their food is good and regular, clothing sufficient and clean, beds and rooms better than they have been accustomed to, and however punished, they must necessarily feel themselves in good quarters. The truth of these remarks may be confirmed by the words of a lad, who when advised to go to the workhouse after his imprisonment here, replied that they should not keep him there, he would run away, as he preferred the prison where he was better fed;" and when on the point of leaving the gaol, when the same lad was asked what course he intended to take, he said, " I will get work in the brick-croft during the summer, and come in here in the winter !"

The very prevalent conviction now existing of the uselessness of the gaol as a reformatory institution for children on the one hand, and the carelessness with which hardened young culprits regard it on the other, have, in the next place, a very injurious effect on society, by rendering the consequences of juvenile crime very uncertain, and by lowering the dignity of justice. The feeling that a child is branded for a life of crime by a first imprisonment, prevents persons of ordinary kindness of heart from prosecuting. While, in the more favoured circles of society, cases *never* occur in which children are brought into a criminal court, it so often happens, in a lower grade, that crimes are passed by from motives of kindness, as to give great impunity to crime. The case of the boy G., p. 19, is an instance of this. The crime of uttering base coin was clearly brought home to the youth, he was in the keeping of the master, but the lady to whom he attempted to pass the half-sovereign refused to prosecute, feeling that doing so would be an unkind action. The consequence was that this youth was thrown on society with a lost character and encouraged by impunity to pursue his evil course. Had there been any hope in the mind of the lady that he would be reformed by prosecution, Christian benevolence would have led to her putting him in the hands of justice. Instances of the kind might be multiplied, a few only will be selected.

A professional gentleman had in his employment a youth belonging to a respectable family and brought up under religious influences; he never showed any tendency to dishonesty; greatly then was the gentleman grieved and disappointed, when it was discovered that the youth, having been long imitating his handwriting, had, by forging his signature, appropriated some large sums of money, with which he had made his way to Liverpool on his way to the United States. He was discovered there, and the gentleman could easily have apprehended him, but felt that, under the present system, imprisonment would ruin him for life and disgrace an innocent family. He left him therefore to enjoy the fruits of his iniquity.

A respectable bookseller of the city of Bristol has twice within the last year or two been robbed to some amount by boys in his employment. In each case a degree of art was displayed which indicated an adept in crime; in each case no suspicion had been attached to the boy, who continued his course of dishonesty for some time without detection; the parents of both were what is usually termed respectable. In neither instance did the bookseller prosecute, from a strong feeling of the permanent injury which would arise to the boy from such a course. He was compelled to dismiss them, and they were left to the guidance of parents who did not show that degree of displeasure at the dishonesty of their children, which would lead to the hope of their being reclaimed. It is worthy of remark, that this bookseller had employed at different times three boys from a neighbouring Ragged School, two of whom belonged to criminal families, yet he had never discovered in them the least dishonesty.

A printer in the same city in the present month of November discovered that a little boy of 12 in his employment had robbed him, and investigation proved that he had for some time been frequently doing so, spending the money in toys. The boy was taken to the station, where he manifested a very hardened feeling, and seemed quite indifferent to his situation. Had the master believed that his prosecuting the boy would have been the means of placing him under reformatory discipline, he would gladly have done it; but he could not expose him to a public trial, and to a period of imprisonment which would only have the effect of hardening him, and branding both him and his parents, who are poor but holding a good character. The boy was therefore discharged; the father appeared to have tried every means in his power to correct him; gentle persuasion and punishment seemed equally unavailing; he would gladly pay whatever his means permitted to have the boy removed from his bad associates, and placed for a time in a Reformatory School.

In all the foregoing cases the individual injured was a religious and benevolent person, who abstained from prosecuting from a sense of justice to the offender, for he felt that doing so would be inflicting an injury, very disproportionate to that which he had received, without effecting reformation. A sentiment of compassion for a young child, even without any higher motive, often leads to a similar course, and it is in general, therefore, those children who are most uncared for by society, who become marked by the police, and who come into collision with persons of low and selfish character, a class of children therefore peculiarly needing Christian influence, who are subjected to magisterial treatment. A similar feeling of the injustice of dealing with the faults of children as if they were men, not unfrequently influences magistrates themselves to endeavour to find some excuse for merely reprimanding and discharging young boys brought before them. The police reports during the fruit season afford frequent illustrations of this. The uncertainty of punishment thus created, must surely diminish in the minds of children and of the public, the belief that suffering must justly follow transgression.

Another consequence, not less injurious, follows from the present state of the law as respects children; the dignity of the administration of justice must be greatly lessened by the frequent admissions publicly made by those who execute it, that the course pursued is useless and injurious, and the perplexity expressed by magistrates, when compelled to deal with the offences of children. We have already alluded to the testimony borne by the Recorder of Bristol to the Grand Jury, that the punishments he had inflicted on such culprits had not had the effect intended, and had not checked juvenile crime. ("Ref. Sch." pp. 270, 271.) The Recorder of Birmingham expressed himself yet more strongly when addressing the conference assembled in that town in December, 1851, on the subject of Preventive and Reformatory Schools. "We must endure," says Mr. M. D. Hill, " to behold these little creatures,— to see them on tiptoe raising their eyes over the bar and meeting the gaze of the pitying spectator with an indifference revolting at any age, but doubly painful to witness at this early period. And while we are but too conscious for our own peace of mind that their fate is placed in our hands, we feel that we are compelled to carry into operation *an ignorant and vengeful system, which augments to a fearful extent the very evil it was framed to correct.*" In the very courts of justice a mockery is enacted, for most frequently do judges pass sentence of the highest secondary punishment, one which was intended to strike the greatest terror into the minds of offenders, and to break the spirit of the most contumacious, on children of 14, 12, or even 10 years of age; and this is done with the avowed intention of having them sent to what is supposed to be a good Reformatory School, which can be entered only by those who have received such a sentence. Surely this is making the law of none effect.

Magistrates on the bench are continually heard to express their perplexity how to act towards these young offenders, the law directing them to one course, their own sense of right and their natural feelings suggesting another. The following is a scene which took place in Manchester; it is recorded in the *Manchester Guardian*, Jan. 10, 1852, in a paragraph headed, "An Unfortunate Young Thief:"

"A little boy, apparently between 11 and 12 years of age, was brought up for stealing some old keys and a pair of scissors, when a conversation of which the following is an abstract, took place between the Magistrate and the boy. 'You were here last week, weren't you?' 'Yes, Sir,' 'And what was done to you?' 'Got three days.' 'Any thing else?' 'Yes, Sir, whipped.' 'And it has done you no good, it seems.' 'Yes, sir, it has, but I couldn't get home. A policeman took me home, *but my father wouldn't let me in.*' The poor young prisoner confessed that he sold the keys, for which 1½*d.* was received, but said he did not know they were stolen. *Magistrate,* (to the prisoner,) 'Well, I don't know what I can do, but send you before the Recorder.' 'Well, what must I do? I did my best to stop at home; I'd be glad to stop in the workhouse if you'd send me.' 'I don't mean to say you are not to be pitied, but certainly you're a very bad lad.' The superintendent of police said that the prisoner's father was a very decent man, but time after time the boy had been brought to the station, and his father now refused to have him home, as he said he could do nothing for him. *Magistrate.* 'It may be very probable that the boy is wayward, *but if his father will not look after him, what is the boy to do? It's really a miserable case.*' The superintendent said he believed the prisoner went home when he came out of prison last week, but his father would not have him. *The prisoner was then committed for trial at the Sessions.*"

It does not appear that even a reprimand was given to the father for thus almost compelling his child to be an injury to society at large, or a burden to it in gaol; the magistrate perhaps felt that he had no legal authority for doing so. But is it longer to be endured, that a magistrate shall be forced to send a child to a public trial, acknowledging from the bench that the child could do nothing else, because the father chose to neglect his duty? Such cases are not uncommon. We find the following cases among many in the Police Reports of the *Bristol Mercury:*

"May 31, 1852. Emma G., a child about 10 years old, was charged with stealing 3½d. from the person, which, on being detected she dropped on the floor of the shop. The policeman swore to the identity of a woman who was looking outside the shop, as being her mother. The fact of the theft having been proved, the magistrate *said he was sorry there was no help for it but the child must be committed!* She was removed crying bitterly, the mother on the contrary *evincing the greatest indifference.*"

This little girl was one of those for whom 23 gentlemen were summoned from their business to find a true bill against her. The result of all the formidable apparatus of constables, a bench of magistrates, the gaol, gaoler, and turnkeys, a court of justice formally assembled, a learned recorder sent for from a distance, was fourteen days' imprisonment! This was indeed a virtual acknowledgment of the injustice and absurdity of the whole proceeding. The mother, the real offender, was untouched.

"March, 1852. William L., a boy, was charged with having been found concealed in a shop. The prisoner has only just been discharged from Bridewell, where he had undergone *two months' imprisonment for a similar offence.* The magistrate said *that as two months' imprisonment had done him no good, he would try the effect of a longer term,* and he committed the prisoner for three months' imprisonment with hard labour."

Such a scene as the following cannot much contribute to the dignity of justice:

"Feb., 1852. Thomas V., an incorrigible *little* vagabond, who was only liberated from Bridewell yesterday, was charged with stealing a piece of bacon. The prisoner took the bacon from a shop, and being followed, when hard pressed, threw the stolen article at the pursuer's head; 'a course however,' *the magistrate remarked,* 'that did not save his bacon !' The prisoner, who displayed the coolest hardihood of demeanour, was sentenced to six weeks hard labour, *with the piquant addition of a whipping.*"

Here the self-reliance, coolness, of a young child, now hardened by familiarity with crime and its consequences, is able to provoke not only the reporter, but the magistrate himself, to forget the solemnity of the administration of justice. The little boy having thus set the bench of magistrates at defiance, soon renewed his offences after liberation; and was sentenced by the Recorder at the July Sessions to seven years' transportation.

Similar perplexities assail London magistrates, and elicit from them like confessions. The following is copied from the Police Reports of Oct., 1852.

"At the Mansion-house on Wednesday, Alfred H., aged 13 years, was charged with having stolen a pair of boots from a shop in Bishopsgate Street. The prisoner, who has been frequently imprisoned for theft, was dressed like an errand boy, and wore an apron which was tightly tucked round his waist, but could in an instant be let down, and be used as a bag or cover for property of large bulk. An officer said, 'I saw the prisoner, as I was going along, look earnestly through the windows of the shop; and having had him in custody for stealing boots before, I had no doubt of his intention. In a moment he slipped into the shop and was out again with the boots, which he was just going to deposit in his apron when I took him up in my hand, and then he threw down the property.' Alderman Lawrence: 'You have had occasion to apprehend him before?' Officer: 'I caught him before in the act of stealing boots from the next bootmaker's to that where I apprehended him last night. He has been summarily convicted three times for theft. He has been whipped twice, and he has been once tried at the Old Bailey, and sentenced to be imprisoned for three months.' The prisoner: 'No; I have been whipped but once, and sentenced summarily only twice.' Alderman Lawrence: 'Have you father or mother?' Prisoner: 'Yes, both; they live in Spitalfields.' Officer: 'I could not find them. The boy cannot tell the truth. The moment he gets loose from prison he begins to steal.' Alderman Lawrence (to the boy:) 'Why do you not live with your father and mother? They won't have you, I suppose?' The prisoner: 'It's not that; but I live in Brick Lane.' Alderman Lawrence: 'With whom?' The prisoner: 'I am there lodging by myself in one of the lodging-houses. I get my living by jobbing about.' Alderman Lawrence: '*Neither whipping nor imprisonment seems to have any effect upon you, but I must try them both again.* You must go to Bridewell for 21 days, and be there soundly whipped.'

In the following case a boy actually challenges his judge to do his worst, and having practically proved the inability of the law to restrain him, expresses his determination to transgress again, to obtain what he looks upon as a high premium.

" Nov. 15, 1852. At the Middlesex Sessions, on Monday, a boy pleaded guilty to stealing money from a till. It appeared that he had been *summarily convicted eleven times*. The Assistant Judge said the young thief knew that, by pleading guilty, he would be sentenced by the magistrate to three months' imprisonment, and in that way escape the punishment that Court could award, when the previous convictions were within its cognizance. In this case he had not the power to sentence the prisoner to transportation. The prisoner: '*I want to be transported*.' The Assistant Judge: 'I dare say you do; but I am sorry to say you cannot be gratified at present.' Prisoner: 'Oh, very well; *I shall go on the same game again when I'm out, till I do get transported, though*.' The Assistant Judge : 'Well, I promise you that the next time you come here you shall be transported, if guilty. Now, mind that.' He then sentenced the prisoner to nine months' hard labour."

We must not pass by another aspect of this subject, the connection which the administration of the Poor Laws frequently has with juvenile delinquency. The Rev. J. Davis, Ordinary of Newgate, stated to the Lords' Committee, that " There is a very close link between the scum of a workhouse and these juvenile offenders. Many will say, they have no parents whom we have found to have parents; but a number of them are orphans brought up in workhouses, who get among the vicious portion of the inmates of a workhouse, and so fall into vices, and from vices into crimes." This close connection certainly exists, and may be traced among many causes, to two particularly;—the first, the manner in which parish authorities neglect the claims of children who are thus driven into crimes, or in which they free themselves from the care of children who have become chargeable on them; the other, the condition and treatment of children in a large number of our workhouses.

A case illustrative of the first of these positions was given in " Reformatory Schools," p. 285; the subsequent history of the lad A. fully proves it. He remained " wild in the streets," living on occasional jobs, or on plunder, and resisting all attempts to bring him under better influences, until the cold of winter led him to seek the warmth and shelter of the school; he now again desired a home in the workhouse with another little boy; it was *refused to their repeated applications*, and equal disregard was shown to the representations of the schoolmaster, that the lads were utterly destitute, and had shown a true desire for admission. He then accompanied them to the magistrates, who sent an officer to demand their admission, which was now granted. But it was too late, the wild habits were already too deeply rooted; in a few weeks A. left this asylum, and many months did not pass before he was committed for trial, as one who, though young, is an experienced and noted pickpocket. The Recorder awarded him nine months of imprisonment. Can any one who has studied this subject feel the slightest expectation that this punishment will reform him? If not, he will continue to be a burden to the country. And to such a life he has been driven, being without any natural guardians, by the neglect of those who are termed "the guardians of the poor."

A similar case recently occurred in the same city, in which two friendless boys might have been driven to crime by similar treatment, had they not been sheltered in a Ragged School.

"A few evenings since," says a teacher, "two poor boys came to the school, who told the master that they were utterly destitute of food and shelter; one belonged to Manchester, where he had a father living, the other was Irish, and believed he had no parents. The boys were evidently not common vagrants, the Irish boy being decently dressed and well conducted, though uneducated; the other having received a superior education, and his deportment being such as to inspire confidence in his statements. They had applied at the Poor-house the preceding evening, but were refused relief or shelter, and had passed the night in the streets; a teacher went with them to renew their application, but they were again refused any help, though directed to appear the next day before the committee. Then one loaf was given to the English lad, and he was told with that to make his way to Manchester! The Irish lad was peremptorily refused all help, for Bristol claims a right to treat all Irish as aliens. Further inquiries were made about the boys, which proved that the Manchester boy's statements were perfectly correct,—that he was reduced to his present condition through no fault of his own, and had borne an excellent character. He was forwarded to his home through the efforts of friends."

Now had these boys not met with those who cared for them, because they were homeless and destitute, and had they not been so imbued with the fear of God, that the thought of breaking His laws to preserve life, did not appear to have occurred to them, —for one said, "we must have died if we had not been brought to the School,"—what alternative could they have had but to find a certain home in the gaol, and so enlist themselves in the dangerous classes? And who would have driven them to this course?

But, it will be said, that Bristol is a chartered city, and has a prescriptive right to defy the regulations of the English Poor Law,—to set at nought its commissioners,—to turn a deaf ear to the entreaties for succour of the homeless child,—to declare that no one born in our sister island shall ever be naturalized within the ancient boundaries. Be it so, and let it be granted that Bristol is a city peculiar in its privileged immunity from interference, when it chooses to condemn houseless children to the streets, and then to punish them for being found there in the night watches, for of such cases the police reports of magisterial proceedings give almost weekly records;— that it is free to allow children to grow up unchecked in vice, in courts and alleys almost entirely unmolested by its police, and then to present them to its Recorder to be removed from its care by transportation, or immured within the ponderous walls and under the stern discipline of its gaol for a long term of months,—to come forth well fed, increased in stature, and unreformed!

But are other cities, other union workhouses, more innocent of being " accomplices before the fact" in the crimes of these children? Are they better keepers of their younger brethren? Let those who know these things reply! The public papers have told us only in the last year, how the Gaol Chaplain of a neighbouring city, Bath, felt compelled to make it the subject of his official report, that children under his care had been driven to crime by being turned out of the Workhouse. Nor was the matter left unexamined by the Poor Law Commissioners. Nor have the London papers been lately silent respecting similar outrages in the metropolis.

Let us, however, suppose this abuse amended, and that all children who ought to be in a Union School are not only received there, but watchfully detained there; the fact stated by the Reverend Ordinary of Newgate, still remains unaltered, that there is " a close link between the scum of a Workhouse and these juvenile offenders." Whence arises this, that an institution which is intended as a relief from want, should become a nursery of crime? The answer is self-evident as respects those Unions where the young are exposed to direct contamination from persons whose dissolute lives have driven them here to claim national charity. But for the ordinary training here given, we cannot refer to a more valuable authority than to one of H. M. Inspectors of Union Schools, Jelinger C. Symons, Esq., as contained in a letter on District Farm Schools. [London: Clowes and Sons.]

"The bulk of pauperism springs from an indigenous race, for the most part reared and nursed in our Workhouses and Gaols, and on the confines of both. This 'dangerous class' amounts, at the lowest possible estimate, to no less than two-and-a-half millions of the people, who are perpetually preying upon the property, industry, and morals of the country. I regard all reforms as of minor importance which do not attack this leviathan evil. . . Reared in the Workhouse, these children are for the most part accustomed to a livelihood without labour, and are practically taught by habit to regard their status and its daily accompaniments as a natural condition rather than as a degrading necessity A mere fraction of the Workhouse boys in this county (country?) either are, or can be, trained in systematic and habitual labour in the existing Workhouses. When work is given it is usually desultory and unsystematic, consisting of occasional employment and odd jobs. . . Practical lessons on the dignity of labour and the disgrace of idleness, are thus impressed least on the class who needs them most. That which we have engrafted on the green bud remains in the dry. To that dependent state in which we rear the boy, the man naturally reverts: and the system practically results in the perpetuation of a pauper class. A fortnight ago, of the 309 inmates of one of the Workhouses of this county, (Gloucestershire,) 209 had, at previous periods of their lives, been inmates of that or other Workhouses; and if the biography of pauperism were thoroughly investigated, I believe you would find as strong proof of the proverb, that 'what is bred in the flesh will out in the bone,' as the history of mankind can afford."

In a "Memoir relating to the Industrial School, at Quatt," by W. W. Whitmore, Esq., we find this additional testimony :

"It has been remarked that a very large proportion of girls brought up in a Workhouse become abandoned in character. I find in a report of the Guardians of the Poor, in Marylebone, the following striking statement bearing on this point. Speaking of Workhouse management, it says, ' The evil consequences of the present management may be traced in the painful history of the young females who have been sent out of this house within the past nine years, to domestic service, not including apprentices, and whose ages and subsequent history are given as far as they can be ascertained :-

89 leading abandoned lives.

20 chargeable with illegitimate children.

37 having had several situations and outfits, have emigrated.

10 married.

1 passed.

7 dead.

10 receiving relief out of house.

45 supposed in service.
99 nothing known.
 8 taken out by friends.

326

"I believe nearly the same painful story might be told of a similar number of young females brought up in almost any Workhouse."

The importance of this subject requires that a long treatise should be devoted to it alone: but we must now proceed to consider the principle on which the treatment of juvenile delinquents is founded.

The mode of punishment most highly approved by our Legislature, the separate system, is thus spoken of by one of H. M. Inspectors, Col. Jebb, in a letter to the *Times*, Oct. 6, 1852: "A long term of separate confinement is *the most dreaded*, as well as the most salutary, of all inflictions which the humanity of our times permits." Now the salutary influence not existing in the case of children, as has been proved, the principle of *fear* and dread of *physical* suffering alone remains. A forced conformity with a certain external mode of action is all that can be attained in a prison, in the case of children; for in their young minds, which are influenced only by present impressions, the best instructions leave but a faint trace when again exposed to temptation,—they are like "the morning cloud or early dew" which disappear before the noonday heat. We have seen that those who exhibited the greatest apparent improvement when in prison, were influenced only by dread of punishment, and on their release took unto themselves "seven devils worse than before." It is probable that the principle of fear is the only one which a government, as such, can employ in the correction of delinquent children; adopting, then, the parentage of such, if it also undertakes the management of them, it can employ no other as the mainspring of its system. Hence, in establishing the Juvenile Prison at Parkhurst, which was intended to be a very great improvement on the treatment before adopted towards juvenile delinquents, this principle was necessarily very prominently displayed. If an establishment founded on such principle could answer the object of a Reformatory School, that surely would have done so, for it was begun with the best intentions, a healthy and beautiful spot was chosen for its site, pecuniary resources were not limited, and a government usually has at command the best officers that it can select. But to carry out the principle of the employment of physical force and the action of fear on the young convicts, it was necessary to shut out the beautiful island by high walls, to render the labour compulsory, soldiers with loaded guns being on guard to watch the boys, and to appoint military men as officers,—the softening influence of woman being entirely excluded. The experiment has been fairly tried; how has it answered?

In the former work on "Reformatory Schools," especial reference was made to this prison. The establishment was spoken of as excellent in its appointments, furnished with every thing which could minister to the physical and intellectual wants of its inmates, supplying such spiritual nutriment as seemed to its founders most excellent; but, as was proved by infallible signs, egregiously failing in its object from the introduction of the spirit of fear, and from a want of faith in the only spring of action, from which experience shows that real reformation can proceed, love of the child's soul, belief in *the free development of his nature.* The witnesses who furnished these proofs were not casual visitors,—not hearsay reporters,—not prejudiced partizans of a favourite theory,—but one in a high judicial position who gave them in evidence before the House of Lords, and the Governor of Parkhurst himself, both in his evidence on the same occasion, and in his official reports to the Senate of the nation. It would seem superfluous to add a word to opinions and facts emanating from such quarters, but as Parkhurst is still regarded by many as a type of what a Reformatory School should be, it may be well to have a somewhat closer insight into its workings. The following is the impression of a gentleman who has made a recent visit to this juvenile prison, and who had peculiarly excellent opportunities of forming a correct judgment:

" I spent five hours yesterday at Parkhurst, and experience has confirmed me in my views respecting it. What I saw was just what I anticipated. The food excellent, the accommodation excellent; good crops upon the land; plenty of different trades going on;—but almost all the boys working under *fear* instead of kindness. The first field I saw was a picture. There were four gangs at work; *half of the number of boys in each were evidently idle.* To each gang an overseer, not working too, and encouraging the boys in their labour,— but there to look on, to force on the work, and to prevent escapes. And walking along either hedge were soldiers, muskets loaded, and bayonets fixed. How any reformatory process can be expected to go on under such a system is a marvel to me. I was quite tired of the military salute; even the cook capped me in that fashion; and when I came among the brickmakers, who were working under a non-military man, it was quite delightful. I talked to this man about his boys, and how he treats them. 'O sir,' he said, 'I find the right way is to be kind to them; it is much easier to lead than to drive,'—and the man's face showed that he acted on this conviction. He added, 'A boy, if he is put out by being harshly treated, can always find a way of having his revenge; he will turn over his barrow, or spoil his work in some way, and that so cunningly as to make it appear as the result of accident.' I was not surprised to hear that here had never been an attempt to escape on the part of this worthy brickmaker's boys."

Such is the aspect of the place to an ordinary visitor. The official report of the chaplain of the Junior Ward respecting the effect of this system of punishment will be more important. (*Vide* Report of the Directors of Convict Prisons.) "The prisoners placed in the refractory ward belonging to the junior ward, are visited by me. *I cannot say that it has had any beneficial effect upon those who have been placed there in consequence of the fire; they seem still hardened. Several of them have been repeatedly punished since the period of their confinement.* In general I find this ward a very valuable help to us in subduing or restraining the rebellious spirit of these youths." During the year had occurred an attempt made by ten boys in this ward to set on fire the prison. "Seven of these," he says, "were the smallest and youngest in the prison; two of the others were of longer standing, and much older, who urged the plot, though it did not originate with them. During the probationary period of these boys their conduct was very bad, and from the time they joined the junior wards, though under repeated punishment, admonition, and kind advice, they showed a determination to resist every effort on our part to subdue and soften down their stubborn spirit." During the month of January only, he mentions that with about 200 boys the minor offences were 602. During the year the "crimes" reported to the Governor, such as riotous conduct, assaulting officers, damaging prison property, arsony, attempting to escape, &c., were 175. Parkhurst presents a solitary instance of an intended Reformatory Institution being twice in one year set on fire by its inmates.

These and the official reports before cited will receive striking illustration and confirmation, from the narrative of one who had personally experienced the effect of the system, the youth X., whose early history has been already given. It should be premised that he does not speak in complaint of the system pursued; on the contrary, he evidently feels that his conduct fully deserved all the severity that was exercised against him, and he speaks gratefully of the instruction given him. But the facts he states, are of importance in our present inquiry as exhibiting in a striking manner the effects of such a system of treatment on a hardened offender. The narrative also proves how impossible it is, even under the strictest discipline, to prevent contamination and the grossest violation of duty, where a number of boys are congregated together, whose spirit is not kindled to join themselves in the work of reformation.

After being six months at Milbank, during which time he was only kept from rebellion through fear and dread of punishment, he was transferred to Parkhurst. Owing to the badness of his conduct, he was kept six months in the probationary ward; there he began to attend to his schooling, to learn hymns and collects, to read the Bible, having but very few books, and the minister exhorted him to prayer; but he felt utterly unable to understand the Bible. "I used," he says, "to throw the sacred book on the floor in an agony, and say that it was of no use of me trying to understand such a piece of stuff." He thus continues his narrative: "I had not been out in the general ward long, before I began to get into disgrace, and that of a very serious character. Previous to this, I thought that there was no rogue so sharp as myself, but I was greatly mistaken, for I found myself among a number of boys from every quarter of the United Kingdom, some much younger, and some older, and all appeared to be much sharper than me. I soon got linked in with a school of bad ones, and in direct opposition to the rules of the prison, I began to traffic for trifling things, such as small grammar books, etymologies, and pieces of arithmetic. This all tended to harden me, but I did not stop here. I was next tried if I would gamble, but I did not like that, for it was more than I could stand to gamble on the Sabbath and in the House of God, as some of them did; although I used to sit there without listening to the sermon, or joining in the prayers, gambling in the chapel completely horrified me. I still continued to get harder and harder, and commenced to be very unruly; I began to fight, swear, steal, and be disobedient to my officers, for which I was many times punished. My character had now got so bad, that one day when I had got a black eye with fighting; my officers told me that I was a real blackguard; this cut me to the heart, I resolved once more to rid myself of this bad name and character; but do not mistake me, there was not the least spark of religion in me at the time, for I had now arrived at such a pitch of wickedness, that I, with several others, tried to persuade ourselves that there was no future state after death; this was the means to which I resorted to put conscience to sleep. However, I tried to be more cunning, and I established a bit of a character again. I soon fell back into my old ways, and became a profound sabbath-breaker and a blasphemer. I hated every well-disposed boy, and was hated by them; I lived at enmity with both prisoners and officers, and thus became miserable in the extreme, for I was never out of punishment. This I thought to remedy by running away; I effected my escape, while digging one day on the land, with two more as bad as myself, but we were brought back the same night, placed in the refractory ward, and whipped the next morning; but they might as well have whipped a block of wood as me, for I only laughed at it; it took not the least effect upon my hard heart, and my flesh was now almost as hard with punishment. I remained in close confinement for seventeen days, when I was let out again; I now broke out in open rebellion, plotting, scheming for revenge against the officers who had got me in justice punished. I had not been out above that much longer, when, I was put in again for mutiny in its most ferocious form. Me and another boy entered the refractory on a Monday evening, and before we had been in an hour we began our diabolical conduct, whistling, singing, cursing, and abusing every officer that came to us,—in short doing every thing that was bad, and swearing vengeance against all who came to us, till the officer was actually afraid of coming to us, and no marvel, for we were more demons than human beings. The next morning we were both whipped for our bravery, as it was termed by our companions. When I was tied up to be flogged, I began to pour forth the most horrid blasphemies that ever were uttered by any human tongue against the governor and other officers that stood by, worse than ever I had done before or since. For this horrid conduct I was reported to the Secretary of State, who ordered I should be placed for twenty-one days in close confinement, on 18oz. of bread a day, afterwards to be placed in the penal class, where I was to be kept for three months under strict discipline, without sufficient food to eat. After undergoing all this, you may have some idea what sort of an object I was; if my parents had seen me they would not have known me. I was exceedingly thin, very little beside skin and bone, and racked to pieces with pain and disease, and all this I brought upon myself by my diabolical and fiendish conduct. If I had not been blessed by Almighty God with one of the strongest constitutions, I should have been in the grave long since, for I have suffered enough through my own folly to serve a dozen men. During my stay this time in the refractory, I began to read my Bible, and listen to the voice of my minister. I also began to pray as he directed me; these delightful services gave me great pleasure; they assuaged the pain of body and mind under which I was then labouring, and made me think there was something better in store for me. But, O! so soon as ever I came from under the rod of correction, these delightful thoughts began to fly away like the relics of a dream. One Sabbath forenoon I went to chapel as usual, and the minister preached a beautiful sermon, to which I listened with great attention, but I was now so weak that I could not remain five minutes in one posture. The governor seeing this, ordered me out of the refractory ward to my own ward. On the same Sabbath at dinner time, I had not been from under punishment one hour, before I broke one of the prison rules. I had now been without flesh-meat or any such thing for three months; a boy came and offered me a piece of bread and meat, which I took, though in direct opposition to the rules of the prison. One would have thought that I had had enough of punishment, but no, I had not done yet. All my officers pitied me, and so did my fellow-prisoners, for it was truly heart-rending to see a boy of about 17 years of age, who, but three months before was in good health, as stout and strong as any one in the prison, now a mere skeleton, racked to pieces with pain, and as weak as a little infant."

Surely the law makes sin, when it converts the offering a morsel of meat to a fainting brother into an offence. The poor youth was soon conveyed into the Infirmary, where, he says,—

" I was now so ill, that all who saw me gave me up entirely for death;" the most severe medical treatment was found necessary; "all this time which was three months I did not know whether I should live or die; but for all this there was scarcely a thought about my immortal soul." When he began to recover he was treated with much indulgence, and availed himself of it constantly to break the prison rules, "because I saw," says he, " that they did not wish to punish me, for they knew well that I was not able to stand punishment." He soon began his mutinous conduct again, and subjected himself to repeated punishments; being taught by each only to be " a little more cunning." A circumstance soon after occurred which somewhat awakened his conscience. A theft he committed with many precautions, in order to benefit a companion, was brought home to him in a way which, though apparently accidental, struck him as a divine interference, and yet it was not so clearly proved upon him as to subject him to punishment. He determined once more to try to do better, having been at Parkhurst about two years and a half; for about five months he persevered, got into the evening school, and gained good conduct stripes on his arms; he was taught a trade, but this, he says, proved his destruction, by giving him means of getting unlawful indulgence; for three months, he continues, " I lived the most profligate life; I spent the Sabbath in the most diabolical manner, and during the week days I stole all that I could lay my hands on; till at last me and another made it up to steal one of the workmen's dinners; however we were found out about the matter, and reported to the governor, for which we were both turned out of the evening school, and lost our stripes; however, instead of letting this punishment, which was but small compared with our offence, have some effect on us for good, we both determined to be ten times worse; by and bye, we both made up our minds to run away. My companion lingered, but I had become so miserable that I could not stay any longer. I ran away by night, and determined in my own mind so to commit myself that I might not go to Parkhurst any more."

This strikingly bears out the statements of the Governor in his Report. (*Vide* " Ref. Sch.," p. 320.)

" I broke into a house; the mistress of it heard me; she got up and alarmed one or two of her neighbours. I at once threw myself into their hands, and was retaken to Parkhurst."

Having pleaded guilty on his trial, he was sentenced anew to seven years transportation. Society had done its worst with him. This was the result. Happily he was placed where the dews of Christian kindness softened his hard heart, and opened it to receive the rays of divine grace in a fruitful soil. This is the youth " gentle, earnest, and serious," (p. 20,) whose cell is now the scene of a new life to him, and who hopes, if not in his native land, henceforth to devote himself to the glory of God, and the benefit of his fellow creatures.

Surely no one can read the foregoing narrative without perceiving how utterly hopeless it is to attempt to effect a real reformation or change of heart on these young persons, by the action of fear and the employment of physical force. Such a case is not a solitary one, but the true portraiture of a class.

We shall conclude this chapter with one more illustration of the effects of the present system on those unhappy young persons who have become, to their unspeakable misfortune, the " children of the State." It is derived from the last Report of the Chaplain of the Manchester Gaol. It needs no comment.

" I may quote here as a mournful illustration of this description," *i. e.* the condition of juvenile delinquents, " a case that occurred in this gaol during the past year, and which, I fear, *may be taken as a sample of many others.* A boy, only 12 years of age, who had already been eight times in the New Bailey, was committed to the Borough Gaol. His father was dead; his mother-lived in a cellar in one of the lowest streets of the town, and endeavoured to earn a scanty subsistence by selling pipeclay. She could just support herself, and left the boy to pick up a living as he best could. As may be presumed from such a state of things, the boy was utterly destitute of all means of instruction, and grew up, not only ignorant, but sullen, obstinate, and mischievous. His behaviour towards the officers of the gaol was dogged or insolent. The expression of his countenance dark and repulsive—the very index of the stubborn will and evil passions within—but to myself he was uniformly docile, and even gentle; would listen to my instructions and assent to my wishes in everything; and I was often struck with the change of expression that would soften and light up his otherwise hard features as I talked to him. Going into his cell one day shortly before his term of imprisonment expired, I inquired into his condition and prospects, and feeling painfully how hopeless they were, and how impossible that the lad could escape the life of misery and crime to which his very circumstances seemed to oblige him, I paced his cell for a few moments, anxiously deliberating what was to be done; at last, pausing, and looking the boy full in the face, I said to him, ' If I could obtain some sort of situation for you, where you could earn an honest living, would you try to do better ?' The boy, who was never known to give way to any softened feelings before, burst into tears and sobbed convulsively, as he assured me I should never have cause to repent it. I left the cell, assuring him I would do what I could for him, and that, so far as I had any means to prevent it, he should not be lost. My hope was to have got him into an institution for destitute children near London, but £20 was required; and after an unsuccessful appeal to two or three individuals, I was unable to obtain it, and the boy was discharged. Two days after I opened the door of a cell, and to my surprise found him again an inmate. My first exclamation of sorrow and surprise was,—'What B., you here again?' He hung down his head, as though unwilling to meet my eye, and after a few moments of silence, he suddenly raised it, and looking at me with an appealing and hopeless expression of anguish I can never forget, he said, with an almost passionate emphasis, 'Sir, what *could* I do?" and then told me his tale thus: 'On leaving the gaol, he went directly to look for his mother, in the cellar where he had left her. She was not there, gone, the neighbours said, into the workhouse. Penniless and houseless, he wandered about all day and all night in the streets, and the next day, driven by hunger, he stole some bread, and was committed for the offence. He said he knew not what to do, and everything was better than his condition outside. Shortly after, an officer looked into his cell, one Sunday afternoon, and found him lying on his bed, which he had unrolled contrary to orders, reading his Bible. The officer reproved him, and desired him to roll it up till the proper hour. To his surprise, the boy rose immediately, and without a word, or a look of anger and defiance,—his usual answer on such occasions,—quietly obeyed the order. The same officer, passing the cell not long after, looked in again, and found the unhappy boy suspended by a hammock girth to the gas-pipe,—and *dead!*"

Of whom will the blood of this child be required?

" INASMUCH AS YE DID IT NOT UNTO ONE OF THE LEAST OF THESE MY BRETHREN, YE DID IT NOT TO ME!"

CHAPTER VI.

AMERICAN EXPERIENCE.

We may now, it is hoped, be permitted to assume it as a proposition sufficiently proved, that the present treatment of juvenile offenders is useless as a remedy of the evil, injurious as regards both the individual and society, and besides exceedingly costly,—as indeed everything bad must be. A different system was distinctly pointed out in the preceding work, which was shown to be effective as a remedy, highly beneficial as regards the individual and society, and consequently far less costly.

That if such a system is so effective *it ought* to be adopted, few will deny. " But CAN it be carried out ?" say politicians and economists. We will not answer that everything that *ought* to be done, *can* be done by those who have faith—who, like the grain of mustard seed, will, with steady, patient aim, spread forth their roots deep and their branches high, nourished by heaven's sun and rain; who have thus gained a strength to which the Saviour's promise is granted, that it shall remove mountains. But we shall now proceed to show *how* the principles which are here advocated have been *practically* carried out in other countries, and shall commence with that one most allied to ourselves, by race, by language, by habits of thought,—the United States.

The principles which we wish to show thus practically developed, are,

First, That children who have been brought under necessary legal interference by their infringement of the laws, should be dealt with in Reformatory Asylums rather than by ordinary imprisonment; the punishment in such Asylums being hardly more than what is implied in confinement and restraint; reformation and industrial training being the main features of the process. This was the principle set forth in the Lords' Report of 1847.

Secondly, That such schools or asylums to effect the desired end, must be under the guidance of enlightened Christian benevolence, sanctioned and mainly supported by government inspection and aid. [" Ref. Sch." p. 349.]

Thirdly, That since it is absolutely impossible that a government, as such, can secure such guidance for these establishments, *voluntary effort must be mainly looked to for the infusion of the true reformatory element into these Asylums,* and therefore must be encouraged, and, as far as possible, called out by the legislature; which, granting the means and the authority to carry out the work, will exercise inspection to ascertain that these are wisely employed. The State will thus retain the authority it has taken from the parent in consequence of his neglect of duty, and will place the charge in the hands of those who can and will discharge it well.

Having exhibited the practical development of these general principles, we shall show how this reformatory action is carried out by those who have successfully attempted it, and finally consider some of the difficulties which arise in the prosecution of the work.

The condition of the juvenile population in America is particularly important to our present inquiry, because it is believed by many that a good system of national education would completely relieve our country from its present load of infant crime.

We have shown that in our own country these neglected children will not avail themselves of the education afforded in the British and National Schools, and that the bulk of the juvenile offenders of the worst class have had abundant means of education offered to them, but have nowise profited by it. Yet still it is supposed that the masses of the "perishing and dangerous" children would be beneficially affected by it. Let us observe the effects of it on such masses elsewhere. The system of National Education in the United States is the pride of that country, and justly so, for in those States where it is fully developed it exhibits features which are not often found in combination, State interference and helps, with voluntary effort,—a government supporting, and a people vigorously working. It needs only to read the laborious, searching, and enlightened Common School Reports which reach us from that sister land, to show us that individual minds are there actively engaged in the work; and that intellects of the first order throw their power into what is a great public undertaking. These schools are freely open to all, none are so mean or low that they may not receive admittance there;— except indeed that persecuted race, who, for wearing a skin of the colour which God gave them, are condemned by their white brethren to exclusion from such intellectual privileges as they possess. With such exception, one which we trust will not long disgrace a free and enlightened country, the Common Schools, affording intellectual training of a very high order, are accessible to all. Let us now hear the testimony of an American to the influence which these free schools have on the class from which spring juvenile delinquents.*

"Our own system of Free Schools stands out in striking contrast with the provision made for popular education in the Old World. And when we remember the number and character of our Free Schools, thrown open without distinction to the whole people, when we know that this system has been improving for years, that the amount of money raised by taxation in this commonwealth has increased three-fold within fourteen years, being the last year upwards of 915,000 dollars, a gain of more than half a million; that in the same period there has been an increase of more than a thousand schools, with an

---

* Christian Examiner, May, 1852. Art., "Juvenile Depravity and Reformatory Schools, pp. 399—401. Boston: Crosby and Nichols."

addition of 2,733 teachers, and that there are no less than 200,000 children that improve these privileges; we are forced to feel that honourable means for public instruction has been provided by the State. When we know that in the city of Boston alone, between 20,000 and 30,000 children attend the public schools, in addition to 2,000 others who attend private seminaries, we cannot but feel thankful that we live in a community in which the young are looked upon with such wise solicitude, and where they are so ready to reap the advantages they enjoy. *Still, all this should not blind us to painful realities.* From a late School Report we extract the following: '*Does the instruction provided by the city reach all those persons for whom it is intended?*' This question suggests itself to every one who observes the apparently great numbers of children at large in school-hours in almost every part of the city. It is not difficult to find out what are the occupations of many of these children. They are hawkers of papers, or sellers of matches, most of the time occupied in selling and gambling. They are beggars, male and female; strolling from street to street, through lanes, highways, and alleys, *practising the elementary lessons of pilfering, lying, deception, and theft.* They may be seen wherever wooden structures are in the process of building, repairing, or tearing down, seeking for fragments of wood, to which they evidently feel they have a very questionable right. They are the loafers on wharves, *and practised in all the modes of juvenile vice. Are these children in the way to become honest citizens? Are they not in a course of education for worthlessness and crime?*

"Let us turn from this to the records of the Courts of Justice, and the Reports of the Police. It has been officially stated that there are upwards of 800 boys in Boston *connected with Grammar Schools alone, whose names are on the police-lists as truants or vagrants.* A late report of the Grand Jury says, 'The Jury have been pained to see the large number of minors, *frequently amounting to more than half the cases,* who are brought before them, generally for larcenies. It is stated by Beaumont and De Tocqueville, in their report upon the penitentiary system of our country, that of all the convicts in the

United States, one in every ten is under the age of 20 years.' From the City Marshal's Report we take the following: 'Allow me to renew my appeal in regard to the young in this city, and *to the large and increasing number of poor and destitute children of both sexes, who are growing up in vice and crime.*' In an investigation made to ascertain the number thus exposed, between the ages of 6 and 16,—1064 were found, 882 males, 182 females. My opinion is,' says the Report, ' that, of the whole number, from 8 to 900, from neglect and bad habits, *are not fit to enter any of our present schools.* From the best information which I can obtain, I am satisfied that the whole number in the city at the present time, including the above number, is not less than 1500 of the same class as those described.' And he adds: ' I earnestly call your attention to them, and the necessity of providing some means to have these children properly brought up, either at public or private expense; for I am satisfied that *it will cost the state and the city more for police-courts, and prisons, if they are suffered to go at large, than it would to take them now, maintain them, and make them useful citizens.*'

" No one," truly remarks the reviewer, "will be insensible to the startling character of these facts, and the justice of the conclusions. *Every such child as is here alluded to, is a plea for extended Christian effort. Our public school system is accomplishing incalculable good, but here we see a class springing up among us, who come not under its influence.* It is the beginning of a state of things which exists on a large scale in the Old World."

Nor is it only a beginning. *The New York Christian Inquirer,* in a recent number, thus speaks of its actual existence : " The condition of our street boys has been often described, but we suppose that few realized either its depths or its heights. That they are generally destitute, ignorant, profane, lying, thieving, fighting-scholars in the school of life, is taken for granted." And twenty years ago the same condition of a class untouched by a national education, was forcibly pointed out by the late Rev. Dr. Tuckerman, who was the originator of Domestic Missions in that country, and probably in our own. His warm Christian sympathy for the forsaken and outcast led him to seek to discover the true cause of the great existing evil; the results of his extensive experience, embodied in his reports, point to the same conclusions as have here been laid down. He thus shows the little effect of a National Education on the class we are considering:

"Before the establishment of the House of Refuge in New York, more than 500 young persons were annually committed in that state, either as criminals or vagrants; and we learn from the Superintendent of the Penitentiary at Bellevue, that of the children committed there, not more than one in eight could read and write at the time of committal. . . . . From the 1st Jan. to 31st of Dec., 1830, the number of children received into the House of Refuge in New York, was 144. Of this number 71 could not read, and 20 of these did not know a letter, 33 of the 144 were all that knew anything of arithmetic, and of these 22 were in addition only. The average age of these children was 11 years 6 months; and of the 144 only 60 were of American parentage. This institution was opened in 1825. . . . . The House of Refuge in Philadelphia was opened in 1828; the whole number who have been received into it, is 289 boys and 93 girls. Of the 289 boys, 182 could not read, and only 31 knew anything of arithmetic. Their average age was near 15 years. 70 of these boys had previously been in prison. . . . . In a memorial of the Pennsylvania Society for Promotion of Public Schools, presented to the Legislature of that State in 1830, it is said, 'there are at least 400,000 in Pennsylvania, between the ages of 5 and 14; and of these not 150,000 were in all the schools of the State.' This fact, I am aware will hardly be thought to be credible; but it has been reported to the Legislature, with at least an apparent belief in its truth by the Governor of Pennsylvania. . . . In the Prison of Wethersfield, Connecticut, there are a few less than 200; of these 42 per cent. cannot write; 16 per cent. cannot read. . . . . Of 300 men who have been in the Sunday School of the Auburn State Prison, Massachusetts, 85 did not know the alphabet; and 200 were able to read only in easy lessons for children, and by spelling some of the words!"

It is evident, then, that the mere providing of abundance of schools is not of itself sufficient to raise the people. But further, Dr. Tuckerman states his conviction, that while hundreds of young children were infesting the streets, and entirely neglecting the numerous excellent free-schools provided by the city, "*as they now are, they cannot, and ought not to be admitted into the public schools, and they must be prepared for them by schools adapted by private Christian kindness to their present circumstances.* The character and condition of the bad boys of this city is the most pitiable, the most deplorable which can well be imagined. And they have strong claims upon us, because, in truth, *their own is not the heaviest part of the responsibility for their character and for their offences.* Reared amidst the worst examples, they never knew the kindly influence of religious and affectionate interest in their welfare and happiness; *never can they know it, but through the sympathy of those who will seek them that they may save them.*"

In development of such an idea, a School of Reformation was opened in South Boston, in 1826, to which the magistrates should send children convicted of crimes; shortly after, the Rev. Mr. Wells was appointed to undertake its management. That gentleman entered on his work with a firm conviction that it could be accomplished by the means indicated by Dr. Tuckerman. "Most people imagine," he says, "when they see or hear of bad boys, that they are a worse kind of boys, worse by nature than others. If my observation be of any value on this subject, it is not so; for though at first there be strong sproutings of evil principle and passion to be lopped off, *we often find him as good a stock, and as rich a soil as in other cases.* .... However bad a boy may be, he can always be reformed while he is under 15 years old, and very often after that age; and he who has been reckoned and treated as if incapable of any thing like honesty and honour, may be worthy of the most entire confidence. .... We live together as a family of brethren, cheerful, happy, confiding, and, I trust, to a great or less degree pious." To this "family" the magistrates of Boston did not fear to intrust delinquent children.

But young persons, however dangerous, however morally perishing, could not be sent to this school without legal conviction. Many there are who might be rescued without their incurring a legal taint; many parents are there, who, feeling their inability to exercise the necessary control over their children, would gladly consign their authority to those who would well exercise it, at the same time contributing to the support of the child. To supply this need a society was formed which asked for no pecuniary aid from the state, but solely for authority and power to carry out its operations. In March, 1833, the Boston Farm School Society was incorporated, having for its object, " the education and reformation of boys, who, from the loss of their parents and other causes, are in danger of becoming vicious and dangerous, or useless members of society." A certain degree of exposure to vice and criminal delinquency constituted, as it were, qualifying requisites to entitle to its assistance; and though not directly connected with the criminal courts, or under their cognizance or supervision, this school was designed to have an intimate affinity with them, and be their voluntary aid and ally. (*Vide* Reports for 1847 and 1849.) This Society, uniting with that of the " Boston Asylum for Indigent Boys," received from the state a corporate act in 1835, on its establishment in Thompson's Island, but was otherwise wholly disconnected from public support or administration. This act gave to the Corporation " power to admit into their Institution any indigent boy above the age of 5, at the request of his parent or guardian; and to accept from him a surrender in writing of any such boy to the care and direction of said Corporation." It likewise gave " authority to the Corporation to retain and employ such boys on their farm, after they are of suitable age to be bound out, until the age of 21 years: or they may bind out such boys, when of suitable age, in virtuous families, or as apprentices at any reputable trade, until the age of 21 years, in like manner, and on the same conditions, as overseers of the poor may by law bind out the children of poor persons settled in their respective towns." The Institution receives, however, not only such children, but also others, morally exposed, or exhibiting tendencies to evil, whose parents desire to place them only temporarily under its care and reformatory training, paying towards their maintenance. For these it is in the act provided, "that any such boy, who shall not have been surrendered to said Corporation in the manner herein provided, may be withdrawn from the Institution, or the person to whom he is bound, by his parent or guardian, upon payment to said Corporation of the expenses incurred by them in the relief, support, and instruction of such boy."

This Farm School is still conducted on these principles, with only an increasing conviction on the part of its supporters and friends of the importance of such a school of moral training for the rescue of those who must otherwise almost inevitably fall into vice. It is unnecessary to detail its general plan of management, because it does not differ in any important feature from others that will be described in this work.

With respect to results, the managers state, after an experience of more than twenty years, that " they cannot doubt that these have been highly beneficial."

In reference to the age and character of the boys admitted, some important facts may be gathered from the Reports. Though boys of 5 years of age are admissible, and all may be retained until 21, practically, few or none are admitted under 8, or remain beyond 16, before which time they are apprenticed out. In 1849 the number of boys was 85; of these 15 were between 8 and 10; 31 between 10 and 12; 34 between 12 and 14; 3 between 14 and 15; and 1, 15 years old." It is found by experience undesirable to admit to this school " boys of maturer age, and already confirmed in bad habits;" these exercise an injurious influence over the younger members, " initiate them into tricks and vices before unknown to them, and impart the same spirit of discontent and insubordination by which they are themselves actuated. By avoiding boys of this character, and selecting for admission chiefly such as are friendless and destitute, and those morally exposed to ruin, but as yet only in the incipient stages of delinquency, the managers have been able to secure good order, good morals, and contentment. Boys are often truant and unmanageable by their parents, who are not really vicious, but who, being taken from their haunts of idleness, and placed at the Farm School, become orderly, docile, and good boys. It is such as these that are 'snatched as brands from the burning.' " From this Institution thus the boys go forth into the world without any criminal taint in public estimation; it is designed, not to supersede " State Reform Schools," but to prevent the necessity for them.

The principles developed in the preceding extracts have now become so fully acknowledged in the United States, that in many of them we already find Reformatory Schools taking the place of Prisons for juvenile delinquents.

In the city of New York, March 29, 1824, an Act was passed "to incorporate a Society for the Reformation of Juvenile Delinquents." It thus opens:

"Whereas, by the petition of several of the inhabitants of the city of New York, it is represented that they are desirous of establishing a Society and House of Refuge for the reformation of Juvenile Delinquents in the said city, and have prayed to be incorporated; *Therefore*, be it enacted by the people of the State of New York, represented in Senate and Assembly: *that all such persons as now are, or hereafter shall become subscribers to the said association, pursuant to the by-laws thereof, shall be, and hereby are constituted a body corporate and politic by the name of the* Managers of the Society for the Reformation of Juvenile Delinquency in the city of New York; and by that name they shall have perpetual succession, and being in law capable of suing and being sued, &c. It is observable then that any individual who feels sufficient interest in the object to subscribe to it, is henceforth one of the managers. It is further enacted, 'that the estate and concerns of the said corporation shall be conducted by a board of 30 managers, to be elected by a plurality of ballots of the members resident in the city of New York, being subscribers aforesaid, and present at such election yearly.' And again: 'That the said managers shall have power at their discretion to receive and take into the House of Refuge, to be established by them, all such children as shall be taken up or committed as vagrants, or convicted of criminal offences in the said city, as may, in the judgment of the Court of

General Sessions of the peace, or of the Court of Oyer and Terminer in and for the said city, or of the jury before whom any such offender shall be tried, or the police magistrates, or of the commissioners of the Almshouse and Bridewell of the said city, be proper objects; and the said managers shall have power to place the said children committed to their care, during the minority of such children, at such employments, and to cause them to be instructed in such branches of useful knowledge as shall be suited to their years and capacities.' Full power is given to the managers to make all arrangements and regulations respecting the direction of the affairs of the society, the management and control of the children, the appointment of officers, and the designation of their duties; the only condition imposed being, 'that the said managers shall make an annual report to the Legislature, and to the Corporation of the city of New York, of the number of children received by them into the House of Refuge, the disposition which shall be made of the said children by instructing or employing them in the said House of Refuge, or by binding them out as apprentices or servants; the receipts and expenditure of said managers, and generally all such facts and particulars as may tend to exhibit effects, whether advantageous or otherwise, of the said Association.' "

The Legislature of New York thus freely intrusts the care of children whose criminality has placed them at its disposal, to a number of persons who have, in the first place, shown their zeal in the work by making a pecuniary sacrifice, and who have been selected by the free annual choice of the subscribers to form a Board of Managers. The Legislature requires only to *know* what is being done, trusting otherwise to the inspection which those personally interested by giving their money would certainly exercise, and to the anxiety which responsible and removable managers would have to discharge their duty; it reserves to itself only the power that it may at any time hereafter alter, modify, or repeal this act.

An act being thus passed to enable the managers of the House of Refuge to receive and detain juvenile delinquents, a corresponding act was needed to enable judges to send them there; it stands thus:

"Whenever any person under 16 years," (by a subsequent Act this is altered to 17,) "shall be convicted of any felony, the Court, *instead of sentencing such person to imprisonment in a State prison*, may order that he be removed to and confined in the House of Refuge, established by the Society for the Reformation of Juvenile Delinquents in the city of New York; unless notice shall have been received from such society, that there is not room in such house for the reception of further delinquents. Such convicts shall be removed by the sheriff of the county, pursuant to such order, and he shall be allowed the same compensation therefor as is provided for the transportation of convicts to the State prison, to be audited and paid as part of the contingent expenses of the county."

The maintenance of all these children, prevented by State regulations from gaining their own living, could not equitably be thrown on private benevolence; the Senate and Assembly of New York therefore enacted in 1825 that the public treasurer should pay annually to the society for five years, 2,000 dollars; and in 1831, that 4,000 dollars should be paid annually. In addition to this sum, the Commissioners of Health are directed to pay annually 8,000 dollars from funds at their disposal, any deficiency from this sum to be supplied from the public treasury; likewise the proceeds from various specified licenses and fines are to be paid to the treasurer of the House of Refuge, and recoverable by him; and the Commissioners of Emigration are directed to pay to him certain specified sums, a deficiency to be supplied by the State Treasury; likewise the institution was entitled to a share of the Common School funds. [*Vide* Act of Incorporation and Laws relative to the New York House of Refuge, 1849.]

Thus was substantially acknowledged by the State of New York, the principle that it was for the public advantage that such an institution should exist; that it would be most effectively conducted if intrusted freely to the management of voluntary supporters; that it should therefore receive State authority, and be mainly supported by public funds. The twenty-fifth and twenty-sixth reports show how far the experience of a quarter of a century satisfied the public of that State as to the soundness of these principles.

"Thus far," say the Managers in 1850, " our institution has continued prosperously to carry on the great work of reformation. . . The noble example furnished by the city of New York has, we learn, been followed by other cities of the Union. . . . Our own State, now thoroughly convinced of the salutary effects of the system, have granted a charter for a noble Institution in the western part of the State. The beneficial results arising from the discipline and management exercised in the house have been so frequently alluded to in our reports, it seems almost needless to speak of them again, but will refer to the letters in the appendix, received from boys and girls, and parties to whom they have been indentured, for information on this subject."

The letters relate to such facts as these:

"The above boy was committed by the city authorities for sleeping out nights, and committing petty offences, at the age of eight years. He remained two years in the institution, and has now been six years in his place." "This boy was sent to the House for sleeping out nights, and committing petty thefts. He was in the Refuge 12 months, and has now been two years in his present situation." "This boy was committed for drunkenness and petty thefts. He remained in the House 20 months; he has been two years in his situation; his master says he behaves well, and seems very ambitious of future usefulness." "This boy was committed for being incorrigible. All accounts from him since he left the Refuge are favourable." Such is the general character of the letters, and the teacher is able to state in 1851, "We feel a satisfaction in saying that our labour has been rewarded with results more satisfactory than we even anticipated."

The establishment of a House of Refuge in New York was shortly followed by the erection of a similar one in Philadelphia, in 1826, which has been ever since in successful operation. This, likewise, is supported in part by voluntary contributions, in part by appropriations from the State and from the County Treasury. Thus, in each of these great States, the principle is acknowledged, that the public funds, the local treasury, and individual benevolence should all unite in this work of redemption, all being concerned in it. It is worthy of remark, that in both of these institutions public grants do not appear to deaden individual effort, for in both, the treasurer's report exhibits a large balance in favour of the Institution. The labour of the inmates, boys and girls, forms in both an important item in the receipts, and is productive not only of pecuniary but of high moral benefit. This labour is not agricultural, but a great variety of trades are taught,—masters, in the several departments, contracting for the labour of the children.

In these two schools provision is made for both boys and girls, with due regard to their separation; and a system of classification is adopted depending on the conduct of the children, privileges being attached to the higher ones, and badges worn to mark good conduct. In no one of the reports is there any indication that a case has ever occurred in which it has been found necessary to transfer a child from the school to the prison.

The Report of the House of Refuge in Philadelphia, (for juvenile delinquents, both male and female,) is the twenty-fourth presented by its Board of Managers "to the Senate and House of Representatives of the Commonwealth of Pennsylvania, and the contributors of the House of Refuge."

The House of Refuge is designed both for boys and girls; the average number during the year 1851, is as follows: In the "White Department," 197 boys and 56 girls; and in the "Coloured Department," 94 boys and 37 girls. An "Indenturing Committee" provides for the disposal of the children on leaving the Institution, and state that "they continue to receive from the persons to whom the former inmates have been indentured, gratifying evidence of the beneficial effects of the training of the Institution:" 170 were indentured during the year. The increasing importance of the Institution and the inadequacy of the present building, leads to a strong appeal from the managers in behalf of the erection of a new building; to meet the deficiency in the available funds of the Institution, " a memorial has been prepared for presentation to the Legislature of our State, asking an appropriation of 15,000 dollars per annum, for three years, payable from the *Treasury of Philadelphia County,* and 5,000 dollars per annum, for three years, payable *from the State Treasury.*" This application for aid is founded on the long acknowledged importance of such establishments in the United States. "The gratifying evidence," continues the report, "which we have in the *munificence of private individuals, and the liberal aid afforded by public authorities towards the erection of Houses of Refuge in various sections of our Union, that the beneficial influence of Reform Schools is justly appreciated in many parts of our country,* has been adverted to frequently in former Reports of this Board." A great variety of trades is taught to the boys, and various kinds of female labour to the girls. The intellectual education is given with no grudging hand, as is proved by the enumeration of the text books and various scholastic apparatus, as well as the books circulated among the children.

To this the master attaches much importance, remarking in his report, " Only those who, receiving knowledge, begin to feel that they are gifted with new powers for rising to respectability in the world, hold on their way when the protecting walls of the Refuge no longer guard them from temptation." Four hours per diem are allotted to school instruction, and an additional hour for those least advanced in their studies. The teachers speak highly of the value of the visits of the Ladies' Committee, as a means of stimulating the girls, and infusing a good spirit into them, and the " Board tender their thanks to the teachers who have kindly lent their aid to the work of Sunday School instruction." " Religious exercises have also been regularly conducted in the chapels on the Sabbath. For the gratuitous services of the *Ministers of the Gospel of various denominations so kindly tendered*, the Board beg to return their thanks." These points are very important; they prove that not only in pecuniary contributions, but in a large amount of voluntary aid, is the Institution greatly indebted to voluntary effort.

In these Reform Schools mechanical trades only are taught. An Agricultural Reform School has been recently established at Westborough, near Boston, Mass., on similar principles. Extracts from the fifth report of the committee will give some idea of its success and of public appreciation of it:

" When we first commenced our operations, it was predicted, and by some of those, too, who had had experience in the case of juvenile delinquents, that high walls and close fences would be found indispensable to our success, and that very few, if any, of the boys could be safely trusted to labour in the open field. We preferred to try, at least, another experiment, and we think the result has proved that, to trust with some degree of confidence such boys even as these, is the best way to inspire faithfulness, and that, in very few instances, out of the great number in whom we have placed it, has this confidence been abused; while the few escapes that have occurred, (only four out of so many hundreds,) have been from the number confined within the walls of the building, and not from the boys who have been permitted to go beyond them."

What a contrast this to the thirty who escaped in one year from the walls and sentinels of Parkhurst, and of whom the Governor remarks, that they have so thorough a dislike of the place that they seem to consider any change to be for the better, even to a prison!

"The greater part of the boys who have been placed out as apprentices," continues the report, "have, by their subsequent good conduct and deportment, answered the expectations which had been formed of them, as the letters and documents published at the close of this report will, in several cases, abundantly prove. To these documents, and *the evidence which they afford of the usefulness of this institution, the attention of the government is particularly invited.* It is true there have been a few instances in which boys have been returned by their masters, as proving unworthy and unsuitable to be retained, but they have been so few as to stand only as exceptions to a general good report. . . . The Reform School has been now for three years in, may we not say, successful operation. Has it not, in its healing and restoring influences, accomplished as much as, in so short a time, its reasonable friends could have anticipated, and much more than its doubting and hesitating ones expected? *We think it has.* In some cases it may have failed to effect any perceptible improvement. This was surely to be expected. In others, the improvement may have been less marked, or more slow and doubtful in its progress, than the guardians and friends of the Institution could have wished. But in another class of cases, and we rejoice in believing that this class is not a small one, evidences of radical and thorough reformation have been afforded not to be mistaken, such as we believe will bear the test of time, bringing no relapses to dishearten or disappoint us."

The principles acknowledged in these Institutions are now generally recognised in the United States, and public opinion is entirely enlisted in the work. Similar Schools are being established in other districts, embracing in their object not only convicted children, but those who are morally destitute. Such is the Baltimore House of Refuge, opened at the commencement of the present year.

The acts of the Legislature bring under the control of the Managers of this Institution, with powers of apprenticing at the time the stay in the Refuge is over:

1. Children convicted of criminal offences.
2. Those who are committed as street-beggars or vagrants.
3. Children whose parents ask their admission for incorrigible habits or vicious conduct.
4. Those whose parents, from moral depravity or otherwise, are incapable or unwilling to take care of them.

From the opening address we may make the following extracts:

"The virtue and consequent social order of a community are not to be achieved by interdicts or terror of the law. That process gives but a frail tenure to civil security—the end and glory of all government. Intercept vice, and do so by checking and by forestalling vicious habits. *Infuse inclinations and tastes whose current tends to good, and, for that, invite to occupations that wean and lure from mischievous plots and yearnings.* The ranks of marauders and of the licentious will here have no material to fill or to keep them up;—and society will know a peace pledged and fortified for its best safeguard upon the love, or the habit of virtue.

"Our Sister States are daily rallying to these truths, and enroll these refuges as primary and commanding muniments of the public order,—not dealing with them as benignant experiments, or play-grounds of philanthropy, to gratify humane humours,—*but as essential resources*, and as dedications and structures of sacred duty.

"*What is individual duty is no less the obligation of the State.* 'They judge not the cause of the fatherless, yet they prosper; *the right of the needy* they do not judge. Shall not my soul be avenged on such a nation as this?'"

That the success of these institutions is not exaggerated, we have an important testimony. In the months of November and December, 1848, a deputation appointed by the Governor-General of Canada, visited the principal cities of the United States, to examine the penitentiary and other systems of criminal punishment;—the following is an extract from the report of that Commission relative to juvenile offenders:

"Of scarcely less urgency than the reform of the gaols, is the necessity of some immediate action on behalf of the youthful delinquents. *It is distressing to think that no distinction is now made between the child who has strayed for the first time from the path of honesty, or who perhaps has never been taught the meaning of sin, and the hardened offender of mature years.* All are consigned together to the unutterable contamination of a common gaol, and by the lessons there learnt, soon become inmates of the Penitentiary.

"*We recommend to your Excellency the immediate erection of one or more Houses of Refuge for the reformation of juvenile delinquents.* Such an establishment might be economically built on the Penitentiary lot at Kingston, and be governed by the same inspectors; but the expense of transporting children to so great a distance from the extreme point of the province seems to make it necessary that there should be a House of Refuge for both divisions of the province; one at Montreal or Quebec, and the other at Toronto or Hamilton.

"We recommend that such House of Refuge consist of two departments, one for children whose parents or guardians, by vagrancy or vicious conduct, are unwilling or incapable of exercising proper care and discipline over them; and for children whose parents and guardians make complaint to the proper authority that from the incorrigible conduct of such children they are unable to control them; and the other for children who have been convicted of crime."

It appears in this recommendation to be forgotten that children ought not to be thrown upon the State for support and training merely because parents are "unwilling" to discharge the duties which nature has assigned to them. Likewise it may be remarked, that if any classification is adopted, it surely should depend on the actual condition of the child, not on antecedent circumstances. If any difference is made in the position of the child from the cause of his being placed there, surely the children voluntarily consigned by anxious parents should not be placed with those of the vagrant and the vicious, who have been criminally thrown on the State.

"The control of the discipline, and business affairs of such House of Refuge, might be advantageously placed in the hands of the Penitentiary Inspectors. The weekly visiting, the apprenticing of children, and the general carrying out of the philanthropic objects of the Institution, might be vested in a large board of managers, to be appointed by Government, or, as in the United States, *in a society of benevolent persons formed with this view.*

"All criminal courts of the province might be empowered to commit children to the House of Refuge, and any two justices of the peace, or city magistrate, on a case being shown.

"The Managers of the Institution should have the control of all children so committed, during their minority; and they should be empowered to place them at such employments, and cause them to be instructed in such branches of useful knowledge, as may be suited to their years and capacities. They should also have power to indenture such children as apprentices to such persons, and to learn such trades or other employments, as in their estimation will be most conducive to their reformation and amendment, and will tend to the future benefit and advantage of the children. During the continuation of his apprenticeship the youth to remain still under the control of the Managers, and in case of irregular conduct, the Managers to have the power of bringing him back to the House of Refuge. The children in the two departments to be kept strictly apart, but the system to be the same, namely, *a combination of education, labour, and healthful exercise.*"—[Twenty-fifth Report of the New York House of Refuge.]

In this Report are embodied most of the principles which have been here advocated respecting the establishment of Reformatory Schools for Juvenile Offenders : the recommendations here given are in full accordance with those embodied in the Report of the Lords' Committee for 1847 ; they are founded not on theory only, nor on hearsay evidence, nor even on official reports,—evidence which we also have at this remote distance,—but on the personal examination of a deputation appointed by the highest authority in our colonial territory in North America. Surely such recommendations, founded on convictions so attained, are entitled to very serious consideration.

Another view of the subject presents itself, which shows that the United States have advanced before us in their legislative enactments respecting delinquent children. We have endeavoured to prove that while those only who have been legally convicted are usually termed Juvenile Delinquents, yet that a large number of children are morally culpable at least to an equal degree, and are therefore " dangerous;" that a still larger number are in a condition of spiritual destitution, " perishing " from lack of true knowledge. Over the first the law has asserted a claim, but in England it has abstained from interfering with the condition of the last, lest it should in any way endanger the " liberty of the subject." Sheriff Watson and his fellow-workers have indeed dared to go beyond the strict letter of the law in their mode of dealing with the perishing children around them; but until such a proceeding is legalized it is not likely that it will be generally imitated, however beneficial it may prove to be. Such a course has been already sanctioned by the Legislature of Massachusetts. Now whatever faults may be found with the Constitution of the New England States, they surely cannot be accused of want of tenacious attachment to personal liberty. Yet we find that the existence of evils similar to those of the Old Country, has led in the New to legislative enactments similar to those recommended by the late Conference at Birmingham, to enable the benevolent to apply an efficacious remedy to the juvenile vagrancy which is now preparing the way for juvenile crime. The following are extracts from the "General Laws and Resolves passed by the Legislature of Massachusetts, in the year 1850."

"[Chap. 294.] An Act concerning Truant Children and Absentees from Schools.

"Be it enacted, &c., as follows:—

"Section 1. Each of the several cities and towns in the Commonwealth, is hereby authorized and empowered to make all needful provisions and arrangements concerning habitual truants, and children not attending School, without any regular and lawful occupation, growing up in ignorance, between the ages of 6 and 15 years; and also all such ordinances and by-laws, respecting such children, as shall be deemed most conducive to their welfare, and the good order of such city or town; and there shall be annexed to such ordinances, suitable penalties, not exceeding for any breach, a fine of twenty dollars; *provided* that said ordinances and by-laws shall be approved by the Court of Common Pleas for the county, and shall not be repugnant to the laws of the Commonwealth.

"Section 2. The several cities and towns, availing themselves of the provisions of this act, shall appoint, at the annual meetings of said towns, or annually by the mayor and aldermen of said cities, three or more persons, who alone shall be authorized to make the complaints, in every case of violation of said ordinances or by-laws, to the justice of the peace, or other judicial officer, who, by said ordinances, shall have jurisdiction in the matter, which persons, thus appointed, shall alone have authority to carry into execution the judgments of said justices of the peace, or other judicial officers.

"Section 3. The said justices of the peace, or other judicial officers, shall, in all cases, at their discretion, in the place of the fine aforesaid, be authorized to order children, proved before them to be growing up in truancy, and without the benefit of the education provided for them by law, to be placed, for such periods of time as they may judge expedient, in such institution of instruction or house of reformation, or other suitable situation, as may be assigned or provided for the purpose, under the authority conveyed by the first section of this act, in each city or town availing itself of the powers herein granted."

[Approved May 3, 1850.]

This law has not remained a dead letter, as will be shown by the following extract from a recent Boston paper :

"The enforcement of the 'Truant Law' in this city is beginning to show good results. The following paragraphs are from an article in the *Transcript*. The statistics were derived from the officer appointed to make complaints according to the statute.

"This officer has induced, within the past six weeks, 140 children to attend school regularly. Of this number 54 were absentees, and 95 were habitual truants. Of the absentees 19 were girls, and 35 boys. Of the truants 7 were girls, and 88 boys. Of the whole number 121 were children of foreign parents, and 28 were children of Americans.

"Two of the habitual truants have been sentenced to the House of Reformation for six months, by the judicial officer appointed to try these cases. Another truant has been sentenced for three months. One boy has been sent to the Reform School during his minority. One has been admitted to the Farm School, and another has been taken in charge by the Overseers of the Poor.

"Seven of the children whose cases have received attention from this officer, have parents in the House of Correction. Five were orphans without any home, the fathers of two are in the State Prison, and one child has been abandoned by its parents."

Such is a brief view of the provisions actually made in the United States for the class we are considering: it is hoped that our own country will not long delay to recognise the principles on which they are founded.

CHAPTER VII.

CONTINENTAL EXPERIENCE.

Having considered the development of the principles of Reformatory Schools in the United States, and shown from the experience of that country, their practicability and usefulness, we proceed to inquire into their acceptance among our continental neighbours.

There are at present in France Forty-one Home Colonies for children and young persons, of which twelve are penitentiary or reformatory colonies, founded and directed by private individuals; four are penitentiary colonies, directed by the State; twenty-five, including two in Algeria, are colonies of orphan foundlings, deserted and pauper children only. Two of these last, however, have recently made an engagement with the government for the admission of a certain number of young offenders, acquitted as having acted "sans discernement." These colonies have generally had their origin in private charity, seconded, to a certain extent, by the administration of the several departments or communes, and aided by grants from the government.

The Reformatory " Colonies" were originated by that of Mettray, founded in 1839, which has been the type and example of most of the agricultural colonies that have been formed in France during the last ten years. Details of the management of this institution were given in " Reformatory Schools," pp. 324—329; we shall therefore now only consider the relation which such schools bear to the legislature.

The " Colonies " or Reformatory Schools, to which convicted children are consigned by the French government, are under the management of private individuals. That of Mettray owed its origin entirely to the efforts and generosity of MM. Demetz and de Brétignères de Courteilles. They were seconded by a society of benevolent individuals, styling themselves the " Société Paternelle," a name which well indicated the spirit of its operations.

The object of the " Société Paternelle" is thus expressed in the first article of its statutes:

"The Paternal Society has the following aim:

" Firstly, to exercise a benevolent guardianship over the children *acquitted* as having acted without discernment, who should be confided to it by the administration, in the execution of the ministerial instruction of the 3rd December, 1832; to procure for these children, *placed in a condition of provisional liberty, and collected into an agricultural colony*, (school,) a moral and religious education, as well as primary religious instruction; to have them taught a trade, to accustom them to the labours of agriculture, and then to place them in the country, with artizans or farmers.

" Secondly, to watch over the conduct of these children, and to aid them with its patronage, as long as they have need of it."

The principle on which this ministerial instruction is founded, is contained in article 66 of the Penal Code; it is as follows:

"When the accused shall be less than 16 years of age, if it is decided that he has acted *sans discernement*, he shall be *acquitted;* but he shall be, according to circumstances, given in charge to his parents, or conducted into a house of correction, to be there brought up and detained during the number of years which the sentence shall determine, which however shall not exceed the period when he shall have completed his twentieth year."

In article 67 it is added:

"If it is decided that he has acted *avec discernement*, (*i. e.* with a full understanding of the criminality of the action,) the penalties shall be pronounced as follows:

"If he has incurred the penalty of death, of forced labour for life, of transportation, he shall be condemned to from 10 to 20 years of imprisonment in a house of correction.

"If he has incurred the penalty of forced labour for a limited time of detention, or of seclusion, he shall be condemned to be confined in a house of correction for a time, equal to a third at least, or to a half at most, of that to which he would otherwise have been condemned."*

It appears, then, that an important principle has been for some time recognised by the French law, namely, that the same judicial treatment is not applicable to children and to adults; and that if it is shown that the child has acted without a due under-

---

* These extracts from the French law have been communicated to the author by M. Millet, "avocat," who adds, that the period of detention may be always shortened on the application to the administration of the parents or guardians.

standing of the nature of his criminal action, " sans discernement," he is *acquitted* on that ground; if it is proved that he acted with full comprehension of his fault, he is still, in consideration of his immature age and unformed experience, sentenced to only one-half, or even one-third of the punishment which would be inflicted on an adult. Our English law, while depriving a young person of legal rights until the age of 21, treats him even in the most tender years as fully deserving the punishment of adults, so soon as he proves to his judge his want of " discernement" of the consequences of actions by the commission of evil; the only difference marked by the law in adjudging a punishment to a child under 14, being that he should have it increased by the disgraceful addition of a whipping! The French law, then, acknowledges that a child under 16, who does not comprehend the nature of his action, is to be held not legally guilty:—he is *acquitted;* but is he to be thrown on the world in this state of moral ignorance, to the injury of himself and society? Is he to be left without a guide? Another important principle is acknowledged in the same law. If the child accused of crime is *acquitted* on the ground of having acted " sans discernement," he is, according to circumstances, either to be restored to his parents or taken to a house of correction, to be detained and brought up, or educated (*élevé*). The care of his education is therefore confided to his parents, or undertaken by the State, according to circumstances;

nothing can appear more reasonable, or more indicative of the paternal character of the government. But when placing acquitted children in the alternative of being under the care of the government or of their parents, as seemed best, it was forgotten that no legislation, as such, can supply to a child the nurture and the kind of correctional discipline which a parent, or one who willingly assumes that office, can afford. Thus the "education" which these poor criminal children were to receive in the " houses of correction" became consignment to prisons of the worst description, in which, during the early years of their establishment these wretched young beings were more than decimated.

During the four first years of the establishment of the Prison of La Roquette, in Paris, for juvenile offenders, the annual ratio of deaths was 121 per 1000! During the whole seven, up to the time of the report, and during the last three of which considerable improvements were made, at once lessening the mortality, the annual ratio was 100 per 1000. The mere statement of what these improvements were, as reported by M. Delessert to the Minister of the Interior, for 1846, will give a fearful picture of the previous condition of the unhappy prisoners. After speaking of the improvement in the diet and clothing of the young prisoners, by giving them woollen instead of cotton garments, and white bread instead of brown, and of the better ventilation and warming of their cells, he mentions that arrangements are now made for their taking exercise, by the formation of solitary walks (*promenoires individuels*) for them in the waste land surrounding the building. The influence of this last measure, he says, " has been immediate, for it has enabled the children every day to take sufficient exercise, and has given the power of completely changing the air of their cells during their walk." M. Delessert " does not hesitate to state that it is principally owing to the development of bodily exercise that he must attribute the diminution of the mortality observable in 1845 and 1846 !" No wonder is it that the poor children were decimated, when confined without sufficiently warm clothing and with coarse food *in unventilated cells, without the power of taking exercise !*

To remedy such a state of things, to point out how such an anomaly in the execution of the law could be altered, M. Demetz and his associates applied themselves. " It is not only," says Dr. Cochin,* " to a moral, useful, and logical work, that the Paternal Society devoted itself; it is not only a need of the country which it satisfied,—its object was to supply a great deficiency in the law, to fulfil a duty of the government. It wished, in reality, to collect the children *acquitted* as having acted 'sans discernement,' but whom the 66th article of the Penal Code permits to be detained in a House of

* "Notice sur Mettray," par Augustin Cochin, Docteur en Droit, Tours.

Correction, to be *brought up,* during a certain number of years. Every one knows how this wise arrangement has been executed: if a very small number of these children were apprenticed, in virtue of recent ministerial circulars, the greater part were shut up in Houses of Correction in double contempt of the law and of justice. Truly, it was a violation of justice! for only the guilty are condemned. And of what were these children guilty? of having committed a fault? but they were declared destitute of discernment between right and wrong; —of being vicious and idle? but they have neither the means of gaining instruction nor the strength to labour;—of being vagabonds? but a child has always the home of his parents. It is a violation of the law! for a measure of policy has been transformed into a penal condemnation; *a child who was acquitted has been punished, and instead of his being educated he has been corrupted.* The judge has been compelled to use this language: ' This child has committed a fault, *sans discernement,* without understanding its nature, we will do our best that he may be able, when he is older, to commit new ones, *avec discernement,* with full understanding.' Yet, notwithstanding, would it not be better to keep him in prison than to send him out on the highway? The establishment of Mettray delivers the magistrates from this perplexity, and society from this scandal; *it restores to the law its true meaning.*"

That the views and principles here stated find

acceptance with the French government and are supported by public opinion, is evidenced by the fact, "that though the events of 1848," says Mr. Fletcher, "caused a passing disturbance in the affairs of these establishments, yet that the vitality of the institution, as a whole, has been sufficient to meet the crisis, which seems even to have called forth new energies."* Nay, more; "modifications of the Mettray system have been introduced into several of the large district prisons, as at Clairvaux, Loos, Gaillon, and Fontrevault," (the State colonies above referred to,) at which latter place a farm of 150 acres was taken into cultivation—70 of the 300 young prisoners confined in the prison being employed on it, with most satisfactory results as to their conduct and the utility and profit of their labour.† "On the whole," continues the Reviewer, "so great have been found to be the advantages of correctional training as thus associated with detention in France, that in 1850 the Assembly agreed to the recommendation of the committee, from whose report we have already quoted," (Rapport du Comité de la chambre des deputés sur les jeunes Detenus, Decembre, 1849,)

* *Vide* " The Farm School System of the Continent, and its applicability to the Preventive and Reformatory Education of Pauper and Criminal Children in England and Wales," by Joseph Fletcher, Esq., H. M. Inspector of Schools.—Harrison and Son, St. Martin's Lane. To this valuable pamphlet the author is indebted for the greater part of the information contained in the following part of this chapter.

† Edinburgh Review, Oct., 1851, p. 426. Art., "Juvenile Delinquency."

"and decreed the national adoption of the system, on a scale large enough to embrace the whole mass of juvenile delinquency which has to be dealt with. The Projet du Loi agreed to by them on this subject, enacts, 1st, That in any preliminary stage of imprisonment the juveniles shall be wholly separated from the adults. 2ndly, All juvenile offenders sentenced to imprisonment for periods between six months and two years, and all such as are sentenced to detention as having acted ' sans discernement,' shall be placed in ' colonies penitentiares,' there to be brought up under strict rules of discipline, and employed in husbandry and its associated employments. 3rdly, That *private associations shall be encouraged to form these colonies penitentiares, the State assisting and co-operating as at Mettray, and that if an adequate number are not established in two years, the Government shall interfere, and found as many as are needed at the national cost.* 4thly, That *penal* colonies shall be established in Algeria for young offenders sentenced to more than two years' imprisonment, and for those who, after being admitted into the Reformatory School, prove themselves unworthy of its advantages."

Such is the confidence felt in this system in France. The encouragement given to individual and voluntary effort has not failed in its results. Experiments are being tried in different parts of that country, and thus the circumstances of each locality, and the views of the founders of each institution, lead to that variety of operation, with the same general object in view, which will afford material for an amount of knowledge on this subject that could in no other way be obtained. "In France," says Mr. Fletcher, "where the formation of the greater part of the agricultural colonies has been the work of individuals, their objects are as various as their organization; and they have simply opened a vast field to discovery and experiment of every kind without much care, as yet, for the uniform system to which it will become advisable ultimately to reduce them. . . . The Colonies of France present types of all the forms of Farm School organization employed in the different countries of Europe. In some the occupations are exclusively agricultural, while in several it is endeavoured to combine other industrial occupations with field labour. The combination is the more judicious since it permits some reference to the future vocation of each child, and gives an opportunity of his exercising himself in that which promises to be of most use to him after he has left." In the institution of St. Nicholas, in Paris, again, the industrial occupation is confined to mechanical trades. "The remarkable peculiarity of this School," continues Mr. Fletcher, "is the organization of its industry in workshops, which are hired, together with the apprenticed services of the children, by master-workmen, of approved character, in various trades, such as chasers in bronze, watch-makers, designers for stuffs, makers of mathematical instruments, jewellers in gold and silver, engravers on precious stones and metals, and all the multifarious occupations, half arts, half trades, which supply the numerous articles of refinement which are specially produced at Paris; and all these in addition to the ordinary trades of bakers, shoemakers, tailors, &c. All this industry was grievously disturbed by the revolution of February, but is still sustained."

Equal liberty, and consequently variety, prevails in the religious management of these Farm Schools, while in all, religion seems to have been the original stimulus to the establishment of the Institutions, and to remain the guiding spring of their management. Most of the Schools, like Mettray, are Catholic, several under the direct guidance of ecclesiastics, while in the School of St. Nicholas above mentioned, " although the system of education is essentially religious, the director, in deference to the manners and prejudices of the work-people of Paris, has refrained from giving it any clerical or monastic character; and though the teachers whom he employs are called 'frères,' they are all laymen." Again; " The establishment of Neuhof, near Strasbourg, founded in 1825, is for Protestant children only, on the plan of the Swiss and German Schools, and therefore, for both sexes. . . . The simple and paternal rule, and the admirable order which prevail over the whole economy, are examples which may be imitated with advantage in several of the colonies formed more recently in France. Religion alone," observes Mr. Fletcher, "can accomplish such a work; it is not with a view to worldly advantages alone that men devote themselves, for a trifling salary, to carry out a mission which demands great sacrifices and painful labour every day and every hour. The spirit of true piety which prevails at Neuhof is even touching, and it is from this spirit more especially that the worthy director, and those who aid him, derive their power and their success."

Can any money, any means possessed by a government, secure teachers animated by this spirit?

To aid in preparing such instructors for their work, a society has been instituted, called the "Order of the Agricultural Brothers of St. Vincent de Paul;" it is under the direction of M. Bazin, who founded the agricultural colony of Mesnil St. Firmin, in 1828, and who is supported by other societies, in this Normal School. This religious corporation is composed, nevertheless, entirely of laymen. " Being, above all, *labourers*, the agricultural brothers have no uniform but that of labour; and if they are distinguished from other agriculturalists it is by their self-denial, their devotion to the common cause, and by that internal consciousness of a divine reward which doubles their powers, and fills their hearts with fresh goodness."

The Farm Schools for preventive and reformatory discipline are very numerous in Germany and the Northern States of Europe. Wurtemburg appears to have led the way, as a Reformatory School was established at Stuttgard in 1820; this was speedily followed by others, and in 1843 a return was made of 19 such Schools, many others having been since established. Next to Wurtemburg, Prussia is the most zealously occupied in providing the means of rendering assistance to neglected, abandoned, or vicious children, having commenced the work in 1825. "The Grand Duchy of Baden was not slow to follow the example of the kingdom of Wurtemburg, but with restriction to a more limited class of children. In 1833 an association was formed and subscriptions collected; the institution received the support and countenance of the government; and it has embraced the whole of the Grand Duchy. Its aim is the reformation of children on the road to vice; those whom their parents or teachers have vainly endeavoured to correct; those whom their families might corrupt, and even those under judicial condemnation. . . . In Bavaria the House of Reform at Nuremburg numbers many ladies in the Society who founded and support it; and it receives assistance also from the treasury of the district. Gratuitous admission is only granted to children under the twofold condition of destitution, and want of moral protection." Similar schools are enumerated as existing in the various States of Germany, among which the Rauhe Haus near Hamburg, founded in 1833, may be considered as having served as a model for most of the establishments of the kind since erected. They have extended into Denmark, Norway, and Sweden, and even Russia has followed the example. "The greater part of these institutions are *formed by societies or individuals on a very humble basis,* and only number a few children; some receive children of both sexes, and others only girls or boys." Most of them, however, appear to be receiving government aid and encouragement. "The organization in families generally prevails, as at the Rauhe Haus, which has supplied teachers to many of the schools. Usually the boys are employed in agricultural pursuits and gardening, or other occupations likely to afford them the means of subsistence at their departure." In all the Wurtemburg Schools there are both boys and girls; the average number in the 19 enumerated is about 50, being nearly two-thirds boys, and rather more than one-third girls. Experience has satisfied the minds of the conductors of these establishments of the advantage of such an association of children of both sexes, of course under due watchfulness. In these schools "although children of both sexes be united under the same roof, every necessary precaution is taken that neither impropriety nor danger shall result from this proximity. The girls and boys only meet at meals, in school, and at religious exercises; at other times, during work, in playtime, and above all in the dormitories, they are entirely separate. Each child has its own bed. In each sleeping apartment there is a male or female overseer, who never leaves for an instant, and exercises an especial control over those children whom some peculiar circumstance points out to their attention. Through these precautions, the union of boys and girls in the same family is rendered productive of many advantages, and leave no room for abuses; all the heads of establishments agree on this point, that a too entire separation of families is more prejudicial than useful."

All these German Schools thus illustrate certain principles, which are very important to our present inquiry, and prove the practicability of their general adoption. These principles are:—

First, That such institutions will be best conducted by individual effort and voluntary action.

Secondly, That State support should be given to such schools.

Thirdly, That the family system is the best calculated for such institutions; this may be carried out either by making the establishment small, or, if circumstances render it desirable that a large number should be in the same school, subdividing them into families.

Fourthly, That under due precaution, boys and girls should be associated together, thus placing the children in their natural relation to each other.

The Farm Schools of Flanders and Switzerland had their origin in a want existing in consequence of the deficient arrangements for the support of the poor. "Those in Flanders," says Mr. Fletcher, "have chiefly originated in efforts of private beneficence to deliver the class which inhabits them, by gifts of land and buildings to the several 'bureaux de bienfaisance,' from the barbarous system pursued in some of the communes, and which is not yet extinct, under which the aged, infirm, and orphans dependent on public largess are hired out to individuals, and to obtain the most favourable terms possible for the commune, the price of their maintenance is fixed by a public auction of each of these poor creatures." "These auctions," says M. Van Damme, commissaire of the arrondissement of Roulers Thielt, in a general report to the provincial council of West Flanders, in 1846, " are conducted in much the same manner as the sale of any piece of furniture or beast of burden. Those who have a fancy for the thing, called together by the ordinary modes of public advertisement, attend in considerable numbers to aid in the proceedings. The poor creatures who are to be put out, undergo a sort of public exhibition. Every one is allowed to calculate the disadvantages which infirmity would entail, and the profits to be divided from the remaining strength of each object submitted. Often they are knocked down to the highest bidder amidst the most revolting remarks, and the bargain becomes the subject of mutual jokes or lewd congratulations according as it is deemed advantageous or otherwise for the parties. The paupers thus placed out are for the most part exposed to severer treatment than the greatest criminals in the worst organized prisons." " The orphan child," says a country pastor, appealing to the

Belgian Home Office against this practice, "after being examined like a horse or a negro-slave, is put up, and the rate at which the bargain is struck, is commonly determined by an estimate of the vigour of his health, and the service that can be got from it as an instrument of mendicity."

Such is the cruel disregard of the sacred rights of God's creatures which is exhibited in the face of day,—in a Christian country,—in the nineteenth century! Such are the results of a worship of Mammon! But the very excess of the abuse roused to efforts to remove it. Fermes-hospices were commenced in some districts by individuals, in others by societies; these are in fact little agricultural colonies of the aged and infirm, and of orphan children, helping each other according to the measure of their capacities, under the direction of superintendents, or more commonly of "sœurs de charité." In these asylums it was proved, by the most indisputable facts, that it would not cost more really to give comfort to the aged and the orphan, than to press them to destruction. These experiments having been made, the Belgian Government has led the way in a new and hitherto untried one. "By virtue of a law," says Mr. Fletcher, "which applies to the whole realm, Reformatory Schools have been established which admit to a participation of their benefits every mendicant, pauper, or morally neglected child, found in certain defined circumstances. The design is not merely to come to the rescue of some children only of a given class or locality, but to compass the reform of the whole of a youthful population, heretofore condemned, by the extreme misery, the vices, the thriftlessness of their parents, to be swallowed up and lost in the depôts of mendicity and the prisons. In fine it is boldly attempted to extinguish pauperism in Belgium by the education and apprenticeship of all its mendicant, vagabond, and pauper children; and in the course of this endeavour the highest refinements of discipline and economy have to be brought into practical use. It is the Belgian view that sufficient effect can be produced only by an establishment vast enough to permit every form of experiment in the organization of various works, graduated according to the ages, the powers, the aptitudes, the necessities, and the future objects of the colonists. Such is especially the design of the Reformatory Schools which are being organized at Ruysselede." This great experiment will, when fully tried, afford important material for judgment in the establishment of future schools with a similar object. The management of it is confided to M. Edouard Ducpetiaux, Inspector-General of Prisons and Institutions of Public Charity in Belgium. Mr. Fletcher bases the valuable information contained in his pamphlet on the Report of that gentleman to the Minister of Justice in Belgium, containing the results of inquiries made principally with a view to the guidance of his own judgment, in carrying out the instructions of his government for the organization of the Farm School at Ruysselede.

From a cause similar to that existing in Belgium, the Farm Schools in Switzerland, of which a large number now exist, are intended both for pauper and morally endangered children. Jean Henri Pestalozzi, born at Zurich in 1746, was the first to recognise the impropriety and danger of the gross neglect existing of young children who, if not orphans in its ordinary acceptation, were at any rate "moral orphans." He founded the school at Neuhof, near Strasbourg, of which mention has been already made. He pursued to the end of life, through misapprehension and through scorn, the work of humanity he had undertaken. This was recommenced on a striking scale at Hofwyl in 1799, by M. de Fellenberg, whose views and institutions, so well known to the British public, embraced the education of the highest, as well as the most destitute members of society. The "poor-school" is no longer maintained, but the spirit and views which actuated both de Fellenberg and Pestalozzi are still perpetuated by Werhli, who had been the chief director of the Hofwyl " poor-school," in his normal school of Kreutzlingen, near Constance. "The Swiss Rural Schools erected on the plans of Werhli have increased rapidly. The conditions of admission vary with the nature of the establishment, poverty not being generally held as a sufficient qualification; the want of education and parental care are necessary. Formed by free societies, these schools are principally supported by contributions; to complete their resources, a small annuity is paid by the communes, or by benefactors, in order that a child destitute of all support may be admitted gratuitously." The supervision of each establishment is intrusted to a Committee, who also direct the placing out of the pupils on their departure, and take a benevolent interest in them. The habits of domestic life form the basis upon which these establishments are founded. The superintendence of each of them is ordinarily committed to a married teacher; he fills the office, and bears the title of the Father of the family (*hausvater*); his wife assists him in all that appertains to the housekeeping, and the supervision and industrial instruction of the girls; she bears the title of *hausmutter*. Organized upon the domestic plan, the greater number of these schools receive children of both sexes. The plan of instruction is that adopted at common elementary schools. Agriculture forms the basis of their industry, and various other occupations are usually introduced, to economise the expenditure of the establishment, and to employ the children, when they are prevented from out-door work, or when such is not required. The institutions of agricultural poor-schools," continues Mr. Fletcher, " had proved a great benefit to Switzerland by powerfully contributing to relieve distress, and to stop the progress of pauperism. But experience showed that these establishments alone did not suffice to meet the case of vicious and offending children. When intermingled with others in the poor-school, they are the means of introducing into them the germs of a demoralization which the vigilance of their managers cannot always counteract. *Hence arose the necessity for drawing a line of demarcation between them, and of forming special establishments for the vicious and offending class.* One of the first promoters of this reform, Jean Gaspard Zellweger, of Trogen, submitted a plan on this subject to the general assembly of the 'Swiss Society of Public Usefulness.' This plan was approved, and to hasten its execution, one of the old pupils of Werhli, M. Kuratli, was commissioned to visit the foreign establishments which might serve as a model for the projected institutions. He spent two years in Germany, and after visiting the establishment of Kopf, near Berlin, gave his special care to a study of the organization and methods of the institution for morally neglected children of the Rauhe Haus, at Horn, near Hamburg. On his return to Switzerland, 1840, he was intrusted with the management of the Reform School, which it had been determined, three years before, in 1837, to call into existence. This school is situated at Bächtelen, half a league from Berne, and holds, in some degree, a middle position between a poor-school, properly so called, and a house of correction." The general plan and discipline of this school does not differ from that of the agricultural schools already described, and is particularly founded on the system of organization into families at the Rauhe Haus, the effect of which will be more fully developed in the next chapter. The chief difference is that the number of children confided to one master is only twelve, another teacher being engaged when the increase of numbers requires the addition of another family, and those newly admitted forming for a time a separate section. Thus a strong individual influence is exercised over each child, and so "the work of education is being carried on at every moment; and, in unceasing contact with one or other of the persons in whose charge they are placed, the children cannot escape the good influences which surround them on every side. *Their general conduct leaves nothing to be desired, and their abilities strengthen with their moral progress.* Although the departures have yet been few, the success which has attended the young people augurs well for the future. A committee of patronage has been formed, with a view to procure proper places for the young people going out, and to exercise a kind influence for their welfare."

We have thus taken a brief review of the Schools on the Continent, which are especially intended for the correction of juvenile crime, and are employed instead of the prison in the case of young delinquents. In France we have seen the government distinctly setting forth by a legislative act the principle, that the child ought, when legally an offender, to be treated in a manner quite different from that adopted towards adults, owing to his immature age, and consequent want of "discernement,"—then, having perceived that a government was not adapted to carry out the idea existing in the law, and that private individuals could do so effectually,—it has deputed the assumed care of the child to such individuals, furnishing them with the means of supporting the child. The only instance on the Continent in which a government has itself undertaken to establish a Reformatory School, is that of Belgium, where, for reasons already assigned, a pauper and Reformatory School are united, and the management is committed to one who, to guide his own judgment, has carefully examined practically into all the results of experience already gained in the Swiss and German Farm Schools. Our consideration, limited as it is, of the condition and principles of these and the Wurtemberg Schools, point to the conclusions which Mr. Fletcher's more extended investigations lead him to draw. "The mode," he says, "in which these institutions have been formed, will show the sources from which we must expect analogous movements at home, and yield us the important injunction, *never to clog the springs of voluntary charity or of missionary effort among the people, but, by the hand of authority, merely render aid and assistance wherever it is obviously wanted.* Even all the despotic governments of Europe have already learned this maxim. In Switzerland, and in fact throughout Europe, the agricultural Poor Schools and Reformatory Schools have all the like origin and support, for the most part in private charity and effort, more or less seconded by the public authority. The influences of religion are esteemed an essential condition of their useful existence; and their management is in the hands of local committees, of a more or less public character, according to the degree in which private or public sacrifices take part in their formation and support."

Such is the last testimony of one whose official position and true devotion to the cause entitle his opinion to high respect. He has been called from his work, in our limited view, most prematurely;—may others be raised up to carry on his labours in behalf of the pauper and morally neglected children of our own country!

CHAPTER VIII.

INDIVIDUAL EXPERIENCE.

We have in the last two chapters observed the proceedings of governments, and of associated bodies voluntarily devoting themselves to the work of reformation. We have seen the fruits of the spirit which animated them, but have had only glimpses of the working of that spirit, and of the direct effect of individual influence, and the results of individual effort. These are strikingly developed in the history of the Rauhe Haus established and conducted by M. Wichern, and in a private attempt in the very heart of London to reform some desperate young thieves. This chapter will, then, be devoted to some account of them.

M. Wichern's annual reports form the basis of the following account; they contain the faithful record of his joys and sorrows, his trials, difficulties and disappointments, and his abundant success. His experience will be most valuable to all who are desirous of conducting similar institutions; it will encourage them under failures, warn them against unreasonable expectations, and at the same time prove to them that in due time we shall reap if we faint not.

The commencement of his undertaking was as follows:

"On the 8th of October, 1832, on a Monday, at the house of the schoolmaster, Mr. B., where the members of the male Visiting Society had assembled, the question was raised: 'If the kingdom of Christ is again to be firmly established in our city, it is necessary, among other things, to found a house for the sole object of rescuing the children from sin and disbelief!'

"The assembly consisted almost entirely of men limited in means, and unaccustomed to conduct public undertakings. The next meeting was appointed for November.

"In the meantime it occurred, that as a member of our society was one day sitting at his desk, engaged in his business, a man nearly unknown to him, and wholly unacquainted with our plan, came up to him, with 300 dollars in his hand, and said, 'This shall be yours for the benefit of the poor; but I wish that, if possible, this sum should be expended in a religious institution, and in preference upon a newly founded one.' This happened on the 25th of October.

"It now became necessary, before our November meeting, publicly to acknowledge the receipt of this sum. We were obliged to seek some man of sufficient importance and influence, who might give assurance for its fitting employment. With one voice we proposed Mr. S. H., who acceded to our request, and publicly acknowledged, with us, the receipt of the money, and for the first time the name, 'House of Rescue,' was publicly announced; a riddle to all.

"Nor was this all, A. W. Gehren, of our city, had for some years back been moved to leave by will considerable sums for religious purposes, for example, the erection of a church, the endowment of a ship-preacher, the foundation of a religious lending-library, and lastly, a sum of some thousands for a *House of Rescue;* and Mr. S. H. was appointed executor. He therefore, on joining us, offered us 17,500 dollars for our object. We thus hoped, in the following year, to hire a house and receive some children.

"In January, 1833, several of our friends resolved to issue a popular periodical, for the benefit of the *House*. On the first Saturday in January, when we issued the first number, a female friend, long maternally inclined towards us, was moved to present 100 dollars for the proposed house; and in the following weeks we learned that some maid-servants had joined together to contribute their mite. A poor shoemaker's workman brought to me the whole of his little savings. Many similar gifts followed.

"By July, 1833, after many difficulties and anxieties, we found ourselves in secure possession of the 'Rauhe Haus.' It was the property of Mr. S. H., and was just at this period most unexpectedly and opportunely vacated by the previous tenants. Under its thatched roof were several apartments; by it ran a deep brook, shadowed by the finest chestnut-tree in the neighbourhood; beside it lay a large garden, with a fish-pond. On September 12th, we ventured to call a larger assembly of friends together; when more than a hundred joined hearts and hands, and we might consider the House of Rescue founded. On the 1st November, I and my mother entered on the occupation of it, and immediately received the three first boys."

Thus was sown the small "mustard-seed" which, nourished by heaven's dews, and drawing wholesome juices from God's earth, has spread wide to shelter hundreds, and shed its healing influences all around. It is unnecessary here to give a picture of this establishment, as it has been graphically portrayed by many writers. Attention was first drawn to the Rauhe Haus by Horace Mann, an American writer, in his valuable " Educational Tour ;"* in

* This has been reprinted in England by W. B. Hodgson, Principal of the Mechanics' Institution, Liverpool; 12mo., Simpkin and Marshall.

the "Household Words," and Elihu Burritt's "Bond of Brotherhood," have appeared vivid descriptions of it; this last has been quoted in "Reformatory Schools." The extracts from the reports here given will therefore be selected with a view to illustrate principles, and to show the degree of success which may be hoped for in such schools, rather than to give an historic or descriptive account of this institution.

We learn from M. Wichern's speech at the public meeting held in Hamburg, for the foundation of an "Institution of Rescue," September 12, 1833, two facts of great significance, which, he says, "attest among many others, that here also we need some such institution. First, a distinct prison-school for juvenile criminals has, within the last five years, been found necessary in Hamburg. This institution, opened with 19 children, has, up to this time received more than 200; and many have been refused for want of room. It now contains more than 150. Secondly, no one interested in such matters can deny the increasing depravation of a certain class of our population. How largely the juvenile poor have participated in this general demoralization, is evidenced by the fact, that a special *Penal School* has been obliged to be appended to the poor school."

We find thus existing in Hamburg, at the very time when M. Wichern enforced the necessity of this "House of Rescue," a public pauper-school, which however, was so unsuccessful in its training of the children committed to its care, as to require the addition of a special "penal school;" and a "prison school," in which were at that time 50 children, no inconsiderable number for one town. Why did these not answer the desired object, the prevention and correction of juvenile crime? And why was their very existence regarded as a proof of the necessity of the establishment of another kind of institution? The reason will be obvious to those who have become acquainted with the real condition of delinquent children. A public pauper-school, as such, will never raise above pauperism and vice; it can only do so when elements are thrown into it which can be supplied *only by voluntary effort;* no "*prison* school" can ever enlist the child in the work of its own reformation, and without this it is next to hopeless. M. Wichern felt, then, that a new principle was to be developed: that was to be, the restoration of the child to a healthy moral condition, by placing him, as far as possible, in the position in which the Heavenly Father would have him placed, a well-ordered family, where his best faculties and dispositions should be developed, and where he should be prepared to be a useful self-supporting member of society.

This institution was not to send forth branded convicts, but moral patients, restored to health, and who henceforth should mingle unmarked with those around them. The appropriated designation, "House of Rescue," was therefore dropped, and the new institution took its name from that belonging to the old rough cottage first employed, the "Rauhe Haus." "I particularly recommend," says M. Wichern, "the founders of similar institutions to select some indefinite name, such as Rauhe Haus, the name by which the building had *previously* been known. 'Orphan,' 'vagabond,' &c., are not desirable or appropriate appellations." The child is on admission, at once made to understand that he is now to begin a new life; his former sins will not be remembered against him; there is to be no punishment inflicted on him for former transgressions; he comes as a returning prodigal to a father's house. "A full forgiveness of all *past* is announced to them immediately upon crossing the threshold of the Rauhe Haus." The introduction of a number of new scholars at once into the school at times proved so injurious to the discipline of the whole, that M. Wichern regrets that they had not a separate probationary department, which would probably in many cases be a desirable addition to such a school, for he remarks, " every one does not submit at once to discipline. *But those longer established generally make common cause with the masters, and are the most influential means of reconciling the new comers.*" The children are received at the request of the magistrates, not sent as a punishment, —at the desire of the parents,—or on the application of the children themselves; but in no case are they retained without the permission of the parents.

When the character of the school was established by ten years' trial, even respectable parents were glad to obtain admission for unruly children. "From May 13, 1843, to May 13, 1844," says the report, "73 cases have been announced to us, nearly all suitable. In a great number of these cases, the children were brought to us by *excellent parents*, entreating their admission, *and as much from the better as from the lower classes.*" A list is given of these parents; in all cases the children had been unruly and more or less vicious; some were described by the parents "*as good in general, except an inveterate habit of lying, stealing, and the like;*" in various instances as perfectly brutal, some almost demon-like, both boys and girls. *Very few of them had come under the notice of the police.*

In order to carry out as much as possible the family system, the children are divided into groups of twelve, each independent of the rest in special training and instruction, assembling only on particular occasions. The girls and boys are in separate houses. Each group or family is under the management of an assistant master or "Brother," the whole being under the general superintendance of M. Wichern, who appears to breathe his spirit into the entire establishment. These Brothers, at first selected and appointed especially with a view to this institution only, now form a society which supplies missionaries and teachers to various parts of Germany, from which they are sent here to receive a most admirable preparation for future usefulness. " The assistants of the institution," says the report, " called by the children Brothers, receive no salary, but in its stead such instruction from the superintendent as may enable them hereafter to take the management of similar institutions. They are young men acquainted with some manual trade or with agriculture, or able in other ways to make themselves practically useful, and who are willing, from Christian love, to devote themselves to these destitute children."

M. Wichern's guiding principle in this institution is thus stated by him. "One great cause of demoralization of the lowest class, is the pressure of shameless, self-abandoned poverty. We therefore establish as a principle that the way of life in our institution shall not tend to make the children forget that they belong to this class of the poor; the children on the other hand, shall be trained to feel that *poverty in itself is not an evil, but depends upon the spirit in which it is borne.* According to this principle will be regulated the clothing, and the food, which must be wholesome, but as simple as possible, also the instruction, which will be limited to reading, writing, arithmetic, and singing. The children shall indeed learn to implore their daily bread from their Father in Heaven; but at the same time to earn it from their fellow men honestly and unrepiningly, in the sweat of their brow; and the whole course of life and occupation will have for its aim to prepare them for obtaining by their own energies those comforts and necessaries which some procure with great expense from the labour of others."

Let us now then trace M. Wichern's experience by extracting passages from his annual reports, occupying a period from April, 1835, to the present time. We give his own simple details.

"1834. It has often been asked, how these boys, almost all accustomed to theft, behave in this respect. Every occasional visitor may see, that with regard to our own property we employ no precautions, and suffer no loss. Nor have we had complaints on this point from without, though from the first I have daily sent out many of the children into the town, or for miles into the country around. From the commencement, however, we have expressly excluded them from the kitchen. Their lingering propensity to theft principally takes the form of gluttony, which in some is its only manifestation. Single instances, however, may show the prevailing spirit. Last summer, three boys had plucked three gooseberries in the garden; the others learned it, and would not be satisfied till the three came to me and confessed their fault. Once, after some serious conversation, one, among several others, came to tell me of his having gathered the *pease* of another, and his regret for the vexation and disappointment which he had caused.

"1835. Lying, and a spirit of disorder and indecorum, are the dark side of the picture which we have to present, and often tax severely the most enduring patience. At one period, in consequence of repeated acts of pilfering, &c., I ordered the morning and evening family-worship to be for a time suspended. This produced a powerful effect on the minds of all. And after our regular services had been resumed, I learnt, for the first time, that during their suspension many little associations had been formed among the children, for reading and explaining the Word of God among themselves. One evening, as I was passing through the garden, I heard singing, and found seven or eight boys, who had assembled to hear one of their companions read the Scriptures.

"A party of boys planned and completed a hut similar to that built by D. But they discovered in the timber-work a piece of wood, which one of their number had abstracted without permission from the larger building. This discovery excited them all against G.; and a boy of 12 years, a favourite for his obliging disposition, ran eagerly to fetch an axe, with which, in presence of the offender, he struck so lustily on the laboriously-erected edifice, that the whole was soon a heap of ruins. None of the before delighted builders ever took any farther account of it.

"1837. For a year and a half no child has run away. It has been again proved that for an institution which is pervaded by the right spirit, no wall is precisely the *strongest* wall, and thus such an institution seems enabled to spread an attracting influence, like a net, around it, beyond its local limits. With regard to the children who have left us, all are in the service of artizans, except one who is an errand boy. One girl is in service. Hitherto we have not had any instances of relapse into evil habits; on the contrary, those who have left us persevere in the way of life to which they have been trained. To this their employers bear witness. One master having had a boy from the institution a year in his service, has asked for and engaged a second in addition."

"The progress made by the children in their education is on the whole satisfactory. All the boys, except one, will soon be able to read fluently; this one, 18 years old, will probably never do so. In winter, about 3 hours daily are given to instruction; in summer about $2\frac{1}{2}$. The remaining time, excepting holidays, and prayer-hours, are devoted to labour. We still require a more advanced practical training and employment for those boys whose superior faculties demand further development. I have however always avoided merely mechanical trades. Our object is to call *all* the powers into exercise, in combination with moral aims. The four assistants who have entered since the beginning of 1836, were previously artizans, or practical men in some department.

"Some lads, on visiting their parents, and finding the house unswept, have taken up a broom, and performed voluntarily that to which no compulsion could force them. And when the parents have wished the children to remain with them for the night, the reply has been: 'That will not do; not one of us can be spared, we are all wanted to help each other.'

"Last year 11 or 12 pieces of money were taken from a grown-up member of the family; suspicion could of course fall only upon the boys; but our search was unavailing. After more than six weeks, some of us heard several of the boys, in conversing together, make great use of the word eleven. I accordingly sent for these boys, without letting them know for what purpose, or allowing them to speak to each other. There were five of them. From the first, whom I spoke to in my room, nothing could be extracted; and it was afterwards discovered that he had really not been concerned in the affair. The rest were called in, one by one, and all persisted that they had only been talking of 11 nails. All agreed in referring to an incident that had occurred that day to which the 11 nails bore reference. Nearly half a year afterwards it was discovered that they had really been speaking of the 11 pieces of money, which one of them had stolen; and had been much perplexed at finding themselves overheard. But, while prevented by the presence of an overlooker from *speaking*, one of them had stealthily *pointed* to his hand, then touched with one finger a *nail* in a bench; the other three understood the sign, and all accordingly agreed in one tale.

"I have allowed certain boys, who have proved themselves trustworthy, and who are old enough, to take a share in superintending the others, under the name of *Peace-Boys*. They have no positive authority, either to command or even to reprove; but are only to influence and remind. They are chosen every month, in the family gatherings on Saturday evening; any one who proves himself wholly unworthy, being excluded.

"Any one acquainted with the daily outbreaks among us of rudeness and coarseness, of obstinacy, audacity, and shameless lying, will easily believe that corporal chastisement is sometimes necessary. For serious offences also, I have found *special oversight*, combined with *silence*, extremely effectual. A boy under sentence of silence may not speak to any but the grown-

INDIVIDUAL EXPERIENCE. 269

up residents; he is closely watched both in work and in leisure hours, to maintain this isolation. Against the incredibly numerous instances of *destructiveness*, we have long contended in vain; no oversight, nor even corporal punishment, avails to check them. All is however altered, since I have assigned regular pocket-money to each boy, and deducted, from the fund so applied, part at least in payment of damages. *All destructible articles seem suddenly to have acquired at least a negative worth for all.*

"The state of health has been satisfactory. During the $4\frac{1}{2}$ years since the foundation of the institution, we have had, thank God! no death, among children or elders. The scrofulous tendency, with which most on their entrance are infested, remains our greatest evil. *Accidents* occupy the next place.

"1838. A change of assistants has caused much difficulty. The superintendent of the girls' house had left, and her place was not immediately supplied. The old sin quickly reappeared among them with a few consolatory exceptions. All our regulations, and the efforts of three plain tradesmen's wives, selected one after the other to superintend them, proved unavailing. The utmost that could be attained was superficial decorum, which might have partially deceived me, had I not lived so entirely among the children. The girls' department was like a garden from which the care of the gardener has been withdrawn. Among other bad symptoms were *the gradual cessation of the songs*, before so frequent; *and the extinction of all interest in God's Word.*

"Among the boys the evil took a different form. We need only hint at the disorders resulting among *them* from the irregularities of the girls. Hypocrisy and mutual accusations are other features of the picture, which became daily more gloomy. Frivolity, shamelessness, grievous ingratitude, audacious perverseness, excessive laziness, strife and ill-nature, were the more ordinary manifestations of the inward evil. A certain satiety of bodily food even, no less than of the bread of life, prevailed; and we tried the experiment of enforced abstinence from both. The experiment succeeded to a great extent with a considerable number, but only temporarily. The crisis had not yet arrived.

Several attempts at escape, false accusations, and a series of offences of the most scandalous character, gradually drew attention to two boys as the principal authors of the mischief. One, 19 years old, had for three years abused our patience; the other had been four years with us. Both finally made their escape, and fell into the hands of the police. From this time our community gradually recovered its moral health.

"1843. During the past year we have had eleven attempts at escape, (successful and unsuccessful.) Three of these originating in temporary causes, are of little importance; the other eight were serious, planned deliberately and cunningly by residents of some standing, and accompanied by aggravating circumstances. The majority of the boys showed themselves very zealous in the pursuit. It *has* occurred that a runaway has voluntarily returned; but most have been traced with much difficulty. There have also, of course, been many instances of *underhand* disobedience and bad conduct in the course of the year.

"We now turn to the brighter side; but here the very multiplicity of instances baffles our endeavour to give a just notion of our progress. On the whole, the spirit of obedience, gratitude, industry, reverence for God's Word, and religious ordinances, the spirit of love and truth, reign among our children; so that any one dwelling among them must be happy, notwithstanding occasional temporary disturbances, from which *no* society can be exempt.

"*I instance first the renewed love of the children to their parents and relations.* This is almost always the result of their residence here; and none can fully appreciate the change, without being aware of the dreadful estrangement, or ill-treatment on one side or both, which before existed. Money has more than once been offered me by parents, as the price of their children's amendment.

"——, a girl, who had formerly attacked her mother's life, now sits in tears a whole afternoon, if disappointed of a visit from her. When asked the cause, she replied that when she lived with her mother she did not love her, and often wished to leave her; but that she now loves her infinitely. And her actions prove that love and fidelity, not only to her mother, but to all, have become part of her being. We sometimes overhear (without *listening*, which is wholly forbidden here,) two children talking together of their love for parents and brethren, a feeling before unknown to them. When the 'Brothers' visit the parents on Sunday, they are frequently shown letters received by them from the children, often most expressive of renewed filial love. One young boy had wholly estranged the affection of his parents by his excesses; when he one afternoon went from us to visit them, they wholly ignored his presence, not recognising him by even an angry word. Yet at length a letter from him rejoiced them with the *conviction* of his amendment: the *means* remained a riddle to them. These people were in comparatively easy circumstances. Another mother, excellent but poor, had wholly despaired for her son; *now* this boy is often accessible to no other influence than that exercised on him by the mention of his mother, and after a visit from him she repeated his words, addressed to her: 'How glad I am to have gone to the Rauhe Haus; now if my mother should die, I should not be the cause of it, as I should have been before when I gave her so much trouble.' A gay powerful lad returned weeping from a visit to his parents. His brother had run away from home. When he described his mother's grief, he wept still more violently; but in relating how his father had bade her not trouble herself so much about the lad, his heart seemed ready to break. All night he could not sleep, and next morning insisted on starting off to Hamburg in search of his brother. And this boy when he came to us three years ago, had nearly destroyed his mother by twenty attempts at running away.

"We might go on to speak of those already long dismissed, who have commended their brothers to us, or have supported their families by their own labour.

"We frequently allow the children to go home; last year nearly fifty have sometimes visited their parents on the same afternoon. At certain hours, 7, 7½, or 8, all return punctually, and never but once has any real evil arisen.

"The *mutual* influence of the children on each other is

wonderful. For instance: A very wild intractable boy, of considerable age, entered, after his noviciate, one of the families. A certain gentleness and susceptibility to affection occasionally gleamed through his rude nature. He seemed to suit none of the boys in that house; but another boy, far less developed in all respects, attached himself to him. The intercourse was undisguised, and gave cause for both hope and fear. The younger seemed bound to the elder by some instinct, till his milder nature, without intention on his own part, seems to have *leavened* the whole character of the other.

"We have little difficulty in disposing of our dismissed pupils; on the contrary, it is impossible for us to comply with all the applications from master artizans in Hamburg and its environs, and even more remote districts. At Easter, 1845, 33 such applications were made, and several who had before had apprentices from us.

"Our surveillance of those who have left us is in no respect altered. It is no police superintendance, but a paternal oversight, exercised by the writer of this report, in co-operation with the resident brothers. If necessary we visit the apprentices at their masters' houses *weekly*, but in the ordinary way only once a fortnight; and every fortnight I assemble them on Sunday afternoon or evening, in summer at the Institution, in winter in the town. When on Good Friday 70 of us celebrated the Lord's supper, there were among the number all our apprenticed pupils but one, who was hindered by no fault of his own. It is not to be expected that among so many young people no disorders should arise; but a whole month frequently passes without *any* complaints of the apprentices; and when such do occur, they are mostly of such faults as are common among all apprentices; there are individuals, however, of whom *no* complaint has ever been heard. Our correspondence, were its publication allowable, would be the strongest proof that our labour has not been lost."

The daily routine of the families is thus given in the Report for 1843-4.

"The best houses (unfortunately only three) have the rooms

on the ground floor. Each contains a dwelling-room, with tables, benches, and chests; and a sleeping room adjoining for the 12 children. The 'brother' or 'sister' shares both rooms with them. These three houses have an adjoining kitchen, with apparatus for washing, shoe-cleaning, &c. All the furniture is home-made. Before the house is a play-ground, more or less shaded. Round the play-ground lie the flower beds of the twelve inmates and of the 'brothers;' adjoining is a well-kept kitchen-garden. Such vegetables as are raised by the children's own labour afford the family certain extra delicacies for the table, instead of being merely converted, like the rest, into common soup.

"At half-past four in summer, five in winter, the tower bell rings, and the whole family rises. The brother or sister pronounces a short morning prayer; the beds are made, and all wash and dress. In summer all the boys go to bathe in the pond. The rooms are then arranged, the shoes cleaned, &c. Those who have time sit down to study, or work in the kitchen garden. The brother regulates all. At six the bell again rings, and the family accompany the brother, their bibles under their arm, to the prayer hall, where the whole number are assembled to family devotion. After about an hour the several families return to breakfast in their own dwellings. Then the family is dispersed among the various workshops till twelve (An hour's instruction, however, generally precedes these labours.) At twelve the family reassemble, with the brother. One of them, appointed to that office, has already prepared the table; two others fetch from the 'mother-house' the food prepared in the general kitchen, the brother pronounces a short prayer at the commencement and conclusion, and all eat their meal amid familiar conversation; each having his own plate. Then follows a free interval, in which they play, cultivate their flower-beds, read, &c. The 'table waiters' for the day wash the dishes and arrange the room. An hour from the commencement of the meal the bell rings for work. At half-past four each family reassembles for the evening repast. From five to seven, work and instruction, *not* in the private dwelling. From seven to eight, leisure time, each family circle reassembling;

at eight, the general family devotion; and at a quarter to nine, having supped, each family withdraws to its dwelling, and shortly after, to bed. The brother sleeps in the midst of his family, but goes later to bed. Every Saturday two or three children of each family scour the house thoroughly; and from five to six in the evening, the whole family unite to put their play-ground and kitchen-garden in order."

The weekly conferences and the peculiar occupations of the Sundays and holidays must not be omitted. They are recorded in the reports for 1845 and 1846.

"From six to seven on Saturday evening each family holds a 'weekly discourse;' that is, a 'weekly text' is selected at this hour by the family; and the following Saturday the brother makes this the ground of an address to the children on the domestic occurrences of the past week. Each member is now instructed, by a 'table of occupations,' what employment is allotted to him for the following week; and all those who have had charge of the domestic affairs during that just past, are required to deliver back their various utensils, in good order, to the presiding brother.

"The weekly conferences are as follows: Each brother writes, in the course of the week, a journal, in which he notes everything worthy of remark respecting his children. These papers are delivered to the superior, for careful perusal; and these furnish materials for the conference, at which all the brothers, without exception, are present.

"On Sunday none but indispensable work is done. Clean linen and best clothes are put on. The families take it by turns to go early in the morning, with gardening implements, to the 'Rauhe Haus grave' in the churchyard, where three inmates have reposed for nearly eleven years. The grave is marked by a tall oaken cross, with the words: 'Christ is my life.' The children put the spot in order, weed the flower-bed round the cross, and sometimes hang up a garland. In the afternoon, after the short service, all the families go for a walk,

INDIVIDUAL EXPERIENCE. 275

greeting kindly many whom they meet. A few children are visited by their parents, others go to visit them.

"Many festivals are celebrated. At Advent, the children have each their own *poor* allotted to them; these they visit, with gifts purchased from their savings, or made by themselves. The birthdays of the 'father' and the 'brothers' are generally discovered, however carefully concealed, and gifts are prepared with all possible secrecy in play-hours. One of themselves, on his birthday, is often awakened by the song and greetings of his comrades; and when the family is gathered at table, he has generally a gift from each. One boy, on such an occasion, remained so melancholy as to cause questions; it was found that on that very day twelve months he had tried to escape. Nine days before the present birthday, he had vainly endeavoured to dissuade a new comer from doing the like.

"Every superintendent of a family is confined to his own circle, in which he is in like manner free from the interference of others; while the neighbourly intercourse of the various families is also a peculiar and valuable feature."

Since the foundation of the Institution in 1833, 207 children, 157 boys and 50 girls, have been received into it:

"117 have left us; the condition of these is as follows:

Now under the exclusive care of their parents	21
Emigrated	6
Sailors	9
Day-labourers	8
Agricultural labourers, gardeners, &c.	5
At various trades	48
Student	1
Female servants	13
Dead	6
	117."

Of all of these only five can be deemed failures,

three males and one female having been imprisoned, one female having become a vagrant.

Such are the results of nearly twenty years of patient labour; labour made sweet by the consciousness that it was God's work which was being carried on. The spirit which animated it is manifested in the following address of its founder on one of their anniversaries.

"*For the Anniversary of the Swiss House, July* 20, 1834.

"Yearly, on the 20th July, the Rauhe Haus, with all therein small and great, remembers how on this day, in the year 1834, our dear Swiss House was consecrated to the Saviour, as the good Shepherd; on a Sunday noon, in such bright sunshine that only God's love could shine more brightly.

"But since God has blessed us with rich and manifold blessings through the erection of this house, and since besides this house was the first which the hands of our dear boys aided, strongly and strenuously, to build, for themselves and their succeeding brothers, we will relate among ourselves the history of this house; how it originated, when it was begun, and, how it was finally completed, to God's honour, his creatures' joy, his children's blessing.

"Therefore we thus relate:

"We know of the 12th Sept. 1833, in what spirit and with what aim the Rauhe Haus was founded, and how it was occupied by twelve boys to the end of that year. These twelve boys were our William, Charles, Christian, David I., Edward, John, Cornelius, Nicholas, George I., Thomas, Augustus, Frederick; all of honourable memory among us; who have adorned the Rauhe Haus with many a permanent memorial of their joint industry, not to be forgotten. We will name in this place only one;—the removal of the *wall*, which once surrounded our garden on the west and south. The labour was completed on 25th Jan. 1834. They designed to show thereby to all future comrades and friends for ever, that the Rauhe Haus is a house of free love, which suffers no walls, no bolts; because the love of Christ binds more strongly than either walls or bolts. At times even till late in the night, by lamplight, these boys spared not the sweat of their brow, to accomplish this first united labour, till house and garden lay clear to all eyes; a sign at the same time that our work is not done in a corner, but publicly before the eyes of men, as before God.

"Then came the month of February, and with it the first life of spring in the year 1834. Many blessed and sanctifying days had the Father in heaven already bestowed on his poor family in the Rauhe Haus, to his praise be it said, hope glanced with longing towards our native city, asking whether the faithful God would make it possible that yet other dear children, in our house, should learn to approach Him through His Son. Parents and friends of children in need of help and rescue, knocked at our door, till then scarcely opened but to inmates, and begged for the reception of the children whom they loved.

"What we even then would willingly have done, we could not; for we had no roof to shelter more than the first twelve. But lo! Love soon found the means; we need but to believe in her, and she bestows herself with all her treasures. So the unexpected question could be put to the twelve, whether they would willingly help to build a new house for themselves, and would give up the old to new comrades, twelve boys. What could be more agreeable to the Rauhe Haus' boys than this? and all had already taken up their tools for the new work, when, on the 24th February of that year, the worthy master, Lange, made his appearance, with yard-measure and square, to measure out the site of the future 'Swiss House.'

"He measured the ground according to its present measurement, namely, 48 feet by 24, to the west of the old Rauhe Haus; the front of the new building looking to the south.

"With great energy, the ground was dug out by the twelve young labourers, before Thursday, the 11th March; and on that day, at one o'clock, amid praises and thanksgivings, prayers and supplications, the foundation-stone was laid, at the south-western corner, by the treble hammer stroke of Mr. S. S., of happy memory; whom may God bless for all his love to our house! Now with diligence and joy went on the building from below, under the hands of small and great; while from above, the true Architect in heaven built and blessed; nor were His praises wanting; from the summit of the building and scaffolding echoed far around the lovely songs of those who here saw from day to day a new hut for their own future dwelling arise beneath the labour of their own hands.

"It was on the 16th April, 1834, that the carpenter resolved to erect the gable; the day passed in the severe labour; already the sun was sinking to night in the west, beyond Hamburg, when at length the work was completed. In the Mother-house, we had already twined with ribbons the gay garlands of honour; with song and jubilee the band of builders conducted him to the scaffolding; and quickly he gained the giddy height, surrounded by worthy associates of the carpentring craft, after artisan fashion. Meanwhile, on the firm earth below, the household, and some friends of the neighbourhood, had grouped themselves, looking up to the orator; who, unpractised in oratory, unfortunately began at the end, what we wished to hear from the beginning. He was Rötschinger, the wood-polisher. He uncovered his head, and delivered a poetic address; scanning at one view the beautiful distance of meadows and fields, houses and gardens, the Elbe and the Bill, Hamburg's houses and towers.

"We thanked the carpenter for his address; for he had spoken truly; the Lord had already begun to carry out the blessing, and has more than once shown that He pronounced to this blessing a true amen.

"Without mischance or danger, the work now proceeded to its completion.

"Meanwhile we were seeking some friend of the Lord and of His children, who would be ready to gather round himself, in the new Swiss House, the first family, emigrating for 'the old house,' like a swarm of bees. And before the completion of the building, a young man wandered hither to us from Switzerland, impelled by love of the Lord; and on the 26th June, led by the Lord, he crossed our threshold for the first time. It was Joseph Baumgartner, whom few of our present inmates know personally, but whose remembrance we bless in love.

On the 2nd July, Bickmeyer followed him. Both aided in giving the finishing strokes to the work of adorning and decking the house for the 30th July; because on that day we wished to consecrate to the Saviour this, the first of our children's houses, and to obtain His blessing on it. And the remembrance of that day we to-day especially renew.

"It was on a Sunday noon, on a summer's day, which the love of God had adorned with all the pomp and glory of His light. What we could, we also did, for our dear Swiss House. The upper story was furnished with twelve clean beds for the twelve future inmates. Within and without the new house was richly and ingeniously adorned with flowers and garlands. By about one o'clock, a large number of friends of our house had assembled; they were for the most part those whose love had helped us to build the house. For the first time sounded our organ, a former rich gift from a benefactor already named, and invited by its tones the voices of the assemblage.

"A few words from the Father of the Family explained to the assembled friends the design of the festival; then I turned to you, or rather to the first twelve of our children, who were gathered around us. I still remember well the words in which I then addressed you, from the greatest to the least, from David to Christian, and I think that you all will willingly recall with me a portion of what was then spoken:

"'That you may be helped—for this are you all assembled around us; and that you will let yourselves be helped, you have often promised me with your whole heart. See, now, what has come to pass, and think of these benefits from the Lord, that you may become and remain truly His. Oh, that the Spirit of God might come over you, that you would allow yourselves to be subdued by this love of God! How large a portion has been bestowed on you, your hearts declare; that you feel it, your tears bear witness; but how often you forget it, how often you look backwards, instead of forwards to the goal towards which we strive. My dear, beloved children, does your past way of life in this place bear witness of *this*, or not? However that may be—a new house, a new heart! New benefits, new thanks! New love from God, new giving up of the heart to

Him who gives us all! Shall not this be our vow to-day? Dear children, you vow it to-day before the eyes of many witnesses: of those who have helped us to build the house—from whom you imploringly hope that they will continue to be mindful of our poverty, and will freely show compassion, that you may want for nothing. You know not how to thank men, but I hope—the Lord, who provides for you such benefits from Christian hands—Him you can thank! What better way to do so, than to consecrate yourselves, albeit in great weakness, to your Lord and Saviour, to serve Him in godly fear and filial love all your life long? Begin this to-day afresh; and then we and our friends here present, your benefactors, will devote to God the Swiss House, as we name it; committing it in His name to all the protection and guardianship of His paternal love, &c., &c.

"In heartfelt love, and with uncovered heads, the members of the household now extended to each other the hand of brotherhood, and consecrated themselves, with the new house, to the good Shepherd as his abiding inheritance. We then besought Him, to deign to enter the hut, as guardian and defence; to dwell therein as the lord and owner; to supply us therein perpetually with bodily and spiritual bread: to awaken therein the longing for that far better and eternal abode of peace, which He in yonder fatherland prepares for each one who loves His appearing and patiently expects His salvation.

"The spirit of true joy and religious confidence filled all who were there assembled; in the name of all the beloved pastor of the parish spoke, to direct us once more to Him, who, as the once crucified, now glorified Saviour, had prepared for us this festival. The old became young with the children, the children grave with the old; and all wandered yet again through the beautiful light rooms, in which nothing but simplicity and sufficiency was to be seen, which make rich that poverty which has found its wealth in Christ.

"Among those present was an old lady of 80, a widow, an Anna, who, before this, had often entered with benedictions the circle of you children; a handmaid of the Lord, and who loved me also till her end, with a mother's love. Her heart

INDIVIDUAL EXPERIENCE. 281

was actually broken for joy; overcome by the witnessed fulfilment of her blessing, she was compelled, without seeing more, to hasten home in her carriage. Exhausted, she sought repose, sought it four weeks; then found it in the bosom of the God whom she had served, rather silently than loudly; in the home of peace, of which the consecrated Swiss House had been to us an image. Her memory still remains to us in the benediction, her likeness you see to-day in our house with your own eyes.

"The twelve above mentioned who, on the 21st July, took the Swiss House for their abode, and slept there, for the first time, on the 22nd of July vacated the old house, and so it became possible to assemble the second family. These boys were received from the 31st July to the 15th October, 1834.

"The sweetest, richest experience of God's grace were our portion; and we experienced, for instance, on the first Sunday, that the Lord had remained in the house in blessing. All minds opened to His Spirit and His love, and perhaps in those very days He sowed a seed which—God grant it!—will bring forth abiding fruit to everlasting life. But seldom are such days of *perceptible* blessing vouchsafed to us. Pray, ye of the Swiss House; seek, knock, that you may again find, and hold fast, love and life.

"To-day, on the anniversary of the Swiss House Dedication, all those of the first family of the Swiss House, who then solemnized it with us, have already returned to common life, and are earning their bread as carpenters, tailors, husbandmen, artizans, smiths, sailors, shoemakers, sailmakers, gardeners, &c. Our dear friend, Johann Baumgartner, who assembled here the first boy-family, has already removed to a distance; there, afar off, by his own hearth, to provide for other children home and salvation.

"Upon all these members of the household has God's grace been variously manifested in the Swiss House. May the gracious God still remain with them! And with *them* may He bless anew the house, which we to-day adorn to do Him honour; which to-day we consecrate anew to Him, that *in* and *with* it we may remain confided to His mercy and grace."

We have hitherto considered the reformatory action on juvenile delinquents as carried out in institutions especially adapted to the object; in these great part of the efficacy of the system must be attributed to the entire separation of the youth from his bad associates, and placing him in a healthy moral atmosphere, where all his good feelings were called forth and strengthened. It must be evident to all who have thoughtfully considered the principles from which resulted such satisfactory effects, that in all the cases of reformation, it was not the excellence of the plans, or the adaptation of the arrangements to the proposed objects, which produced the change in the whole character, valuable as these were as aids; *it was the action of soul upon soul.* In every such institution there has been a guiding and pervading spirit of Christian love working for the redemption of an immortal soul, using every means that untiring zeal and wisdom could suggest; in all there has been the endeavour to restore the lost to the healing influences of domestic affection; to make him feel that he is still a member of the human family; the wild and reckless have been roused to work with their teachers for their reformation, and to live under a constant sense of His presence who was formerly to them an "unknown God."

A development of these principles, far more striking, because the experiment was made under less advantageous circumstances, will be found in the following account of the reformation of some young London thieves. For obvious reasons the names of those concerned are not given, but the accuracy of all the facts may be fully relied on, and are derived from personal communication with those concerned. The experiment commenced in connection with a London Ragged School, but was afterwards conducted solely by an individual who was the moving spirit of the whole.

"On the 4th of December, 1848, 15 young men and lads appeared in the B— Street Ragged School before several of the Committee. The Industrial School had commenced with three lads on the 17th of April in that year, and had gradually increased. Their ages were as follows:—A. 25, B. 20, C. 19, D. 20, E. 18, F. 18, G. 19, H. 17, K. 16, L. 16, M. 16, N. 14, O. 12, P. 12, Q. 14. Most of these lads were the vilest of the vile, not only in thieving, but in extreme cruelty, and possibly some of them not free from blood. They were well known to the police, to whom it appeared a perfectly hopeless thing to attempt the reformation of such hardened young villains. The School was now to some extent organized, and in what way is thus described by their teacher and friend.

"On the 7th of Nov. previously, the class met at the master's house, when the following scene took place. The master after giving them a brief sketch of his own life, told them all, very seriously and solemnly, that having had some proof of their honesty and fidelity during the short time he had known them, let the world say what it might he would give them a character, that he would defend that character so long as they deserved it. He then told them it was impossible to be happy or at peace with themselves so long as they violated the laws of their own physical natures; eating and drinking, working and sleeping, &c., must be subordinate to reason; he showed them the nature of the moral law, their obligations to each other; and then concluded by showing them the mercy of God, the beauty of holiness.

He then encouraged these young men to speak freely what they felt and thought on the subject he brought before them.

"A. was the first to rise and speak. He said he was truly grateful that he was where he was that night. At the age of 17 he said he found himself in possession of £1700; father and mother dead; he was then living in the public house where he was brought up. This money he spent in seven months; then borrowed as much as he could of his sister; robbed every one he could during 18 months; was at last detected in robbing a pawnbroker of property to a large amount; was convicted and transported to Gibraltar for 10 years. He said he was now determined to lead an honest life, although he had met his old companions, and 'knowed' of a plant that night of £50; 'but,' added he, 'my lads, we can't lay down happy at nights,—you know it as well as I do, when we go on so. Let us all like one stick together, and do the thing that is right.'

"K. then got up.—'I mean to have my Christmas dinner at home this year. I have had it in prison these last three years. And here is a little stone which me and Jack picked up outside the prison walls when we thought how often we had been inside; and we made up our minds that when we was going to do wrong, we would look at the little stone, and remember what we said outside the prison wall. I have broken into many houses, and gone all over them at the dead of night, and have taken things off the bed where they have been asleep.' 'Suppose they had woke,' said the master. 'It would have been best for them to have kept quiet; they would not have been the first we had settled with the neddy, (life preserver.) I mean to leave it off.'

"F.—'I have been one of the luckiest thieves in London. I have been turned up, (let off,) 16 times at the police station, and up at the office together. I was guilty every time.'

"M.—'Two miles from this place all round, I don't think I could stand on any spot, and be out of sight of places I have robbed. If the houses could speak, one or two or more would say, "you have robbed me." Sometimes I am afraid the school will be shut up.'

"After this very interesting meeting and candid expression,

they commenced making rules to regulate themselves. They formed themselves into a little world; they had their meeting every week, their secretary to take minutes as a chairman. Every rule was well weighed and explained, and all had a voice and a hand in it. Among the rules were such as these: so much work, so much victuals, and at such a time. Fines accordingly. One slice on all the meals stopt, as the circumstances might be. Smoking, swearing, neglect of the Ragged School, being dirty after 9 o'clock on the Sunday morning, fineable. The first blow that was struck, the whole school combined, and bundled the offender out, neck and crop, without judge or jury, and allowed him to be readmitted only on condition that the master and a majority of the boys were in his favour. Such was the beginning of the class."

It is too much to go through the journals from that time to the present, which is nearly three years, but let us see where they all are, and what they are doing now.

"A. is now living with a gentleman as servant, and has been nearly two years there with the greatest credit to himself, and the school he belongs to; is a teacher in the school, and is everything we could wish.

" B. is getting his living by wood-chopping, and this day (May 11, 1851) we have an excellent character of him from his landlady for honesty and industry. (This young man had been in prison 14 times, at the station house 30, and admitted he was not detected once in 20 times.)

" C. is in America.

"D. is now with a first-rate bootmaker, who would not part with him on any account. He was honest, but very destitute when we took him, and is lame in the hip. He is a teacher in the Ragged School.

"E. is in Indiana with a friend of ours, where all our lads have been sent to. He has written a remarkably encouraging letter. Always passed for an honest lad.

" F. is at work with me at shoemaking, and is very industrious, steady, and clever at the business.

"G. is in America.

"H. is with his brother, B., at wood-chopping. He caused the death of a policeman, who died from the blows he received within one month; he has been heard to say, that nothing would give him so sharp an appetite as to cut twelve policemen through every morning.

"K. is a soldier. We have received a letter from him expressing his gratitude, and saying he likes soldiering very well. This is the only lad out of the 15 that has given the policeman the least trouble. He was in prison one month, and the same hour he came out he enlisted; sent for the teacher, and expressed sorrow for bringing a reproach upon the school, bought a bible for 6d. out of the 1s. they gave him for enlisting, and expressed a determination to make the sacred volume his companion, and to be guided by its precepts.

"L., a poor but honest lad. He went from the school to a place, and we believe he is now in Windsor.

"M. is at work shoemaking with me, a real specimen of a reformed thief. This lad's father and mother never meet the benefactors of this school, without shedding tears of gratitude.

"N. is at work, hair-picking in the school.

"O. is at work, shoemaking, doing well. From his childhood he was taught to beg, he was not a thief.

"P. at work, hair-picking in the school. He is very poor, but honest.

"Q.—This lad was brought by his mother to our school, recommended to our notice by a magistrate as an incorrigible thief. We returned him to his parents in a few months, thoroughly convinced of his wickedness, and so far restored."

A friend who was anxious to learn from the teacher himself some particulars respecting the reformation of these boys, gives the following account of two visits paid to him:

"I was desirous of ascertaining the kind of action adopted by Mr. E., especially in reference to the two boys, K. and M., who were then living with him, and who had been before very desperate characters. They had come to the Evening School, where their conduct had been so bad that at the desire of the whole school they were dismissed. 'But I could not dismiss them from my mind,' said Mr. E., 'and I determined to watch for an opportunity of influencing them when alone; I soon after met them, and requested them to come into my own room to talk with me. I made them feel that I was their friend; I put before them the wretchedness of their present mode of life, and its inevitable consequences; I told them that I was willing to help them, if they truly desired to change their mode of life. They were touched, and evidently wished to begin anew. 'Then my lads,' I said, 'if you do really desire to lead a better life, let us ask God's blessing on it.' They knelt down with me, and I poured out my soul in prayer for them. I knew that these poor lads understood not what prayer was, that they could not pray for themselves,—but they did well comprehend that I was imploring Divine aid for them, and their kneeling with me showed that they desired a blessing. From that moment I may date the commencement of a change of heart in them.' M. has continued working with Mr. E. ever since. F. was sent by the help of an emigration society to New York, but found himself too imperfect a workman to succeed, worked his way home, and returned to Mr. E., with whom he desires, he says, always to remain. I saw Mr. E. with his lads at work; they all were earnestly and diligently striving to do their best. I felt desirous of learning how far the change was real which I beheld, and how it had been effected, and asked M. alone with Mr. E. to give me some particulars of his past life. He had been neglected by his parents, and often lived for months away from them, subsisting by predatory habits. The first time he was in prison, he came out feeling more hardened and daring. Again and again he was taken up, but this did not check him; on one occasion he was offered permission to go on his release to Red Hill, but declined, not wishing the restraint. Once when in Newgate he was for nine days out of a month in separate confinement, in the dark hole, as three distinct punishments for insubordination and riotous noise, and he became at last perfectly reckless; though he was so much brought down by this treatment that he came out nearly blinded by the darkness, yet he was soon in prison again. 'But did not you feel,' I said, 'all this time that you were doing wrong? Had you no stings of conscience?' 'No, I had not any feeling that I was doing wrong, and I am sure that the other young thieves do not know it.' 'But surely you knew that you were breaking God's commandments?' 'I did not *know* that there was a God.' 'Yet surely when you were in prison you were taught better.' 'Once the Chaplain made me very unhappy by what he said to me, but I forgot it as soon as I came out of prison.' 'The boys in our school never steal anything in the room or from the teachers, though many of them are thieves;—the policeman told me that showed they knew how wrong it was to steal, do you think so?' 'I am sure, they do not know; I never took anything from any one who was kind to me; if any one did me good I would always do them three times as much.' 'You say that you were not made better by being sent to prison, do you not think that if thieves were sent to Red Hill, they might be reformed?' 'Perhaps so, if they taught them a trade, and were kind to them, but not so well as by being with Mr. E. I wish that all the young thieves could be with him!' 'Do you ever feel inclined to steal now?' He looked at me earnestly and said, 'I *could not* do so;' and when I asked him whether he now believed that there is a God, he uttered a few words of solemn feeling which showed how heartfelt was his conviction. As I looked at this fine independent youth, living in obedience to the laws of God and man, I shuddered at the thought of what society would have done for him, had not a true heart been moved to rescue him. He told Mr. E. after I left, that he saw 'I was one of the right sort, and he thought he should like to tell me the right way, and the only way to reform thieves;' I do not therefore feel that I am betraying confidence in repeating his experience, though no words of mine can convey the impression which he made on me of warm gratitude to his benefactor, and earnest purpose to walk in the right way."

There surely could hardly be a greater transformation of the whole moral being than that which has here actually taken place; it is a change from living without God in the world, to a continual sense of His presence, and an habitual submission to His laws,—from an outer darkness almost incredible in a Christian land, to marvellous light; here indeed the Ethiopian would seem to have changed his skin, and the leopard his spots. By what means this complete alteration in the condition of the whole being has been effected may best be gathered from the words of the master himself in a letter to a friend.

"To God be all the glory for what has been and is being done for and in those lads. But at the same time I see that Jehovah has delegated to, or I might say, lent to man a power that shall suspend, reverse, or alter the present state of man, according to his own faith. I know a man whose looks, and words, and actions, would win the heart of any boy in a few hours; this man's will immediately becomes this boy's law, and any violation of this man's law, (which is mercy and truth met together, mercy being the first and highest principle,) is punished immediately, by an alteration in the looks and words that first made the impression;—the warning, gentle or harsh as the case might be,—loss of privilege or favour, is quite sufficient. Such treatment makes the subjects the image of *their head*. Having thus gained an influence over them, he places them in a free and independent relation to himself, in which they cannot but feel that the obligation is greatly on their side. He employs workmen of talent to instruct them, and pays them according to the quantity of work done, retaining a fair proportion for their board, and laying by a third of the remainder for their future necessities. If by transgressions of God's moral law they incapacitate themselves from working, he is the loser; they know it, and feel it painfully. . . . Boys like mine, who have been notorious for thieving, gambling, fighting, swearing, lying, sabbath-breaking, drunkenness, idleness, &c., would not upon my open system be above falling into some temptation. But my shield and defence is *I try their will*, then we work upon their passions and affections, and you may always know how far they are affected by a certain sort of confession of past sins; the way I test their sincerity is by the degree of their spontaneous sacrifices to serve me, and their own acts of self denial. My lads have often upbraided me by saying, 'Why did not you tell me it was wrong? you should make us do it, we will do what you tell us.' I have always been able to tell when they have done wrong; they look unhappy, they cannot rest until I know it." He lets their past sins be forgotten, unless their own conduct brings them to remembrance. "I make the very most I can of my losses," he writes, "when they are connected with any deviation from the path of rectitude; then, I refer them to the promises they made to do all they could to please me, and I bring to remembrance their former sins, which were buried, but now they all rise up against them to sink them lower than ever, so that it would have been far better never to have known the way of righteousness than to have so departed from it." Religion with him is a daily influence. "The good man's Sabbath is every day; we never eat nor drink without asking for a sanctifying blessing. I know of only one case of any of my lads being the worse for liquor; the temptation was very peculiar, and that has served as a beacon for him and the rest. The influence of these lads and their example is felt for good wherever they go." ["My lads," he says, "would often be glad if I punished them for their faults, they would then feel that they were quits with me, but now they feel that they cannot get rid of their obligation to me. They are bound to me by no indentures, they are under a stronger bond."]

This teacher has here possessed a great advantage in passing his daily life with the objects of his care; having gained their love and confidence they insensibly imbibe his spirit, and they are drawn to that religion which produces in him fruits which they can see and appreciate, for he strives to make even the simplest action an offering of love. "I never forget," he says, "that our Saviour at one time stilled the storm, and at another washed His disciples' feet, and therefore whilst I teach these boys my trade and their duty, I am generally first up in the morning to prepare their breakfast for them."

All cannot, from their circumstances in life or natural character, acquire such ascendency over the minds of others, or, if acquired, so carry out a plan of industrial training as this teacher; yet all, if their own hearts are full of a holy and loving spirit, may find some means of bearing this spirit to the hearts of others. By such influence only can the gospel be brought to shed its regenerating influence on the lost and forsaken.

CHAPTER IX.

PRINCIPLES OF TREATMENT.

We now proceed to consider on what principles we should found a mode of treatment, which may bring into a sound and healthy state the morally diseased children whose condition we have been considering. We have seen these young delinquents exhibiting, in almost every respect, qualities the very reverse of those which we should desire to see in childhood;—we have beheld them independent, self-reliant, advanced in the knowledge of evil, but not of good,—devoid of reverence for God or man,—utterly destitute of any sound guiding principle of action, and of all the commandments obeying probably only that one which was also written on their own hearts, obedience to parents, a commandment which in their case led them, while honouring their parents, to dishonour their Maker. We have perceived that this, their dangerous condition, was the almost inevitable consequence of the circumstances in which they had grown up from their earliest childhood, and most frequently of the culpable neglect or direct criminality of their parents; yet we have discerned, even

PRINCIPLES OF TREATMENT. 293

in the worst, traces of powers which, under a favourable development, might render them useful members of society, occasional indications of the working of the divine spirit within them, and at any rate a susceptibility of good impressions and of kind treatment which promise an abundant recompense of all wise endeavours made in their behalf. Such endeavours have been made, and crowned with success.

It is no empirical system which must be employed towards these children: no well-meant, but misguided sentimental kindness will convert them; nor will a few months, or even a year, generally suffice to eradicate evils which have been the growth of their lives. The system adopted must be one founded on God's own immutable laws; the kindness shown must be in accordance with these, and spring from a deep fountain of love in the heart; the period occupied in the cure must be limited only by the degree in which the remedies employed produce their due effect on the patient.

Let us then consider what is the actual position of the child, physically, morally, and spiritually. The light thrown on this subject by physiologists fully coincides with general experience in representing the child in a perfectly different condition from the man. Every part of his bodily frame is immature; the muscles, says Dr. Symonds, [*Vide* Art. "Age" in the "Cyclopædia of Anatomy and Physiology,"] as well as the bones, are in an incomplete state; they suffice well for the quick and buoyant motions of the lively child, but fail in those violent and prolonged exertions required by the labours of manhood; the brain, though it early equals in bulk that of the adult, is extremely soft, and the same difference exists in the other parts of his frame. Now it is observable that in his growth, the perfection of those organs which connect him passively with the world around him, that is, which enable him to *receive* impressions from the external world, such as the eye and the ear, much more early attain a certain maturity of organization than those which enable him to take an active part, such as the organs of locomotion. For such an arrangement, the author assigns the following reason :

"All the more important motions, important as it regards that world in which man exists as an intelligent and social creature, though less so as it respects their individual being, are the results of a mental condition, no less distinct from sensation than from muscular motion. This state is *desire,* or as it is commonly called, when the antecedent of action, *will* or volition. Probably no mental state is more simple than this, and it may follow any other. *It is therefore the more necessary that it should be preceded by such intellectual changes as will give it a right direction;* in other words that it should come under the direction of certain faculties. *But in early life the faculties to which we allude are very imperfectly developed; those only have attained anything like maturity which are in immediate relation with the senses;* while the reflective faculties, such as comparison, reasoning, abstraction, all in fact that constitutes man a judicious experienced agent, are rudimentary. *The consequence is that the desires or volitions are proverbially vain and dangerous.* Let us observe a child of seven years old; his senses are sufficiently acute for all ordinary purposes, although they are deficient in precision and delicacy; he has seen many attractive objects, he has heard many wonderful stories, and tasted many exquisite delights; he remembers them vividly, he associates them rapidly, and often in shapes very different from those in which they were formerly combined. Desires follow which would prompt him to execute the most ridiculous and mischievous schemes. But happily the muscular system, by which alone he could accomplish them, is too immature and feeble for his puerile purposes. Here then is the final cause that we were in search of; the active corporeal functions of relation must not advance beyond the governing faculty of the mind."

Thus has an experienced and philosophic physician portrayed the condition of childhood, the period during which are unfolding to their full growth in manhood, the physical, intellectual, and spiritual powers of which the germ is in the infant at its birth. This condition is one in which the great Author of all has placed the beings destined by Him to an eternal existence; it is a condition resulting from the gradual development of that frame in which He has enshrined the immortal spirit; of its bones, its muscles, its nervous system, its varied organs whereby the outer world is brought into connection with the inner, all so " curiously and wonderfully made." Such then being by necessity the child's relation to the man, the Father as well as Creator of all has placed him, in the early period of his existence, in a temporal relation to those around him, which is to fit him for an eternal one to Himself. This is well described by an eminent divine.

"The state and condition in which we enter into life, have been so ordered and appointed, that infancy and childhood must needs be to all a perpetual exercise of Faith. During the first years of life we cannot do any thing, we cannot know any thing, we cannot learn any thing, not even to speak, except through Faith. A child's soul lies in Faith as in a nest. He is so fashioned, is brought into *the world in such utter helplessness and dependence, that he cannot do otherwise than put Faith in the wisdom and the love of all around him, especially of his parents, who, in this respect chiefly stand in the stead of God to him.* But every child that comes into the world, is to be trained up not merely as an heir of time, but as an heir of eternity. He is to be trained to live a life of Faith. When we have learned to look at childhood in its true light, as a discipline and exercise of Faith,—when we have recognised the beneficence of the ordinance, that, during our first years, our souls should grow up wholly by breathing the air, and, as it were, sucking the milk of Faith ; we see how rightly, in ages before men were dazzled by the glare of their own ingenuity, it was deemed the fundamental principle of a wholesome education to bring up children in full, strict, unquestioning obedience. *For every act of obedience, if willing and ready, not the result of fear or of constraint,* is an act of Faith ; and that too in one of its higher manifestations."*

It will be at once evident to all who have realized to themselves the condition, physical, moral, and spiritual of the children described in this volume, as well as to those personally and practically acquainted with it, that the childhood of the " perishing and dangerous classes" exhibits features in every respect the reverse of those here described by the physiologist and the divine. The muscular powers, the organs of locomotion, are prematurely developed, and the child discovers in himself the capability as well as the necessity of taking an active and inde-

* From Archdeacon Hare's "Victory of Faith," as quoted in the Preface to " Extracts from the Reports of H. M. Inspectors of Schools."

pendent part in the world around him; the *will* early acquires an unnatural strength from being unchecked and unguided by authority or reason: and all these are far in advance of the " governing faculty of the mind," for the intellectual powers have been exercised only in subservience to the gratification of animal desires, the spiritual nature being almost entirely dormant. That faith or trust, so characteristic of childhood, which springs from a sense of utter helplessness, from a confidence in the superior power and wisdom of those around, and of their loving anxiety for their welfare, scarcely exist in these children; for the instinctive clinging to the parent, which is perhaps hardly ever utterly annihilated, has never been elevated by a perception of what is excellent or worthy of love, and has constantly been checked by the unbridled violence of the passions of the father,—or even of the mother. The *will* therefore of these children, which has early attained a strength disproportionate to their other faculties, is their only guide, though it is peculiarly little adapted to direct them well from being untrained by a principle of duty, by true knowledge, by experience; they do only what is " right in their own eyes," unless compelled to do otherwise. Any kind of real obedience is unknown to them, still less that highest kind, which, " willing and ready, not the result of fear or of constraint," is preparatory to the most exalted faculty of our nature,—faith in the eternal,—the invisible.

Such is, in general, the actual condition of these children,—of even the youngest,—still more so of those who have become hardened in crime, and who have been taught by the treatment they have received from society, only to conceal their true nature with a cloak of conventionalism and hypocrisy. Such is their condition; how is it to be brought back to that which the order of God's providence would have it to be?

It was remarked by the divine above quoted, "Let faith be the primary principle and love will follow, and be dutiful and stedfast." With the children under our present notice the order must be reversed; faith is not the primary principle, does not even exist; love, then, must lead the way,—faith and obedience will follow. The child cannot put faith " in the wisdom and love of those around him, especially of his parents," situated as he is, and yet, that he should do so, is necessary to his future wellbeing; he must be placed where the prevailing principle will be, as far as practicable, carried out,—where he will be gradually restored to the true position of childhood. He must be brought to a sense of dependence by re-awakening in him new and healthy desires which he cannot himself gratify, and by finding that there is a power far greater than his own to which he is indebted for the gratification of these desires. He must perceive by manifestations which he cannot mistake, that this power, while controlling him, is guided by wisdom and love; he must have his affections called forth by the obvious personal interest felt in his own individual well-being by those around him; he must, in short, be placed in *a family*. Faith in those around him being once thoroughly established, he will soon yield his own *will* in ready submission to those who are working for his good: it will thus be gradually subdued and trained, and he will work with them in effecting his reformation, trusting, where he cannot perceive the reason of the measures they adopt to correct or eradicate the evil in him. This, it is apprehended, is the fundamental principle of all true reformatory action with the young, and in every case where striking success has followed such efforts, it will be traceable to the greater development of this principle, to a more true and powerful action on the soul of the child, by those who have assumed towards it the holy duties of a parent.

It cannot be denied that great difficulties exist both in adapting the family principle to any general system of Reformatory Schools, and in wisely carrying out the plan of training in such schools so as to meet individual wants, without deviating too greatly from the necessary rules of the establishment. But we have seen from the experience of our neighbours that the family system can be carried out. If the establishment is small, the master naturally occupies the position of the father; if, as at the Rauhe Haus, or even at Mettray, the numbers are so large as to prevent the possibility of such an arrangement, the same principle is preserved by the formation of a number of families, each perfect in itself, its members closely united together by the tie of mutual responsibility and dependence: all the families having that friendly relation to each other which exists in a well-ordered village, and united by the pervading influence of one master-mind.

The following is the opinion of Mr. Fletcher on this subject, after the close study he had made of the Continental Farm School:

"The classification in families, effected by these institutions themselves, possesses numerous advantages; it facilitates the study of character, and the peculiar treatment, so to speak, of each moral peculiarity; it lightens the weight of surveillance, and makes it more efficacious; it binds the members of the family tighter together by fraternal ties; it permits the separation of those who mutually annoy, and the reunion of those who are agreeable to each other; it stimulates emulation; and it opens the door of Reformatory Schools to certain unfortunates, who, smitten by the hand of justice, are daily excluded from establishments otherwise organized, where, in the absence of classification, the entire population would be exposed to their dangerous contact. But the classification to which we are referring presupposes the existence of a subordinate staff,—first, perfectly capable; and secondly, entailing a proportionate increase of expense."

Should it appear that this system, carried into actual operation in a large Reformatory School, did entail a considerable amount of additional pecuniary outlay, this should not be a reason for abandoning the plan, since the cheapest system in the long run must be that which is the most effective. We will then here assume that as near an approach to the family plan as circumstances permit should be made in all Reformatory Schools, and endeavour to develop our general principle in its application to the practical working of such Schools.

The office which those undertake who propose to stand in the parental relation to such a family, is a most arduous one, fraught with much greater difficulties than those which assail its natural guardians; it must be entered on with no light sense of its responsibilities, with no light feeling of its exalted nature. Such a work is a far higher one than that of the physician; his healing art is to be exerted on the body, his agents are physical means, his hopes of success are founded on certain laws which he can comprehend; but to restore health to the mind diseased is a task to be accomplished by very different agencies. No beating of a pulse can reveal to him the condition of the patient, he must often discover it by symptoms unnoticed by any but the most experienced observer, and must learn even from the cessation of songs the discordant state of the inner nature; he will have to wrestle, not with flesh and blood, " but with the unseen workings of the spirit of evil," and all the means he employs must be in accordance with the divine spirit of all good, and guided by the moral laws of the Ruler of the universe. " Now the noblest influence upon earth," says Dr. Channing of Boston, U. S., " is that exerted on character; and he who puts forth this, does a great work, no matter how narrow or obscure his sphere. The father and mother of an unnoticed family, who in their seclusion awaken the mind of one child to the idea and love of perfect goodness, who awaken in him a strength of will to repel all temptation, and who send him out prepared to profit by the conflicts of life, surpass in influence a Napoleon breaking the world to his sway. And not only is their work higher in kind; who knows but that they are doing a greater work even as to the extent of surface, than the conqueror? Who knows but that the being whom they inspire with holy and disinterested principles, may communicate himself to others; and that by a spreading agency, of which they were the silent origin, improvements may spread through a nation, through the world?" * Such a feeling of high responsibility should pervade the mind of a teacher in a Reformatory School towards every child committed to his care; such a feeling only, blending with a deep-seated religious principle and a love of each child's soul, will kindle that strong individual influence which we have already shown to produce such striking effects; such only will arm to perseverance in patient effort to employ well the means most likely to accomplish these results.

It is unnecessary again to enlarge on the necessity which has been so often dwelt on in this and the former volume, that in the beginning and carrying

* Address on Self-culture, delivered at Boston, U. S., 1832.

on the work, the teacher's mind should be so imbued by a spirit of love, and actuated by a principle of religious duty, that these should pervade the whole system, and bring the child's mind into harmonious action with it. Until the child's *will* is enlisted in the work of reformation, there can be no real progress in it. Religious and moral instruction will of course be a prominent object in all establishments of this kind; that it should be instruction rather of the heart than of the head will be evident; and that it should rather consist in the instilling of sound principles of duty to God and to man, than in the communication of dogmatic instruction, will probably be the experience of all who have practically engaged in the work. So much has been already said in the former volume, both on this subject, and on the importance of making the Bible a living reality to the minds and hearts of the children, that we need not further enlarge on this topic. The intellectual training should be directed rather to the awakening and exciting the mind itself to work on objects higher than those of sense, than to the mere infusing of elements of knowledge. On this subject a teacher will gain valuable aid from a study of the Reports of H. M. Inspectors of Schools already referred to, where are embodied the results of the extensive observation and experience of individuals of enlightened and cultivated minds; also from a valuable little work by Jelinger Symons, Esq., entitled "School Economy;" [London: Parker and

Son;] the chapter especially on "Religious Education and Moral Training" contains much important advice. But while these branches of education will be constantly kept in view, the main feature of the whole plan of the establishment should be *labour*. The degree in which this can be rendered remunerative is doubtless to be considered, but it must be regarded as of secondary importance to the higher objects which it may and ought to subserve. It prepares the child to be in a position in which he *can* " earn his bread by the sweat of his brow," which at present he cannot; it affords full scope and training to the physical powers which God has given him; it imparts a healthy and vigorous feeling to his whole system, which more than anything else puts the child in a disposition to do right; it gives continually a habit of conformity to duty, which is a most valuable aid to the principle which we desire to infuse into him; and it thus directly prepares for the better reception of religious and moral instruction. On this last point it has been well observed by one of considerable experience, "it is by industrial occupation that I wish to convince the children that they are capable of progress, and thus excite a healthy moral energy. There are many and various modes by which truth as a principle can be put forward. Among these, I select labour as tending to develop this important principle. The *youthful mind, especially when uneducated, is incapable of abstract reasoning;* there is perhaps no greater advocate of practical infidelity than idleness." By labour, even a young child may be brought to *feel*, what no reasoning could make him comprehend, his true relation to the world around him, and having practically learnt the natural law, he will be better prepared to receive the revealed one. " Labour may be so performed," again says Dr. Channing, " as to be a high impulse to the mind. Be a man's (or a child's) vocation what it may, his rule should be to do its duties perfectly, to do the best he can, and thus to make perpetual progress in his art. In other words, perfection should be proposed; and this I urge not only for its usefulness to society, but for the sincere pleasure which a man (and even a child) takes in seeing his work well done."

Of all kinds of labour, agricultural employment has been practically found to produce the most beneficial effect, both in engaging the willing exertions of the boys, in producing a good moral influence, and in preparing them for whatever kind of labour they may be hereafter called on to exercise. " There is no knowledge in books," says the experienced Werhli, " like an immediate converse with nature, and those that dig the soil have nearest communion with her."

Dr. Cochin, in his Treatise on Mettray, thus speaks of agricultural labour as applicable to Reformatory Schools:

"It has been said that agriculture is an industrial basis, round which are necessarily grouped many other branches of industrial labour which serve as auxiliaries to it. For the different aptitudes of those who engage in it, it will be easy to have different occupations. It is, besides, a kind of labour for which there is never any dead season, never any superabundance of hands, never any excess of products. This is not all; the health of the poor inhabitants of the towns is destroyed and lost:* field-labour is more healthful, and prepares for the country a more hardy race of men. It is much to have secured to the unfortunate classes whom we have enumerated better conditions of labour and of well-being; but the urgent, essential object, that of the first importance, is to render them moral. Now what occupation has a more healthful moral influence than agriculture? The salutary fatigue of the body removes from the mind evil thoughts, and renders it necessary to devote to repose the hours which in the towns are given to vicious pleasures; the benefits which it procures are never obtained to the injury of others. The necessity of observing the changes of the seasons accustoms to forethought and order; while the spectacle and the continual enjoyment of the riches of the earth, raise the soul towards the all-bountiful Giver. I might insist more on this subject, but I have said enough to show some of the general advantages of agricultural schools, and the earnestness with which the government should be urged to found new ones."

The moral value of agricultural labour is strikingly shown by M. Wichern in his second annual Report of the Rauhe Haus, in 1835.

"The garden and field," he says, "have furnished constant sources of information. I had divided the vegetable ground into equal portions, under the care of the three households, to promote emulation; and we have not been obliged this year to spend one mark on its cultivation. Our cattle and bees have

---

"* A distinguished physician has declared to me that the families of poor mechanics at Paris die away on an average after three generations."

also furnished occupation. *Gardening can scarcely be enough recommended for children of this class,* who love the open air and green trees above all things. This occupation proved last summer most useful to D. D. This lad, now more than 17, had run wild till in his 16th year; twice he had run away; he had learned to sleep on the ice, &c., and had in great measure carried out here also his wild way of life. Raw flesh he eat as willingly as cooked. It was difficult to teach him to count as far as 6. The spring arrived, and I sent him to work in the garden. Shortly his whole being seemed transformed. *His labour led him to value a settled life,* and he appeared from that time to think no more of roving. He concentrated all the scanty powers of his mind on his beds and paths, which soon excited the wonder and delight of all. Instead of being as formerly a mark for ridicule, he now gained such influence, that when the boys went out to labour, those belonging to his circle always waited till D. had settled his task, and frequently allowed themselves to be directed by him. But he found exasperating enemies in the birds which destroyed his seeds. After long waging unsuccessful war against them, he silently resolved to construct a shelter for the protection of his beloved seeds, and after vain attempts of all kinds, at the end of some weeks a pretty little hut of earth really stood there. Before three in the morning he was always to be found there, regardless of all weather; there he stood with a bow and arrows, and had finally the satisfaction of seeing his seeds come up more abundantly than any others in the garden. On shelves in his hut were arrayed gardening implements of all kinds,—a watering pot, a measuring line, and *also the alphabet book,* which, in leisure hours he was wont to take in hand, either by himself, or assisted by some of his companions. Sometimes, while sowing or planting, he induced the others to read over and over to him what they were learning, till it was fixed in his memory."

It will generally be found desirable to introduce various kinds of manual labour into the school arrangements, less with the expectation of teaching the child a trade than to call out and exercise varied powers, to give each one an opportunity of exercising his individual tastes, and to create a spirit of independence, by giving him a knowledge of how to supply his wants in whatever circumstances of life he may be thrown. Such labour will seldom prove sufficiently remunerative to do more than repay the cost of instruction, unless it is made an express object to teach the boys a trade as a means of future support. Then, as we have seen in most of the American "Reform Schools," and at the School of St. Nicholas, at Paris, express arrangements must be made for the purpose, which preclude the full adoption of agricultural employment. The plan of making the last the basis of the Reformatory School training will not be likely to produce an undue number of farm labourers, but will rather afford an excellent preparation for entering on any department of useful labour. It is found that in the Wurtemburg Schools, for instance, "the boys are apprenticed to artizans, and the girls go into service as nursemaids, &c. Very few find their way into rural labour in after life, notwithstanding their early training to it; nearly all obtaining more profitable occupations in the towns."

The industrial occupations of girls in a Reformatory School must necessarily differ much from those of boys: their employment will partake more of the character of household training, such as will prepare them for their future duties in life. Yet they should be arranged on the same general principle as that of the boys; a pleasurable feeling and lively interest in the work should be excited by varied and evidently useful labours, while the powers are called out and strengthened.

But that labour should have this beneficial and reformatory effect, *it must be voluntary*. This is the result of the experience both of those who have had an opportunity of observing the effects of compulsory work, and those who have seen the moral and invigorating influence of voluntary exercise of the powers. In the Reading Gaol the magistrates are so fully satisfied of the uselessness of forced labour that though sentencing offenders to " hard labour," they give them instead idleness, as a more severe punishment, after a time granting them work as a favour. Without discussing the wisdom of the proceeding, the fact is striking which was stated by the Rev. J. Field, Chaplain of that Gaol, to the Lords' Committee in 1847, that of 1900 prisoners who have been there in confinement, only two have refused to work, or have disliked the work given them; and he adds, " This point I would press most strongly, as involving a principle essential to any reformatory system of prison discipline. An observation has been made which my own experience has fully confirmed; it is in the nature of Englishmen to hate anything which is put upon them by force. I am sure therefore that industry, and consequent honesty, will never be promoted by compulsory labour." The

Rev. Sidney Turner, Chaplain of the Philanthropic Farm School, gives a similar testimony before the Committee of the Commons, in 1850. He says, in answer to questions proposed;—

> "The discipline I adopt is dissimilar from that adopted at Parkhurst in this, my boys work with workmen, not under them; they are not under the superintendence of military officers, in fact throughout the whole day, they are led to rely more upon themselves, and to act more upon motives. This system developes the genuine character of the boy; if you can get an ounce of genuine action from the boy, it is worth a whole hundred weight of mere forced action, which will only last while the pressure is upon him."

When labour is forced, it has not the bracing physical effect which voluntary exertion produces. The mind has a very strong influence on the body, especially in children. Every parent knows how completely the ability of a child to execute a task depends on the will. Thus the body, under a continued system of forced labour, becomes less able to resist the effects of cold and physical suffering, and to preserve health a greater amount of personal indulgence is necessary. This has frequently been complained of as an evil arising out of our present system of prison discipline, especially as regards children; and a similar ill effect attends the system, even when that labour is carried on in the open air. Mr. Turner points out, in the same evidence, the difference in the physical comforts of his and the Parkhurst boys; while those under his management are accustomed to brave the inclemencies of the weather, and to be satisfied with hard fare,—

"I may mention," he says, "that when the first number of boys came to us from Parkhurst Prison, in 1846, their complaints were almost endless; they had not the comforts, they said, which they had had before; they wanted more clothing; they wanted mittens, they wanted comforters round their necks, they wanted gruel at night, and cocoa in the morning, and a variety of things of that sort."

While country boys working freely with the energy of youth may be seen warm with healthy exercise, yet with very scanty clothing, in the midst of winter, solicitude for the health of those committed to his charge, induced the medical officer of Parkhurst Prison, [*vide* Reports of Directors of Convict Prisons, 1852] to lay before the directors the necessity of "the addition of a flannel waistcoat with sleeves, as quite essential to the preservation of the prisoners' health." Such an article would be by no means esteemed a necessary for a boy by respectable labouring persons, and the commencement of the use of it early in life might be productive of serious inconvenience. A remarkable fact is stated by the same surgeon, which strikingly shows the effect of forced labour.

"Although the health of the establishment," he says, "is so gratifying, the number of applicants for medical assistance in cold and inclement weather is very great, more than a hundred frequently presenting themselves. It is unnecessary to say that the majority feign disease to avoid labour. The expedients to which they resort are numerous; the most common is soap-eating at the time of washing, which produces sickness and a fevered state of the tongue; it is common also to put lime and other irritating substances to wounds, and troublesome ulcers have sometimes resulted; lime has also been placed under the eyelids to cause inflammation. It is indeed extraordinary what efforts many make to avoid work. As the majority of those confined are from towns, and as most of them have either had no occupation or have laboured in a desultory manner, the steady systematic labour to which they are subjected is to many so repulsive, that I am convinced that numbers would prefer being locked up in their cells, in bad weather, on the lowest diet, if they could by doing so avoid field occupation in the open air."

Such a mode of evading work, would never, we are fully persuaded, be practised by a number of boys engaged in active and voluntary labour

Of not less importance than the hours of work is the right employment of the time allotted for recreation. It is then that the mind of the child most freely developes itself either for good or for evil. Dr. Watts most forcibly points out in the hymn we all learn in childhood an important truth, founded on unerring laws. "Nature abhors a vacuum" in mind as well as in matter. The empty cell of the imprisoned child must be peopled by him with forms of evil, if he has no angel visitants; his mind, his powers, his hands must be employed in inventing and executing mischief, if he has nothing good and agreeable to occupy them; the playground and the hours of relaxation must be badly employed if they are not actually devoted to healthful and innocent sport; the children collected together in playtime, will be sure to be taking from each other lessons in vice if they have no more pleasant recreation. Every judicious parent is practically fully aware of this truth, and how much valuable knowledge may be gained by children from well-devised toys, how much their powers are quickened and their inventive genius called out, not only by the bat and ball and top, but by the simplest articles on which they are permitted freely to exercise their fancies. Hence the toyshop is becoming a magazine of art, and the genius of scientific men is enlisted to supply it. The same principle is only of greater importance in the training of these morally neglected children. It is one which is only beginning to be understood, nor has the due employment of play-hours formed a part of school reports. No mention is made of the occupation of this part of the day in the reports of Parkhurst Prison, but Sergeant Adams, in his evidence before the Lords in 1847, ["Ref. Sch.," p. 318,] gives such an account of the restrictions laid on the amusements of the boys, as renders it not astonishing that they employed their time in planning conflagrations, and the other crimes enumerated by the Chaplain in his Report. The venerable founder of the Wesleyan School at Kingswood, near Bristol, laments, it is recorded in his life, that instead of this school being better than others, as it was intended, it was not so good. "The children," he says, "ought never to be alone, but always in the presence of a master; this is totally neglected: in consequence of which they run up and down the wood, and mix, yea, fight, with the colliers' children. *They ought never to play, but they do every day; yea, even in the school!*" Such will generally be the effect of the repression of the sportive energy of childhood.

A judicious master will, then, study to make the play-hours as much as possible a period of active and innocent enjoyment, and he will so associate himself with the children in their sports, as to make them feel that he truly sympathizes with them. He will thus have a far better opportunity of studying their characters than when they are under more direct control, and the lessons he may incidentally give in the play-ground will be of the most effective kind. All formality should be there discarded, and the master will find that such a course will add to the love, without diminishing the respect of the children. The effect of a contrary system, one of formality and uniform regularity, is well described by an American writer after inspecting a Union school in England.

"While visiting the —— Institution, which we mention as a very perfect specimen of its kind, there was a scepticism of the heart attendant upon our approbation of the mechanical arrangements, which at the time we could not account for, but we believe it was their want of naturalness that was the cause of this unwelcome coldness. The whole scene was too much like the result of a well-ordered gaol robbed of its horrors. We saw that 500 boys were well fed, well clothed, well instructed, humanely cared for in all particulars. But when the hour came for their regular exercise, and when for this purpose they were all turned out, like so many horses, and all in uniform, the idea of children was lost; the whole scene struck our hearts, as the sound of their wooden shoes upon the pavement struck our ears, as something as discordant as unnatural, and failed to excite that glow of sympathy and tender feeling which the sight of a number of children together always produces, when we see them in the position that seems to belong to them, helping, as it were, through our sympathies to guide us in their education. If the children in the —— school could read their wants aright, they would plead for some 'pile of dirt' to ,level, some object to excite and interest their imagination, some crooked tree, some stubborn rock, some old shed, where all was not square and perpendicular, and nicely finished off. The only picturesque thing about them is their ragged clothes, the mending of which has, no doubt, some charms to them as presenting a variety; but the holes and the patches are scanty fare for the freshness and vigour of a child's imagination, especially when these are coupled with the idea of regular task-work. A child looks upon the world as a mystery; and with a more truthful eye than the adult he sees it as a mystery, he puts no limits to its wonders, to him it stretches out to infinity, for he has not shut it in by a selfish life, and bounded it by views made narrow through sordid calculations."

The general plan of discipline recommended for adoption in all such schools as these, which have moral training as an especial object, has been sufficiently developed in the preceding volume. Yet it will be supposed by many that even if in a day school corporal punishment can be dispensed with, in one where the whole education of the child is conducted, and a paternal relation sustained, it will form a necessary part of the discipline. Without venturing to say that there will never occur a case in which such punishment may be salutary, we would express a strong conviction that the less it is employed the better, and for reasons which will be evident after a perusal of the following anecdote.

This passage in Eadmer's life of Anselm is quoted by one of H. M. Inspectors of Schools in his Report to the Committee of Council on Education, in illustration of the effect produced by habitual severity, and the use of corporal punishment, especially on boys subject to "peculiar wilfulness," a feature characteristic of the class we are considering.

"Eadmer relates," he says, "that Anselm, being at a monastery, the abbot consulted him as to the education of the boys there, complaining, at the same time, that they were sadly perverse, indeed incorrigible, and yet day and night they were continually beating them, *but still they grew worse and worse.* At which Anselm, being astonished, said, 'Do you never give over beating them? When they grow up to be men, how do they turn out?' 'Dull and brutish,' (hebetes et bestiales,) was the reply. On which Anselm observed, that it was but a poor return for all the pains and expense they were at in the education and maintenance of these children, if the end attained were the transmutation of human beings into brutes. 'But,' rejoined the abbot, 'what must we do then? we keep them as tight as we can, yet we do not succeed.' 'Keep them tight!' said Anselm, 'suppose you were to use the young trees in your garden thus, and allow them no freedom, what sort of timber would you get?' 'None, but what was crooked and useless.' 'Are you not,' rejoined Anselm, 'producing the same effects on your boys? As they do not observe any love or kindness in your dealings with them, *they think that you have no other motives in your discipline than envy and hatred, and so it turns out, most unhappily, that they grow up full of hatred and suspicion. He who is but young needs gentle treatment,* he must be fed with milk; *cheerfulness, kindness, and love are the means whereby such are to be won to God;*' on which it is recorded that the abbot fell on his face, and confessed his error, and asked pardon of God."

It is not to be inferred that if this constant severity is reprobated, undue indulgence is advocated. We have seen that in those establishments where the spirit of love is the ruling principle, the most strict attention to duty is required, and neglect of it punished. But these punishments are so inflicted as to be perceived by the child to be the natural and inevitable effect of transgression, and to be given with a sorrowing heart by the teacher. Likewise the general order of the school should be such as to make the discharge of ordinary duties as natural and easy as possible, while a well-arranged superintendence and constant personal influence, such as we have seen at Mettray and the Rauhe Haus, should, imperceptibly to the child, diminish his temptation to do wrong, while his principles are as yet unformed, and his power of resisting evil weak. Such watchfulness must be quite distinct from espionage, nor must it interfere with that manifestation of confidence in the child which, even if disappointed, will do more for him in the work of reformation than any suspicious control; but it must especially be exercised over that part of his character in which he has hitherto shown himself so deficient, a true and practical understanding of the rights of others, and a regard for their property. How is this to be communicated, so as to have a regulating influence on the future conduct of the child? The mere inculcation of the laws of God or of man on this subject is notoriously inefficient, or we should never meet with a thief who had been a weekly attendant at our churches, or who had, when a child, learnt the ten commandments as one of his earliest lessons; we should not discover so frequently in the world grossly fraudulent transactions, which are palpable violations of our Saviour's golden rule. The State attempts to enforce this lesson by the infliction of punishment in case of violation of these laws; pains and penalties are multiplied, the theft of three apples has been punished with imprisonment for three months, and yet statistical records furnish no data on which to found the belief that the law, "Thou shalt not steal," is better observed in our country. The experience gained in Ragged Schools, as detailed in the former volume, and the history of the London thieves recorded in the last Chapter, both point to the principle on which we may most surely begin to found a regard for the property of others. The child will not steal from those whom he loves; even the hardened pickpocket will abstain from touching the property of one who has shown him a kindness. The awakening a reciprocity of love in the child will be the first step towards enabling him practically to understand our Saviour's golden rule, on which hangs the whole law of our relations to those around us. But the habit of pilfering once acquired is with difficulty broken, and is often committed from mere thoughtlessness, especially in an institution where all that the children see around them being for their own benefit, they with difficulty acquire a feeling of individual property. The plan adopted by M. Wichern, after numerous ineffectual attempts to check a growing disregard of property, was founded on a deep knowledge of human nature. He gave the boys property of their own, and the value they attached to it enabled them to realize the importance of that of others; the care which they took of what belonged to themselves taught them what they owed to those around them. The intelligent master of a Union School has been heard strongly to regret that the circumstances of the children under his care prevented their having this important branch of moral training, and that never having been able to call any thing *their own*, they would be unprepared to understand what was *not* their own.

The age at which children should be received into such establishments must vary with circumstances. It is evident that the younger a child is the more probability will there be of his reformation; but if very young he must probably remain a longer time in the establishment, and his labour will be less remunerative. It is likewise difficult to fix a limit of age for admission, because children differ very much in the precocity of their powers, and in their knowledge of evil. " He knows more than a man," said a poor woman of a young boy who was living with a bad mother in the same house. " He knows more than a man," she repeated with bitterness, "and he is worse than a husband!" Such a boy, thrown freely among others younger, might do irreparable mischief, and would require special watchfulness, while others more advanced in age may be like young children in knowledge of evil.

While, then, the age of 16 would probably be the limit at which young persons should be admitted into a Reformatory School, it would be far better that they should be sent at an earlier age. If the system were to become general, and a young child were committed to it as soon as he showed a tendency to vice which could not be controlled at home, older Juvenile Delinquents would be less common. It is evident that if boys and girls are in the same establishment, the age should be fixed younger, and that special arrangements should be made for older offenders.

The length of time during which a child should remain in the establishment, can be less easily determined than the period necessary for the cure of a patient who enters an infirmary. In the Rauhe Haus the average period of residence is from four to five years, while in the American Reform Schools it is only between one and two. Much must depend on the amount of previous training of the child, and his probable position on leaving the establishment. But in any case, *it should depend on the progress he has made towards reformation.* Though his will must be enlisted in this work, and it is desirable, if possible, that he should enter the institution voluntarily, yet we know that those who most need it must at first feel *obliged* to submit to the necessary restraint, or they will not do so. The condition of dependence is the natural one for a child, and by no means interferes with its happiness or the due exercise of his powers, if kindly enforced. This is the experience of the American Reform Schools, as stated in the twenty-seventh report of that at New York: " *Did they know for a certainty,* that they must stay till signs of reformation appear, they would settle down into a calm, quiet frame of mind; give up their time and attention to mental culture, and their reformation would be rapid."

In all that has been here said the principles of treatment are equally applicable to children of both sexes. If the family system is thoroughly carried out, it necessarily follows that boys and girls should be trained in the same establishment and under the same general management, with such modification as may be needful for each sex. Where there cannot be exercised in the household the constant watchfulness of parental care, such an arrangement would be most undesirable and dangerous; but where this can be secured, and where the children are sent young to the school, it is believed that a far higher moral influence may be exercised by this true development of the family system, than by the complete separation of boys and girls, which has been often found to lead to results exactly the reverse of those contemplated. The opinions of Mr. Fletcher, derived both from his own experience, and from observation of that of the German Schools will be of weight.

"This union of girls and boys under the same roof is somewhat contrary to received usages, and one might dread its giving rise to some inconveniences. But experience has proved, and proves every day, that these inconveniences are more apparent than real. It is observed, on the contrary, that the imaginations of children are more excited when the sexes are separate than when united, and fraternal and daily relations have been established between them. In a village, the habitual contact of girls and boys, under the general surveillance of the parents, forms the rule, and it has never occurred to the mind of any person to seek to restrain it. The rural school destined to represent, in a minor degree, domestic life and village routine, can, and ought to admit of the like toleration, provided that the necessary precautions are taken that the intercourse shall not degenerate into abuse. Amongst these precautions may be mentioned—

"1. The vigilant supervision of the mothers and fathers of the family.

"2. The admission only of children under 12 years of age, and their dismissal at 17.

"3. The separation of the dormitories appropriated to children of each sex.

"Subject to these precautions, which even common sense dictates, the union of children of both sexes in the same establishments presents numerous advantages, viz.:

"1. In respect of economy of management.

"2. In respect of a judicious distribution of labour, as being suited to the capacities of either sex.

"3. In respect of instruction and education, by softening the disposition, creating emulation, and strengthening the fraternal ties which should unite the members of one family."

Such being the advantages derivable from the

true family system, where facilities exist for trying it, it will be advantageous to adopt it. But in this, as well as in the working of every other part of the system, it must never be forgotten that it is the spirit alone which quickeneth, and that it is earnest, faithful, loving, long-suffering devotion to the child's highest good which only can bring forth good fruits, and help to make him wise unto salvation. With this as a guiding principle, and with the adoption of wise means, under the Divine blessing, much good may be confidently hoped for.

Among the young delinquents brought under our notice in the first Chapter, we have seen some left through mistaken kindness to continue their career of vice unchecked; others hardened by repeated imprisonments until they were prepared to receive the highest secondary punishment the law can inflict; others, again, brought under the influence of Christian kindness, drawn by the strong cords of love from their evil ways, and restored to be useful members of society. We have looked into deep gulfs of human misery and vice, the surface of which only could hardly be contemplated without horror; we have heard from thence arise faint cries for help, when at last the wretched little victims knew that they were suffering. We have seen nations, one after another, rising to remove this fearful evil; and governments thankfully and willingly aiding those who would give their lives to this work of regeneration. Results have followed from such a course undeniable as to their unmingled good. Under Providence, the means employed have effected in a large proportion of cases an entire change of life, in many a transformation hardly credible.

Shall our own country still remain unmoved, and with cold, suspicious air, refuse its aid in the work?

CHAPTER X.

APPLICATION OF PRINCIPLES.

We have been gazing on a vast mass of juvenile crime. We have not sought from tables of statistics the annual number of convictions of young delinquents in our country, or endeavoured to compute, by comparing these with the increase of population, the relative proportion which juvenile delinquency bears now to that of former years. These sources of information have not been made the basis of our inquiries, for reasons which must be evident to those who have thoughtfully perused the mournful narratives which have been interspersed throughout this volume. The actual number of convictions, or even of commitments of each individual, affords but a very inaccurate indication of the amount of crime which he has committed against society; the enumeration of crimes legally proved against children, points but faintly to the multitudes who are beginning their life, and are likely to continue it, in a state of utter ignorance of the laws of God and man, and consequent disregard of them. An attempt has been made to classify those who are commonly called Juvenile Delinquents; it has been shown that the mere fact of a child's having been branded as a felon by a legal sentence, does not prove that he is guilty of such an amount of moral criminality as would render him necessarily injurious to society, if subjected to wise treatment; and that while the children of one class may require for their reformation only temporary corrective treatment, or even simple removal from their evil associations, into a condition of active and morally healthful occupation, others would need long years of careful training before they could be restored to society with any hope of their becoming useful members of it. We have thus seen that the simple fact of a conviction of dishonesty by no means indicates the degree in which a child is morally diseased; it does not show that he is really worse than hundreds or thousands of children in all grades of society who have manifested equal regardlessness of the rights of others; it proves only, that he is beyond the pale of Christian care, either through the neglect or vice of his natural guardians, or through being without such guardians, and consequently dependent on society, which also has neglected him. But beyond these Juvenile Delinquents pointed out to us by the "Law of the Land," innumerable multitudes of children have been discovered to us by the Christian philanthropist, and by the disclosures of their associates; some swarming in our large cities and haunting all its by-ways,—others wandering over the country,—all growing up in the thickest Egyptian darkness, in utter ignorance of everything that might profit their immortal souls. No statistics have been needed to force upon us the dreadful conviction that this amount of moral evil of the most dangerous kind must go on increasing, if comprehensive and effectual measures are not taken to arrest its course.

Some consideration of the amount of juvenile crime, and the efficacy of the means at present adopted to check it, formed a part of the investigations of the " Select Committee of the House of Lords, appointed to inquire into the execution of the Criminal Law, especially respecting Juvenile Offenders and Transportation;" the Report of that Committee has been already quoted, bearing witness to the necessity of establishing " Reformatory Asylums" for young offenders, "the punishment in such asylums being hardly more than what is implied in confinement and restraint, and reformation and industrial training being the main features of the process." This report was founded on the concurring testimony of " Recorders of Cities and Boroughs, Judges of Local Jurisdiction, Magistrates, Governors and Chaplains of Gaols and Penitentiaries, Prison Inspectors, and others having the care of convicts at home and in the colonies." In addition to this weight of evidence, " answers to questions circulated were likewise obtained from thirty-three learned Judges of the United Kingdom, exercising criminal jurisdiction." These questions were framed with a view to elicit the opinion of these gentlemen, whose high legal position and experience rendered their views of weight, respecting the effect of the present treatment and the most probable means not only of killing the seed, but of checking the growth of juvenile crime. All these Judges fully concurred in the belief that good moral and religious education, commencing with infancy, is the only means which can be resorted to with any hope of success in reforming the rising generation; it was forcibly pointed out by Mr. Justice Coleridge, " that education to produce such effects, must *be really good; something very superior to that generally given.*" Chief Baron Pigot added to the expression of his opinion of the importance of early training the conviction that " any system of education designed to produce a considerable effect on the amount of crime, must be so applied as to embrace the whole population, including, *as the class to which in this view, it is most important to extend the boon of knowledge, the very lowest and most destitute of our people.*" And Lord Denman's high standing lends weight to the expression of his " sanguine hope, that moral training, followed by the means of obtaining a decent livelihood, will so materially diminish the amount of crime as to make it a rare exception even among the lowest classes, *instead of threatening, as it now does, to become the rule.*"

Years passed by, and no legislative movement

APPLICATION OF PRINCIPLES.

followed this expression of the strong opinion of our rulers.

The same subject received incidental consideration in the "Select Committee on Prison Discipline" in the House of Commons, which sat in 1850; but the Report states that "on the interesting question of what system of prison discipline is best adapted to juvenile offenders, this Committee has not received sufficient evidence to enable them to offer distinct recommendations."

But the condition of the "Perishing and Dangerous Classes of Children" and of Juvenile Delinquents, could not be banished from the hearts of those whose daily life brought them into close and most painful contact with them. Ministers to the poor, domestic missionaries, must meet them face to face in their dismal abodes; managers of Ragged and Industrial Schools must constantly witness an amount of physical and spiritual destitution which the machinery they possessed was utterly inadequate to remove, and they must be toiling on hopelessly, —if faith can ever be hopeless,—unless more effective means are adopted; those who have laboured long in asylums for the convicted young, saw by what had been already done, how much might be effected if the government would only believe the palpable facts which they could lay before it;—recorders, legal men of every kind, perceived the fatal inconsistency of our law as regards children, and when forced to condemn these poor young creatures in a solemn sentence, felt themselves obliged to do that which was most repugnant to common sense, to the law of nature; chaplains and governors of gaols, were daily harrowed by the sight of evil which they could not remove, and hardly lessen by the means they were compelled to use; the coroner felt the same, in fine, who had been called to hold his inquest over the corpse of a poor child, who by his own hands had thus freed himself from those of justice. Such persons as these, earnestly desiring that some effective steps should be taken to meet the existing evil, assembled in conference at Birmingham, from all parts of the kingdom, in December of the past year. They did so, on the requisition of forty-five gentlemen of the classes above described, who thus spoke:

"We earnestly request your attendance at a Conference, to be held at Birmingham, on Wednesday, December 10th, for the object set forth on the annexed page.

"From our personal knowledge of the state of the 'perishing and dangerous classes' of children, we are persuaded that the most effectual means of checking the progress of crime is by adopting the plans here suggested. We further believe, that the combined efforts of all those interested in the present condition of such children can alone arouse the Legislature to the necessity of granting the required measures."

The object of this Conference on "Preventive and Reformatory Schools," is thus stated in the circular:

"A Consideration of the Condition and Treatment of the 'Perishing and Dangerous Classes' of Children and Juvenile Offenders, with a view of Procuring such Legislative Enactments as may produce a beneficial change in their Actual Condition and their Prospects.

"THE CHILDREN WHOSE CONDITION REQUIRES THE NOTICE OF THE CONFERENCE, ARE—

"First, *Those who have not yet subjected themselves to the grasp of the law*, but who, by reason of the vice, neglect, or extreme poverty of their parents, are inadmissible to the existing School Establishments, and consequently must grow up without any Education; almost inevitably forming part of the 'perishing and dangerous classes,' and ultimately becoming criminal.

"Secondly, *Those who are already subjecting themselves to police interference*, by vagrancy, mendicancy, or petty infringement of the law.

"Thirdly, *Those who have been convicted of felony*, or such misdemeanour as involves dishonesty.

"THE PROVISIONS TO BE MADE FOR THESE THREE CLASSES, ARE—

"For the first, *Free Day Schools*.

"For the second, *Industrial Feeding Schools*, with compulsory attendance.

"For the third, *Penal Reformatory Schools*.

"THE LEGISLATIVE ENACTMENTS NEEDED TO BRING SUCH SCHOOLS INTO OPERATION, ARE—

"For the Free Day Schools, *such extension of the present Governmental Grants, from the Committee of Council on Education, as may secure their maintenance in an effective condition*, they being by their nature at present excluded from aid, yet requiring it in a far higher degree than those on whom it is conferred.

"For the Industrial Feeding Schools, *authority to Magistrates to enforce attendance at such Schools, on children of the second class, and to require payment to the supporters of the School for each child from the parish in which the child resides, with a power to the parish officer to obtain the outlay from the parent, except in cases of inability.*

"For the Penal Reformatory Schools, *authority to Magistrates and Judges to commit juvenile offenders to such Schools instead of to Prison, with power of detention to the Governor during the appointed period, the charge of maintenance being enforced as above.*

"In this statement of the object of the Conference it is assumed that society has a right to protect itself from the injury and loss which it at present suffers from this class of children;—that the existing system does not so deter or reform as to protect society,—and that EDUCATION, including both instruction and training, is the only means of effecting any material diminution of juvenile crime.

"Also, that in *all* the Schools above named, the object in view is, not so much to give a certain amount of secular knowledge, or to enforce a temporary restraint, as to train up useful and self-supporting members of society, acting on a religious principle; hence, *they will be best conducted by individual bodies, with close and rigid inspection by the State as to their effective working.*

"The parent has a double duty to discharge towards his child; first, to supply him with the means of subsistence; secondly, to train him in the way he should go. It is, therefore, further assumed, that, by neglecting the second part of his responsibility, he ought not to be permitted to escape the first."

The important testimonies delivered on that occasion are known to the public through the "Report of the Conference," [Longman and Co.] The resolutions unanimously passed by it were as follow:

"1. That the present condition and treatment of the perishing and dangerous classes of children and juvenile offenders deserve the consideration of every member of a Christian community.

"2. That the means at present available for the reformation

APPLICATION OF PRINCIPLES. 333

of these children have been found totally inadequate to check the spread of juvenile delinquency, partly owing to the want of proper industrial, correctional, and reformatory schools, and partly to the want of authority iu magistrates to compel attendance at such schools.

"3. That the adoption of a somewhat altered and extended course of proceeding on the part of the Committee of Privy Council is earnestly to be desired for those children who have not yet made themselves amenable to the law, but who by reason of the vice, neglect, or extreme poverty of their parents, are not admitted into the existing day schools.

"4. That for those children who are not attending any schools, and have subjected themselves to police interference by vagrancy, mendicancy, or petty infringements of the law, legislative enactments are urgently required in order to aid or establish industrial feeding schools, at which the attendance of such children should be enforced by magistrates, and payments made for their maintenance, in the first instance, from some public fund, power being given to the proper authorities to recover the outlay from the parents of the children.

"5. That legislative enactments are also required in order to establish correctional and reformatory schools for those children who have been convicted of felony or such misdemeanours as involve dishonesty, and to confer on magistrates power to commit juvenile offenders to such schools, instead of to prison.

"6. That the following gentlemen form a committee, with power to add to their number, to adopt such measures as they may think desirable in order to obtain the requisite parliamentary enactments, as well as to prepare a memorial to the Committee of Privy Council, and for the attainment of the specific objects laid down in the foregoing resolutions."

The object of this Conference, then, embraced all "morally destitute" children, whether convicted or unconvicted. A superficial view of the subject would perhaps lead to the supposition that the government grants already made for educational purposes are attainable by all who need them, and hence that no alteration in the existing system is needed to enable the unconvicted children, however low, to receive an equal share of aid, should there be found Christian workers who would carry the benefits of education to them; and it was doubtless the intention of the Legislature in making the grant, that all classes of Her Majesty's subjects should equally share it. But the Ragged School movement has been organized since that time, and the regulations of the committee, well adapted to meet the wants of the labouring population, did not meet these; "the boon of knowledge" has *not* been extended "to the very lowest and most destitute of our people." It therefore became an object of the Conference Committee to point out to the Committee of Council on Education this want, and to request an extension of the grant, so as to include schools of all kinds. The following memorial has been, with this view, submitted by the Conference Committee to the Educational Committee of the Privy Council:

"Your lordships' memorialists respectfully beg to represent, That an increasingly large class of schools, called the Ragged Schools, or Free Day Schools for the Destitute, intended for those children who, by reason of the vice, neglect, or extreme poverty of their parents, are inadmissible to the existing School Establishments recognised by your lordships, *do not* and *cannot* receive any fair proportion of the Parliamentary Grant for public education, under the existing regulations, yet, that for their maintenance in an effective condition, they require it in a far higher degree.

"They cannot, at present, receive such aid for the following reasons:

"1st. The neglected condition of the children requires very peculiar qualifications in the master, and not only would it be impossible for many an excellent Ragged School master to go through the examination required by your lordships for certified teachers in ordinary schools, but were he able to do so, such capabilities would by no means test his fitness for his peculiar duties, while other qualifications of a very different kind are indispensable. The masters, therefore, are not aided.

"2nd. The arrangements respecting pupil teachers and stipendiary monitors are inapplicable in Ragged Schools. Such arrangements are devised for the purpose of training teachers. It cannot be your lordships' desire to train teachers for the next generation from the most degraded children of this; and were it so desired to form teachers from this class of society, the want of early training, no less than the character of the instruction given in Ragged Schools, would render the children trained in them unable to pass the examination which is required.

"3rd. The industrial training given in Ragged Schools, which is a most important part of their system, tends to form habits of industry rather than to teach a trade, and though its results have been found to be very beneficial, yet the fluctuating nature of such schools prevents that progress which your lordships' regulations require in the case of ordinary schools.

"4th. The buildings for such schools are necessarily in poor parts of towns, and however well adapted they may be for the purpose, they will seldom be such as would receive a grant from the Committee of Council under the existing regulations.

"5th. The schools themselves must necessarily be in such an educational condition, that they would hardly be considered entitled to receive grants of books and apparatus under your lordships' present regulations. Ragged Schools, or Free Day Schools, are therefore at present virtually excluded from aid. They perform, however, a very important work, by acting on a class as yet uninfluenced by religious or general education. But such schools, to be of use, must be efficiently conducted.

To be so, a much larger amount of support is required, than suffices for the maintenance of ordinary Day Schools, inasmuch as no pence are paid by the children, and a larger staff of teachers, many of them industrial, is required.

"The most strenuous efforts on the part of benevolent persons have hitherto failed to raise an adequate income for such schools, or to carry them on as they would desire.

"Your memorialists would therefore respectfully, but earnestly, pray,

"1st. That masters who give satisfactory proof that they are fitted to carry out the objects of Ragged Schools, be aided by a grant from your lordships.

"2nd. That monitors articled for two or three years, and undergoing an examination calculated to test their fitness for assisting in these schools, should receive, as in ordinary schools, a reasonable payment for their services, and that a greater number of them should be allowed.

"3rd. That your lordships' conditions in respect of buildings, industrial training, and apparatus should be so modified as to meet the circumstances of such schools."

The prayer of this Memorial is in full accordance with the suggestions repeatedly made to the Privy Council by the late Joseph Fletcher, Esq., in his reports, and especially in the last; they were suggestions founded on a close study of the relative positions of different classes of schools, and the means by which their varied requirements might be met. Should the prayer be granted, a means will be afforded of bringing to bear on the "perishing classes" of children a far higher kind of education than has been yet generally attempted in our Ragged Schools, while the inspection which forms so important a part of the government aid, will in no way interfere with what is so jealously guarded by the

APPLICATION OF PRINCIPLES. 337

Ragged School Teacher, religious instruction, that being left as it is at present in Dissenting Schools, to the management of the Committee of each School. It is to be hoped that the managers of these Free Day Schools, feeling their need of more certain and effective help than they at present receive, will support this memorial by their own petitions.

But, were Free Day Schools extensively established in all large towns, we have seen, from the experience of the United States, that their mere existence would not meet the evil; we know from our own, that a large amount of persevering Christian effort is needed, to make such schools really supply the existing want. Let us suppose this effort made, and sustained by the untiring zeal of the master and of voluntary teachers, will they effect the end proposed, and to what extent? They alone do not; this was shown in the preceding volume, and further demonstrated by experienced speakers at the Birmingham Conference. They do, indeed, supply a great want to a portion of our population which would otherwise have been untouched by any educational instrumentalities, and thus confer a great benefit on the neighbourhood. Yet scarcely less good is done by their revealing wants which they cannot supply, by disclosing a class which they cannot reach. The following statement, made by a teacher in that Bristol Ragged School, which formed the subject of several of Mr. Fletcher's reports, will illustrate this:

"An experienced visitor from a distance, who one day came to our school, remarked, 'you have done much good by showing *what you cannot do.*' The remark encouraged me, for it proved that the speaker understood our difficulties, and saw the need of a more effective remedy than we could apply. Here are some of the cases which show what we have not been able to do, and what we cannot do by any exertion we can make. Of the very first scholars whom I remember in our school at its commencement six years ago, almost all have been since in prison, one has been transported; the instruction given them during a few hours in the day could not counteract the hourly influences to evil under which they had been brought up. They had all bad mothers, and I have never known children grow up in virtuous habits when the mother was bad. Our efforts with six of these boys particularly have been unceasing, but we have found it impossible ever to induce them to attend school regularly, nor could we produce any sensible effect on one of them, until they were removed from their parents. We have not been able to arrest the progress of crime in the family of the C—s; the father kept a little shop near the school, and boasted of his connections and of the good society in which he was received; the children had had a tolerable education, and should have been above the Ragged School, but their deportment and moral tone were below even that of our children; the father's dissolute habits prepared the children for vice; the second son gloried in being spoken of in the newspapers as the head of the gang of juvenile thieves in the neighbourhood; his younger brother followed his example, and the school, which could produce no restraining effect upon them, was greatly benefited as they were severally taken up, or left the city. Nor were we able to exercise a sufficient restraint over Z. and V., both clever, spirited, and energetic boys, to keep them aloof from the tempters that assailed them at every turn; they both were in prison more than once; when in the school and under our influence they manifested good qualities which induced us to make an effort to remove them from the town, to a distance, where they showed readiness to work and gained a good character. With their younger brothers we are beginning earlier,

APPLICATION OF PRINCIPLES.

and have every hope that they may turn out well. Nor have we been able to effect any real reformation on many other boys, occasional attendants, who might have grown up honest men under different circumstances, but whom we have had the pain of seeing one after another joining the ranks of the notoriously hardened young thieves. Many in our neighbourhood who are now transported, *would not* come within the school; one of these, now by a commutation of sentence at the Philanthropic Farm School, the master distinctly remembers as a boy who, by his derisive taunts, used to keep away younger ones, and who often disturbed the school by his yells and abuse; nor would three brothers who were sentenced at the last assizes,—their mother is known to be a receiver of stolen goods;—poor A. we could at last exercise no control over, and were thankful, for the sake of the school, when he was thrown into gaol. If the school has not been able to check effectually those who were falling rapidly into the criminal class, equally little has it been able to do in drawing away the mendicants from their trade. We fed the four young L—s for six months in winter, as their father was ill, and hoped to make them so attached to the school that they would continue to attend,—in the summer they all left; I have continually seen them since in the streets begging with their mother or alone, and no persuasions can induce them to attend. The same has been often the case with Irish children; though pleading cold and starvation they will not yield their liberty even with the offer of warmth and food, they prefer their begging life in the streets. We have been equally unsuccessful in the case of parents who are utterly regardless of their children's welfare; in one week the Master lost twelve children from one very bad street; he called on the parents, and the only answer he could get was that the children did not care about coming to school; so they were left in the streets to hear and see every possible kind of wickedness. Many are the families whom we can thus mark growing up from infancy, trained to nothing but vice; though the means of instruction are within their reach, they will not avail themselves of them. Such a family is that of the K—s; there are two older girls, bold and bad, who have never come within the school, and six fine boys varying from five to twelve years of age; they are children of whom any parent might be proud, if only they were trained; but they make the streets their nursery as soon as they can run, and after a time accompany the older ones on match-selling expeditions. They are growing up ignorant little barbarians *for whom we can do nothing."*

Numerous cases similar to these last were recorded in " Reformatory Schools," Chap. iv.; where Christian effort has done its utmost, and has failed to influence, the alternative is, either that the children shall grow up to ignorance and vice, society tacitly consenting, since it sees and does not interfere;—or that a vigilant police surveillance of the street shall, under magisterial authority, compel attendance at an Industrial Feeding School, on all such children as infest the streets, thus necessarily growing up to be injurious to society. In such cases the expense of their food should be borne by the parents where practicable, in others by the parish; the Educational Grant aiding in the expenses of instruction, as proposed in the Ragged Schools. How completely such a plan answers the end proposed of checking mendicancy and petty pilfering, and securing the elements of religious and moral education to the most low and degraded, has been fully proved at Aberdeen, where it has also been shown how little alteration is required in the law to make such a proceeding, instead of being an exception, the ordinary duty of magisterial bodies. This branch of our subject, where we have to deal with children who are not absolutely criminal in the eye of the law, involves perhaps greater legal difficulties than the treatment of those who are already in the hands of the State, from being acknowledged as Juvenile Delinquents. We have seen that our Transatlantic neighbours approach it fearlessly, and that their experience has hitherto been satisfactory.

The Committee of the Conference has, however, been relieved from the necessity of taking any steps to bring before the government the condition and treatment of these "perishing and dangerous" classes of children, by the appointment, near the close of the last session, of a Committee of Inquiry into the Condition of "Criminal and Destitute Juveniles." This Committee is resuming its sittings with an evident earnestness of purpose, which gives rise to the hope that the subject will ere long be brought directly before the legislature.

In the mean time let us briefly consider some of the difficulties which are felt by many to stand in the way of the adoption of plans which otherwise are acknowledged to be good. Our Continental neighbours and our brethren in the United States have yielded the initiative to individuals who have listened only to the voice of benevolence, and what they conceived to be the dictates of common sense, without considering the objections that might be raised by political economists; the respective governments saw that their labours were wise and good, therefore they aided and supported them. But in our own country it appears necessary first to weigh well all imaginable objections, and to secure the favourable attention of the government, before the effort is extensively tried. We fear not, however, to meet all difficulties boldly, certain that they cannot really stand in the way of what is just and true.

The objections usually alleged to the treatment of juvenile delinquents here advocated, are of two kinds, moral and political. We shall consider them separately.

The first and most prevalent is that by our efforts for the reformation of delinquent children, we are acting unjustly towards honest persons, who would gladly receive the same benefits for their offspring, and who deserve it more. Now, we believe that it is scarcely possible to fall into a more dangerous error, or one more glaringly opposed to the dictates of common sense, as well as to the plainest facts, than the supposition that by judicious efforts to reform the children who are growing up in uncontrolled viciousness, and to train them so that they may become useful members of society, we are acting unjustly towards respectable parents, who require not our help to train their offspring, because they can do it far more effectively themselves. If, indeed, we perceive that the independent and self-supporting poor do need also some of that Christian kindness which we are showing to these more destitute ones, let us give it; let us bestow ungrudgingly on them some of that superior knowledge of which circumstances have made us possessors. And such efforts are made in behalf of the respectable labouring portion of society, as is testified in every large town by our Mechanics' Institutions, our Athenæums, our Mechanics' Reading-rooms, in the originating and support of which the highest minds lend their willing aid; by our public schools, established and conducted by voluntary Christian effort, aided by the Government, where, for a few weekly pence, children often receive an education superior to that for which elsewhere as many shillings are paid. What is actually done for the labouring classes is generally overlooked, when the complaint is made that we are injuring them by helping to raise from their degradation those beneath them. But, without regard to this, we would fearlessly assert that we are conferring a great and direct benefit on the labouring classes by every well-directed effort to reclaim the children of the perishing and dangerous ones; and further, that so far from placing such children, as it is said, in a better position than those of the respectable and well-conducted parents, we cannot do so even were it our desire.

With respect to the first of these positions, we would ask whether it is not an equal injustice to decent labouring persons who are striving in sickness to pay for medical aid, and tenderly to nurse the sick members of the family, to provide for others who in time of need have not these advantages, far superior and gratuitous medical aid in the infirmary, with attendance and diet beyond the reach of the poor man? Is it just to the respectable labourer who preserves his health by a strict observance of God's laws, to afford to one broken down by diseases which are the direct effect of his disregard of them, indulgences which are far beyond his reach? Was it right when the cholera was raging, to bestow blankets, food, and all manner of sanitary appliances, on the squalid, degraded inhabitants of low districts, that they might thus be defended from that infectious disease, which, if once it gained ground among them, would spread its ravages among the decent poor in their immediate neighbourhood, and reach at length the more favoured portion of society? In such cases who would hesitate? none would dare to say that man should be more just than his Maker, who "maketh His sun to rise on the evil and on the good, who sendeth His rain on the just and on the unjust;" especially when the Saviour has laid the same law upon us, by his command, "Be ye therefore perfect, *even as* your Father which is in heaven is perfect." We must strive to remove evil wherever we find it, by the best means that lie in our power, otherwise, we become participators in it, for "whoso knoweth to do good, and doeth it not, to him it is sin." If this reasoning be correct with respect to physical evil, still more so is it with respect to that which is moral and spiritual. This is forcibly shown by Dr. Channing.*

* *Vide* Sermon on the "Obligation of a City to watch over the Moral Health of its Members."

"How little may it profit you, my friends," he says, "that you labour at home, if in the next street amidst haunts of vice, the incendiary, the thief, the ruffian, is learning his lesson, or preparing his instruments of destruction? How little may it profit you, that you are striving to educate your children, if around you the children of others are neglected, are contaminated with evil principles or impure passions? Where is it that our sons often receive the most powerful impulses? In the street, at school, from associates. Their ruin may be sealed by a young woman brought up in the haunts of vice. Their first oaths may be echoes of profaneness which they hear from the sons of the abandoned. What is the great obstruction to our efforts for educating our children? It is the corruption around us. That corruption steals into our homes, and neutralizes the influences of home. We hope to keep our little circle pure amidst general impurity. This is like striving to keep our particular houses healthy, when infection is raging around us. If an accumulation of filth in our neighbourhood were sending forth foul stench and pestilential vapours on every side, we should not plead as a reason for letting it remain, that we were striving to prevent a like accumulation within our own doors. Disease would not less certainly invade us, because the source of it was not prepared by ourselves. *The infection of moral evil is as perilous as that of the plague. If any member of the social body suffers, all must suffer with it. This is God's ordination, and His merciful ordination. It is thus that He summons us to watch over our brother for His good."*

This is a universal principle directly bearing on the question at issue. It would be easy to show in detail the application of it to the particular circumstances of the classes we are considering, but must limit ourselves to the effects on schools. The following is the testimony of a master of an Infant School in one of the worst localities in Bristol, to the effect produced on his own school by the establishment of two Ragged Schools, and a Free School for the children of the Irish poor, in his immediate neighbourhood.

"One effect," he says, "of these schools, has been, combined with some temporary causes, to produce a small decrease of about ten per cent. in the average attendance for the past year; this has not been so much by children leaving the Infant School to go to these schools, as by preventing the influx of particular classes at particular times. Formerly, a considerable number of the children of the Irish migratory class, whose parents were engaged in selling fruit, &c., attended my Infant School during the summer months, the *attendance of each child, however, not averaging more than three weeks*. Besides this there was a fluctuating and irregular mass of the children of improvident parents, whose earnings gave them full ability to pay for their children's education, but who would not sacrifice the indulgence of their appetites for the benefit of their offspring, in order to keep them at all regular or decent. The effect of the establishment of the Ragged Schools on my own, has been, by preventing to a considerable extent the influx of the above classes, to reduce considerably the attendance during the summer months, but at the same time to render the general attendance far more steady and regular; the range of numbers a few years since was from about 60 in the winter to 180 in the summer, whereas the range during the present year has been from about 90 in winter to 145 in summer. *I need not state that the efficiency of the school has advanced in the same proportion.*"

Here we see that while the education of nearly 200 children in neighbouring Ragged Schools has removed contaminating influences from the children of the respectable poor who attend the Infant School, it also renders their education of a superior character, and extends it to a larger number. The experienced master of a British School in another equally bad locality in the same city, expresses his conviction, that "the establishment of a Feeding Industrial School for older children, with compulsory attendance, would prove highly beneficial to his own school. With respect to numbers, the very few that might be withdrawn from his by the desire of a gratuitous education, would be more than compensated by the numbers who are now kept away by their parents, from the fear of the contamination they would be exposed to in their approach to the school, while an increased educational stimulus would be given to the class attending his school, by the upward pressure of that below."

The assertion is made, in the second place, that the children who have had a vicious home and passed a neglected childhood, *cannot* be placed, by any benevolent efforts in their behalf, in a position equally desirable with that of children who have been carefully reared in a virtuous home, and that the parents of such as are thus aided, are not raised, and cannot be raised into a better position than the virtuous and striving.

Who that reads Burns's exquisite picture of a Cottar's Saturday Night, will say that such holy and happy influences can ever exist in a Reformatory School,—that any work of man can equal the work of God's own hands? Who that watches a little boy proudly attempting to handle a spade at his father's side, or sees him gradually trained to exercise his father's craft by working daily with him, and learning what no mere hireling could teach, will think that such instruction could be supplied by the best industrial training in a school? Who would not choose to engage in domestic service a girl brought up by a careful mother to understand household duties, rather than one reared in the most excellent charity school? What master would not choose as an apprentice a boy who has early imbibed good principles from the precepts and example of his parents, rather than one who has afterwards only had them implanted by kind instructors? What poor mother, striving by great self-denial and effort to send her children neat and clean to school, carrying regularly to the master their weekly pence, does not feel that she is in a far higher position than her careless neighbour who sends hers dirty and ragged to a Free Day School? It is impossible for us by any human effort to subvert the law of Providence,

APPLICATION OF PRINCIPLES.

that as a man soweth, so he must reap, that evil must follow disobedience to God's commands; all that we can do is to endeavour to avert suffering from innocent heads.

Two illustrations from the records of a visitor of the poor may add to the weight of argument.

"Yesterday, Mrs. C. called on me to tell me of the departure of her eldest son for Australia. Her maternal feelings quite overpowered her when she told me how she had walked down to the mouth of the river to watch him on the deck to the very last, and how lonely the house seemed without him; how he entreated that his brother and sister would join him as soon as he was settled, for he cared for no one but his own dear family; and how she and her husband must then go with them, for how could she live without her children, who were all in the world to her; and then what advice he gave to his sister to be sure to gain as much knowledge as possible in every way, for when she had finished her term, and he was fixed, she might come over and make a first-rate schoolmistress. Then she said, with a quiet pride in which I greatly sympathized, that they had raised £30 among them, that he might have a very complete outfit, that she had made all his shirts herself, and that he had quite a pile of books. They had indeed been obliged to stint themselves, but they did not mind that; his brother had first proposed the plan, and borrowed £10, which he was paying back at 5s. a week out of his earnings of 14s. a week; his sister gave up her year's wages as pupil teacher; she and her husband did not care what they deprived themselves of to make up the rest. And for whom was this amount of loving sacrifice made? For one who had been a returning prodigal; who some years before had agonized his parents' hearts by falling into bad company and absconding from his employers, defrauding them of £5; for above a year he was not heard of; the mother was inconsolable at the loss of her first-born, the father was bowed down by shame at the dishonour cast upon him. The youth returned weakened with a dangerous illness, and for a long time was a burden on his parents, who, besides, were paying back the money he had taken; but the lost was found, that was enough for them; for many years he had shown his repentance by his conduct, and his mother was sure he would do well, for his principles were good; she had watched him, and observed that he was strictly honest. Mrs. C. is a fresh happy looking woman, always neatly though plainly dressed, such a wife as any labouring man might be proud of, and her husband knows it well. When I first knew them, some fifteen years ago, they were living in a single room in the midst of the very worst part of * * * *; Mr. C.'s earnings were only 12s. a week, and his wife gained enough besides to pay for the education of her children in a good Infant School in the neighbourhood; she could not earn more, for her own family provided her with abundance of occupation. They never pawned, drank, or got into debt, the children were always neat and clean, the husband loved his home. The parents had had but little education, but desired more for their children, and one after another their good conduct obtained their admission into charity schools where they had a superior education. This is the only assistance they have ever received. They cannot now be called poor, for they have all that they really want, and they are among those whom I truly respect."

Now in the immediate neighbourhood of the former residence of this family are others who with the power of earning higher wages are always in the depths of poverty; far from paying for their children at school, it is with difficulty that they can be induced to send them occasionally to a Free School. Children of fine powers and naturally good dispositions fall into crime, and summary punishment is inflicted on them by the law; this has no effect in reforming them, and there is no truly parental home for the wanderers; a Christian hand is held out if possible to save them, by giving them some moral training, and bringing them under some healing influences; they are then removed to a distant land to begin a new life, but with principles as yet half-formed and untried, and though the ties of family affection are still strong, they are not such as to be a stimulus to a virtuous course. Who will say that such youths begin life with advantages at all to be compared to those enjoyed by the former? Who will say that the Christian hand should not have been stretched out to rescue such youths as brands from the burning? Who can believe that injustice is done to those who are in the rich enjoyment of true blessings, and who are respected in their independence? Certainly not the honest poor themselves; not those who by such Christian efforts are relieved by a heavy tax from a noxious plague!

In the same neighbourhood, in the midst of the very worst part of Bristol, lives another family, which affords an illustration of the same truth.

"Mrs. P." says a visitor, "is a widow whom I have known for many years, her sons strikingly prove how completely good home influences, particularly the love and watchfulness of a mother, and the early instilling of good principles, are a safeguard against temptation and surrounding evil. Though these children had to pass through one of the worst streets in the city to go to school, they never made acquaintance with any of the bad boys who were even their next-door neighbours. Mrs. P. had unfortunately a drunken husband, and was obliged to depend mainly on her own labours to pay for her children's education, but she thankfully toiled at extra work to pay for them at a good Infant School, and as they grew older their conduct obtained them admission into a Charity School, where they had very superior instruction. When her husband died, she had five children depending on her, the two older ones earning but very small wages, but she struggled on without parochial aid, always providing them with decent clothes, though their fare was very hard. She gives her sons a comfortable and happy home, and they repay her by their dutiful affection, bringing her willingly all their earnings, growing up respected by all, and loving their home. She is proud of her children, and well she may be. At the end of a dirty narrow passage near her house, in a low, unhealthy room, which has no opening to the outer air, live Mr. and Mrs. R., they are inoffensive persons of decent character. Mr. R. has worked many years for the same master; but they have never exercised any control over their children, who have grown up in the streets, and have not gone to school *because they would not*. The eldest of the three sons was twice in prison for violent conduct to his parents, and then enlisted as a soldier; the second, (V. already mentioned), though a boy of fine natural powers, has been several times in the hands of justice, though he did not manifest any dishonesty of disposition when under good influences, and treated with confidence; he has been removed to a Reformatory School at a distance, by the efforts of friends; the youngest, T. who had resisted all attempts to induce him to come to school, and had already become acquainted with the police station, is placed in a Reformatory School near Bristol. The mother is truly grateful for the efforts made to remedy the want of early training in her children."

It is evident from this narrative that the sons of the last-mentioned parents cost the city much in the damage done and in the expense of their punishment, and that great effort and expenditure is being now bestowed on them;—but are these parents better off than the poor widow who has her sons around her, happy and respectable? or will the R—s ever take the same position in society as the P—s? Will the poor widow feel aggrieved by the pains that are taken with her neighbour's sons, or will she not rather rejoice that they are removed from being an annoyance to hers? And will she not thankfully feel that her children, preserving their independence, have had aids and advantages that could not have been bestowed on the others?

We are, then, conferring a benefit on the industrious poor by all judicious attempts to reform the degraded and vicious, who can never by our utmost efforts be raised to an equally advantageous position with them.

The next objection will require briefer consideration, as it has already been adverted to in "Reformatory Schools;" it is, that the proposed plan is a "premium on crime." This premium is supposed to be to the parent for leaving his child to become a criminal, to the child for becoming so; such premium existing, it is argued, the dread of the consequences of crime would be removed from the juvenile portion of society.

To hold out in any way a "premium on crime" is unquestionably a very serious evil. We would, however, briefly answer, that the *present* system does this to a very great degree, and that the *proposed* one would not. At present the parent is relieved from the maintenance of his child for a few months, and has him shortly returned to him in a better physical condition; his legal rights over him are untouched. "We would ask those," says the writer in the *Edinburgh Review* already quoted, "who are so vividly impressed with the notion that a reformatory system of correction will present so dangerous a premium on parental neglect, to consider what a direct premium, not only on the neglect, but on the depravation of the boy, the present merely penal system of correction offers. This is too little thought of. But let our readers remember that vicious parents have now only to leave their child uncared for and exposed to vile associates, to at once have him maintained for half of his boyhood at the public cost in prison; while during the intervals of his imprisonments they can have him with them at home, and can profit by the produce of his thefts, and be partially maintained by the plunder which, during his months of liberty he is free to gather from the shops or pockets of their neighbours. Let it be considered also, that such parents have no horror of what our philanthropic writers call 'the prison brand.' To have been in Newgate or Tothill Fields is, in their eyes, no disgrace; and they have the consolation to fall back upon, that the boy will be educated and provided for by the Govèrnment at Parkhurst at last. Surely the penal school, and its entire separation of the boy for years, at an earlier and more hopeful stage, can offer no greater bribe than this."

The substitution for a short confinement in Gaol of a long detention in a Reformatory School, and a compulsory separation of the child from his parent, especially if he be removed to a distance, would be regarded as a severe punishment by both. That it would be so, is asserted by Sergeant Adams in his evidence befor the Lords' Committee. " The entire separation of the child from the parent," he says, " seems to be viewed with dread even by the most worthless parent. Whilst I have had constant applications from parents to get their children into the Philanthropic, the Refuge, and other charities in England, I never found, whilst the Children's Friend Society was in existence, by which children were sent out as apprentices or hired servants to the Cape of Good Hope, and other places abroad, I never received one application from any parent to have his child sent to that charity; but, on the contrary, I have had several applications from parents to beg that their children might not be sent there." Though the separation may not be, as in this case, by the removal of the child from the kingdom, yet the feeling would be nearly the same, if the child were completely and compulsorily taken from the parents. In the American " Reform Schools," it appears to be regarded as a sufficient punishment to parents for their culpable neglect, to withdraw from them all legal right over an offending child during his minority; we have seen that in the Boston " Farm School," to which children are voluntarily consigned by their natural guardians, this right is preserved to such as pay a stipulated sum towards their maintenance.

If, then, the parent both loses his right over his child, is separate from him, and is still obliged to contribute towards his maintenance, or to suffer for non-payment, *he* surely receives no reward for the injury he has done to society.

But is it a great premium to a child for his misdoings to be sent to such a school? Those who believe that it will be so regarded by him, show they know but little of the nature of children generally, and of that of these children in particular.

" I think," says Mr. M. D. Hill before the Lords' Committee, " the mere confinement and restraint of personal liberty would be of itself a punishment, and have a deterring effect upon children of idle and vagrant habits. The experience of all ages and countries shows that a vagrant habit once established, is a very high pleasure to the individual, one that he would not forego. As, for instance, when Indians are brought to towns, and treated with great kindness, clothed and fed, and put into habitations, yet in the end they generally strip off their clothes, and run back to the woods." This we find completely borne out by experience, for, to leave out of account the case of Parkhurst, where in spite of abundance of physical comforts efforts to escape are so common, the great difficulty experienced by all who conduct such schools, is to keep the children there, especially at first while their wild habits have still a hold upon them. A regular supply of food and clothing are nothing to a boy in comparison with his beloved liberty, with the free gratification of his desires.

> "The cases in which the young refuse to make use of an asylum when it is offered to them during imprisonment, are so numerous that the conclusion is forced on the mind, that it is useless to expect that Reformatory Schools, filled by volunteers, can ever be fully available. We have looked into the books of a London prison, in order to see how the case stood in this respect; and we find that in the course of 1851, 28 juvenile offenders, out of a total number of 80, refused the offer of an asylum on their own account, while the parents of one other refused their consent, and 13 others availed themselves of the refuge. . . . . It is quite easy to understand why parents often refuse to allow a child to go to an asylum. It is quite as easy to understand why the boys themselves are unwilling to go. Confinement in an asylum appears to them as a punishment."*

If even while suffering the consequences of transgressions, the young offender, careless about the future and not comprehending it, has so small a desire to place himself in a position in which he may change his past evil mode of life, how little will one at liberty wish to resign his vicious indulgences, and to submit to regular training? The benefits to be derived from it are not understood by him, he has never experienced them,—he has no pleasure in cleanliness, order and regularity, he is debarred from innumerable gratifications which, to him, are of the

* English Review, July 1852. Art. "Juvenile Offenders."

highest value. "I called to persuade Margaret D.," says the Master of a Ragged School, "to return to the Asylum provided for her. She had been in prison three times; on the last occasion her father was there too; her mother is a notorious drunkard, her home is squalid to the lowest degree, nothing but vice and misery is before her;—the home which had been found for her afforded her every comfort, she made no complaint of it, but she had run away from it, and would not go back. But when I paid this visit early on Saturday morning, I did not wonder at her reluctance. In the midst of the utmost dirt and confusion she was seated perfectly at her ease by a blazing fire in the midst of her family; the table was laden with abundance of food, not forgetting strong tea and herrings; such luxuries were not to be found at the Asylum, and she preferred to its restraint her liberty, and an occasional feast like this. It was not until I made the father sensible of the responsibility which rested on him, which he exerted by violently saying to her, 'Then you *shall* go,' that she yielded to what she now felt was a necessity."

"But of all the evils attendant on crime," (we again quote the *English Review*,) "the boy thief knows next to nothing; his calling,—for to a London pickpocket picking pockets is as a calling,—has its own peculiar inducements. The risks inseparable from it sweeten it not a little to him. It is a vast mistake to regard such a boy as one whose daily work is unmixed misery. It is by no means so. *He takes considerable pleasure in it.* He is not excited only by the hope of the shilling or eighteen pence which he may get for the handkerchief worth five or seven shillings, or by the idea of a successful inroad on the pocket of some unprotected female; the very pursuit of his game affords him no small excitement. The dodging a visible policeman round the corner of a street; the detecting a well-nigh invisible detective by dint of his own acuteness; the leading these gentry a long and well-ordered chase; the exercising his calling in the self-governing city of London, and then being off into Middlesex when he sees an eye upon him; the initiating into the arcana of the trade one younger or less practised than himself; the meeting with his comrades in all kinds of dark alleys; the keeping a careful and judicious look-out when others are acting; the ready receiving of stolen property the moment it has passed from the rightful owner;—these, and many such dodges, *do afford to the young street-thief an amount of real excitement*, which keeps him at his work fully as much as any hope of gain, and which operates on him far more strongly than it does on the man. And as the work by which he lives excites him, so also it is true that the fear of punishment is with him a deterring motive of much less power than it is with the man. The idea of loss of character molests him but slightly. If he has not been taught at all, or has been ill taught, it is not likely to trouble him. But if he has been well taught,—and many a London thief has,—experience has not taught him, as it has shown his senior, how great an evil this is. You may talk to him about the value of character as long as you please; but generally the excitement of his work, and his liking of his companions will be far too strong for you; and till he has begun to be sorry that he cannot get work, in order to which he must of course first wish to get it, he will care very little for any lectures that you may read him on the loss of his good name. The same class of remarks applies forcibly to juvenile offenders of the female sex. They, too, know fearfully well what is the excitement of a vicious life. They, too, care extremely little for character, grievously as they often atone for the loss of it."

It may, then, be safely asserted that the compulsory removal of a Juvenile Delinquent from liberty to a Reformatory School would be regarded both by him and by his companions as a far more serious punishment than a few months' imprisonment, which is now treated lightly by the hardened among them; as stated by Mr. Hill to the Lords' Committee, " a child being taken away by the arm of the law, and secluded from other children, they knowing that he is taken for punishment, and not seeing him again in his usual haunts, would have as much deterring effect upon them as you can expect from punishment."

Another objection may be more quickly disposed of, viz., that it would be cruel and unjust to parents who really are striving to keep their children from vice, to deprive them from the charge of them on the detection of an offence.

In all cases of Juvenile Delinquency, a considerable discretionary power would remain with the magistrate or judge, such as is in fact now exercised. The course adopted to a considerable extent by the Recorder of Birmingham, in discharging boys on a first offence upon taking the recognizances of their parents or masters for their good behaviour, has been already referred to, and is spoken of favourably in the Lords' Report. A similar course is continually followed by magistrates on the bench. It would not be difficult for an experienced person to decide whether a first detected offence is the indication of a long habit of vice, or whether it is the result of accidental temptation; whether the parent is able and willing to restrain him from future evil, or whether he is unable through vice or incapacity. But, in general, a parent truly desirous of the welfare of his child will be thankful to have him removed for a time to a care more efficient than his own, with a view to his reformation, and will esteem it no hardship to contribute to his maintenance. One who is not so desirous, deserves not our compassion. Such scenes as the following would, under a different system, soon cease to disgrace our police-courts. In the *Bristol Mercury* we find that in the first week in June occurred the following :

"B. was charged with stealing a cotton handkerchief, the property of his *stepfather, the complainant*. He had behaved in a rebellious and spendthrift manner, and took the handkerchief from the house. Remanded for two days.

"J. M. charged with *stealing a coat from his father*. The mother stated that the boy had got into bad company, and had lately taken several things from home; the coat was found at a lodging-house where the prisoner had gone to lodge the preceding Saturday, with the coat on him. Remanded."

Nor would a poor widow have in vain to ask advice from the magistrates, and to entreat their protection against her own boy, as in the following "Painful Case." [*Vide Bristol Mercury*, Sept. 17, 1852.]

"James R., a boy of 14 years old, was charged with stealing a quantity of wearing apparel from the house of his mother. The complainant, who appeared much affected, a hard-working widow-woman, stated that the prisoner was her only son, she having, since the death of her husband, buried three of her offspring. She had used all her efforts to bring him up respectably, and had got him situations as an errand boy. Latterly he had picked up with a bad companion, incited by whom he on Thursday last went to her house during her absence at work, and carried off a suit of wearing apparel belonging to himself, some gowns and other property. She saw nothing of him from that time till Saturday evening, when he was taken into custody. A pawnbroker produced one of the stolen gowns, which had been pledged by the other boy, F., the 'bad companion,' who was not forthcoming. The complainant stated that F. was a very bad boy, who had been repeatedly in the habit of *robbing his own father, who had not properly corrected him.* He had also induced other boys to commit thefts. *Magistrate,* 'I am afraid he is a very bad boy.' Another charge appeared against R., for attempting to pick the pocket of a Mrs. L. Mrs. R. said, ' Mrs. L. *did not intend to appear, out of regard to her feelings.*' *Mag.,* 'What do you wish the magistrates to do with him?' Mrs. R., ' I wish your worships to protect me; I am a poor widow-woman.' *Mag.,* 'We will remand him till Thursday to allow the police to catch the other boy. *A good whipping will do him good, and I think he will have it then.*' The boy was remanded, but brought up the next day with his bad companion who had been 'caught.' Both were discharged for the offence, the prosecutrix not pressing the case."

With what idea of justice, with what fear of the law, will these two lads, thus publicly threatened and discharged, go forth to their companions? Would not this poor hard-working woman have joyfully toiled to make a small weekly payment towards the support of her boy in an asylum, where he might be removed from the evil examples around him, and trained to an industrious and virtuous life with a wisdom which she did not possess? Thus might her only son have been restored to his mother, and she, a widow, to lead a new life, to be her protector and support in old age.

It is hoped that the foregoing considerations will have removed, in anticipation, from the minds of those who have carefully perused them, a last and stronger objection, existing in the minds of many, to such Reformatory Schools as have been advocated in this volume;—yet it requires here to be thoroughly examined, because it involves a principle, which, if admitted, might prove fatal to any extensive plan for the reformation of Juvenile Delinquents.

It is argued that such establishments, designed for young offenders, can only be considered as another kind of gaol, a corrective as well as reformatory principle being adopted, such correction being regulated by the age of the criminal, his or her position when the crime was committed, and the nature of the crime; that as a crime has been committed, punishment must be awarded; and that the adoption of any other principle would strike a blow at the very foundation of our social economy.

Now it is probable that many who hold this language differ only in words from those who would at once place the child who has rendered himself hurtful to society by breaking the laws of his country, in a position where he shall learn to obey them, and to be a useful member of the community. Every school which is truly reformatory must be corrective; no crime CAN pass without its punishment; and a severe penalty will have followed it in the minds of the parents, the child, and his companions, when his misdoing has been followed by a train of consequences which in the outset are most repugnant to his natural inclinations. Yet this does not satisfy the minds of some who say, "The magistrate must not bear the sword in vain," forgetting that when he wields it in vengeance against these children he has borne it in vain, he has made it of none effect;—who recollect not that he who " sinneth without law " will be judged very differently from those who have possessed it; that the Saviour has declared that " they who know not their Lord's will and do it not, shall be beaten with few stripes;" and that if society can at any time justly demand satisfaction for offences, it is of those who have been taught to discern between good and evil, not of ignorant, uneducated children.

It is believed by persons who hold these views, that a distinct retributive penalty should be attached to every detected violation of the law, which may be peculiarly designated a *"punishment,"* as being irrespective of the future conduct of the offender. Of the effect of such " punishment" on offenders in general, we have the testimony of one whose experience qualifies him to form a judgment, the Rev. J. Field, Chaplain of the Reading Gaol. *"I should look very little to reformation being effected by punishment,"* he says in his evidence before the Lords' Committee in 1847. " I look upon the law not as ever designed to be vindictive, but most certainly as appointing punishment intended to be exemplary to a great extent. I submit, therefore, that we have no right to inflict punishment merely for the sake of avenging wrong, or simply with a view to its deterring effects on others, without bearing in mind at the same time the reformation of the criminal. It is not smarting from punishment that will prevent future crimes. *I believe that the mere dread of punishment as threatened by any law, either human or divine, very seldom prevents crime.* Offences are restrained far more by the correction of a criminal; but they are increased by the hardening process of ineffectual punishment. In order to punishment being corrective, it must be based on sound principles, and accompanied with scriptural instruction, which cannot be given without some considerable space of time."

If this is the general effect of pain arbitrarily inflicted, in contradistinction to that which is the inevitable and natural effect of misdoing, still more so is it in the case of children whose reasoning powers and experience have been too little developed for them to be able to understand its real meaning. In them we have already seen that it excites only a vindictive feeling and has a hardening effect, which is utterly inconsistent with any real reformation, for it puts them in a state of antagonism with those who would effect it. The principle of the reformatory system here advocated is admirably set forth in a paper delivered in by Mr. M. D. Hill to the Lords' Committee in 1847. It forms a part of a "Draft Report on the Principles of Punishment, presented to the Committee on Criminal Law appointed by the Law Amendment Society, in December, 1846."

"By a reformatory system we mean one in which all the pain endured strictly arises from the means found necessary to effect a moral cure.

"A prison (or Reformatory School) thus becomes a hospital for the treatment of moral diseases.

"The prisoner may be called a patient, while the various officers of the prison will gradually attain the position in his mind of persons exercising the healing art, and be no longer regarded as the agents of vindictive powers. Hence they will cease to excite his hostility, and an alliance may be formed between him and them, offering the most important aids towards his cure.

"A steady adherence to such a system will produce a state of opinion withoutside the prison walls as well as within, that the good of the patient is the sole aim of every part of the treatment to which he is subjected; and such being the impression on the public mind, the application of any amount of pain absolutely necessary to the object in view, will not encounter the disapprobation of society.

"But so long as pain is inflicted on the individual, not with reference to his own ultimate advantage, but on the ground that by his sufferings others will be benefited, so long there will be a strong, perhaps a wholesome jealousy abroad, which will operate to keep down the amount of pain to some supposed equality between the particular offence for which he is imprisoned and its punishment.

"This appears to be the secret of the numberless illusory sentences which are daily awarded in our courts.

"When, however, gaols become considered as hospitals, and when consequently they and all prisons connected with them are relieved from the degrading associations which have ever connected themselves with the mere inflictors of pain, any amount of suffering which is felt to be essential to the reformatory process, would no more excite jealousy of the law or dislike towards those who administer it, than is now felt towards a surgeon, who amputates a limb, or performs any other painful operation.

"Nevertheless it is evident the patient will have much to endure.

"Criminals arrive in prison," (and juvenile delinquents in Reformatory Schools,) "under the influence of habits which must instantly be set at nought. They must at once take leave of every indulgence, however intolerable inveterate use may have made the deprivation. No quarter is to be given to their prevailing vice, indolence. They are shut out from the society of their companions, and indeed from all except that from which, until the work of reformation has proceeded through several stages, they are not likely to derive much pleasure.

"As their minds become informed, they find retrospection upon their past courses a humiliating task.

"They have to feel their own weakness. They find that even when the desire to do right has been created, their habits act as formidable enemies, and their failures convince them that the day of liberty is yet far distant.

"That no sentient and reflective being can be placed under circumstances like these, without encountering great and profound suffering, must be evident."

It is evident, then, that in advocating the reformatory principle, and representing it as the *only* one which can be the basis of any system by which juvenile crime can be effectually checked, we do not obliterate the distinction between right and wrong, and thus endanger the whole existence of society. Happiness can be enjoyed solely and exclusively in conformity with God's holy will. *Suffering must and ever will be the consequence of the violation of*

God's immutable laws. Even the physical order of the universe cannot be infringed without appalling consequences; did the world need yet to learn this all-pervading truth, the fearful desolating floods, swallowing up or sweeping away hundreds through the forgetfulness of the mighty powers of the elements even in this very year, might abundantly prove it. The moral government of the world exhibits universally the same great truth; though the wicked may seem to flourish for a season, yet, even in this world, the history of nations as well as of individuals abundantly testifies that sin and suffering are inseparable. And throughout the sacred Book which contains God's message to man, the same revelation is everywhere made, that " whatsoever a man soweth, that shall he also reap." Nor would we, even if we could, attempt to alter this allwise decree; we would rather strive " as fellow-workers with God," to enable the diseased heart to *feel* its own wretchedness, that so it may be healed; we would put the erring child into a condition in which he would painfully perceive the evil of the things wherein he delighted; we would submit him to restraints and privations most repugnant to his present nature, that he may be brought into the way in which God would have him to walk. But all punishment, to be salutary, and therefore to effect the end aimed at, must be the *natural consequence* of the sin, and administered with the same loving hand with which the Heavenly Father corrects His erring children. While he who doeth wrong must, and always will, suffer for the wrong he has done, that suffering, to have a corrective or reformatory effect, must be, as in the order of Divine providence, the *natural result* of his violation of God's laws, not an arbitrary infliction. A *vindictive* element entering in any way into chastisement for evil-doing, excites in the mind of him who receives it, especially of the child, a rebellious and vindictive feeling in return; he has borne the penalty of his sin, he has paid the debt of justice,—he is free,—happy only if he can escape it in future; his sorrow is that of the world, which "worketh death." Such punishment defeats, then, its object; and it must do so, for it is contrary to the Divine law, it usurps the place of the Supreme, for " *Vengeance is mine, I will repay, saith the Lord.*" Let, then, all *punishment* be God's punishment; let it be the working of His own laws, and let us strive to make all suffering attendant on violation of them, conduce to the reformation of the offender, in conformity with the revealed word of Him who "willeth not that any should perish, but rather that he should turn from his wickedness and live."

Other difficulties and objections may arise to hinder the work of regeneration to which we would devote ourselves, but let us only with true hearts set ourselves to it, and we shall find the means of overcoming them. But we must believe and feel, to give us perseverance in our efforts, that it is God's work, and that each individual of society has a certain responsibility resting on him for the performance of it.. He has made man one great family; He has closely bound together those living in one country, —in one city,—by the ties of mutual dependence, for if one member suffer, all must suffer.

"I would that as a city," says Dr. Channing,* "we might understand and feel how far we are chargeable with much of the crime and misery around us, of which we complain. Is it not an acknowledged moral truth, that we are answerable for all evil which we are able, but have failed to prevent? Were Providence to put us in possession of a remedy for a man dying at our feet, and should we withhold it, would not the guilt of his death lie at our door? Are we not accessory to the destruction of the blind man, who, in our sight, approaches a precipice, and whom we do not warn of his danger? On the same ground, much of the guilt and misery around us, must be imputed to ourselves. Why is it that so many children in a large city grow up in ignorance and vice? *Because that city abandons them to ruinous influences, from which it might and ought to rescue them.* Why is beggary so often transmitted from parent to child? Because the public, and because individuals do little or nothing to break the fatal inheritance. Whence come many of the darkest crimes? From despondency, recklessness, and a pressure of suffering which sympathy would have lightened. Human sympathy, Christian sympathy, were it to penetrate the dwellings of the ignorant, poor and suffering, were its voice lifted up to encourage, guide, and console, and its arms stretched out to sustain, what a new world would it call into being! What a new city should we live in! How many victims of stern justice would become the living, joyful witnesses of the regenerating power of a wise Christian love.

---

* "On the Obligation of a City to Care for and Watch over the Moral Health of its Members," a sermon delivered on occasion of the death of the Rev. Dr. Tuckerman, Jan., 1841.

. . . Let society especially protect the exposed child. *There is a paramount duty which no community has yet fulfilled.* If the child be left to grow up in utter ignorance of duty, of its Maker, of its relation to society, to grow up in an atmosphere of profaneness and intemperance, and in the practice of falsehood and fraud, let not the community complain of his crime. It has quietly looked on and seen him, year after year, arming himself against its order and peace; and who is most to blame when he deals the guilty blow? *A moral care over the tempted and ignorant portion of the state is a primary duty of society.*"

If, then, this is part of God's law, we need not ask whether there can be any insurmountable difficulty in carrying its principles into human law, for it is certain that sound political economy being founded on the natural law, *i. e.* on the moral and physical order of the universe ordained by God, can never be at variance with it. There is perfect unity and consistency in all God's laws, and on these political economy must be founded, or it is false. And indeed as a Christian nation a regard is always acknowledged to the laws of Him who is the only Ruler of the Universe. This we find explicitly set forth in legal documents.

Comyn, in his " Digest of the Laws of England," thus defines the " Original and Ground of the Common Law."

" The Foundations of the Common Law are,— 1. *The Law of Nature or Reason.* 2. *The Divine Law.* 3. General Customs. 4. Divers Principles or Maxims. 5. Several Particular Customs. And it was called '*The Common Law,*' because the Code of Laws collected by Edward the Confessor, out of the Laws before used in the several Provinces during the Heptarchy, was common to the whole Realm." It appears, then, that the highest laws of our Realm, yield in authority to that of Nature, of Reason, of God.

We cannot, therefore, be surprised to find that this moral responsibility resting on society forms a distinct part of the ancient laws of our realm, and is acknowledged by the spirit of our laws at the present time. This is well shown in an article by David Power, Esq., Recorder of Ipswich, in the " Law Review," Feb., 1852, art. "Juvenile Delinquency :" "Wherever a number of persons are gathered together, so as to form a community, whether in a village or a town, it is their Christian duty to take care that none of their younger members are growing up untrained, and therefore under circumstances to their becoming criminal; and if such be their duty, the consequences of its breach should fall upon those who commit it and upon no others. . . The inhabitants of at own are reduced by fever and are thus taught to adopt sanitary measures, so as to avoid a recurrence of the pestilence which has been so destructive to them. What if one district had to bear the effects of the bad drainage of another? Crime is a moral pestilence; its causes we are beginning to understand; and if each district had to bear the burden of the crime committed within it, the inhabitants of that district would be induced to take steps to prevent its commission. Our ancestors were wiser in their legislation in this respect than we have been. By the old law of Frankpledge, the existence of which has been traced nearly to king Alfred's time, the freeholders of a tithing were sureties, or free pledges, to the king for the good behaviour of each other, and if any offence were committed in their district, they were bound to have the offender forthcoming; and therefore no man was suffered to abide in England forty days, unless he were enrolled in some tithing or deanery. (Black. Com. vol. i., p. 114.) The law which still prevails by which a remedy is given against the hundred to the owner of property riotously destroyed by a mob, is a familiar instance of the same principle."

The law of Frankpledge, as set forth in one of the laws of Edward the Confessor, is said to consist in this, "that in all the vills throughout the kingdom, all men are bound to be in a guarantee by tens, so that if one of the ten offend, the other nine may hold him to right." (Kemble's Saxons in England, vol. ii., p. 250-1.)

The ancient Common Law of England laid great stress on the responsibility which the inhabitants of a district had respecting the good order of the district, and subjected to a general fine under certain circumstances offences committed within it. The minute particularity with which all kinds of annoyances by which one individual interferes with the well-being of another in the same district are specified, is most striking, as set forth in Comyn's

Digest of the Laws of England, vol. iv., under the article "Leet."

"The Leet," we there find, "is so called of the Saxon word *gelethian, convenire*. And it is named the View of Frankpledge, because all resiants within the Leet were divided in *decennies*, viz., Corps of ten families, *and each of the decennie was pledge for the other, quod staret legi, &c.* Whence the chief of the principal family was named Capitalis Plegius, the others, Franci Plegii; and the court where they appeared, Visus Franci Plegii. The Sheriff's Leet, or the Tourn, (out of which all other Leets are derived,) is the most ancient court." This Leet had not only power to "inquire and determine of all felonies, except homicide," and of high misdemeanours, but even, by the stat. 18 Edward II., "of haunters of taverns, *if they have not wherewithal to live;* of haunters of alehouses; of those who travel by night, and sleep in the day; of vagabonds and hazarders." It was not, then, in the days of our forefathers, thought an undue interference with the liberty of the subject, that the local court of justice should inquire and determine respecting all such persons as were leading a course of life which must necessarily make them a burden to the district. The surveillance over the personal safety and even comfort of each individual was carried so far, that the Leet was even to inquire, "of evesdroppers, who stand under walls or windows by night or by day, to hear tales, and carry them to make debate

APPLICATION OF PRINCIPLES. 375

between their neighbours; of scolds or brawlers;" and " a common nuisance may be inquired of at the Leet." In cases where a crime had been committed, and there was an uncertainty respecting the offender, " a fine may be imposed upon the whole town, hundred, or county." But in the awarding of fines, a certain discretionary power was recognised; " an amerciament *must be reasonable, otherwise the lord shall not have an action for it.*" The Divine Law was also acknowledged as superseding that of man; " if the writ abates *by the act of God,* and not by the default of the party, the demandant or plaintiff shall not be amerced." It almost necessarily follows from this, what we find to be the fact, that since children are " by the act of God," irresponsible, they are, in general, to be exceptions, in the case of penalties awarded. " The king or queen shall never be amerced; nor an infant, generally, for the entry shall be,—*sed nihil de misericordiâ quia infans;* and if an amerciament be entered against an infant, he shall be pardoned, *of course,* and the entry shall be,—*Ideo in misericordiâ, sed pardonatur quia infans.*" This ancient law has been strangely forgotten in our day, for we read in the *Edinburgh News* during this very year (1852):

" A strange, but absurd, case was brought before William L. Colquhoun, Esq., of Clachick, a Justice of the Peace for the County of Perth, at Crieff, on the 10th inst., (ult.,) at the instance of Lord and Lady Willoughby de Eresby and Louis

Kennedy, their factor, as their mandatory, against two children of Mr. Middlemiss, labourer, Muthill, *of the respective ages of two and six years. The youngest child attended the learned justice carried in his mother's arms.* The charge brought against them was, that they had been found in the act of laying snares, for the purpose of catching game, in an adjoining field to the village of Muthill." The crime was proved, at least to the satisfaction of the magistrate, for the evil doers were fined each £1 6s. 10d., including expenses, or, failing payment, thirty days' imprisonment!

Surely, we require to return to first principles, and to learn from our Saxon ancestors, as well as from our French neighbours, that a child acts without discernment of the true nature of his crime, and *" shall be pardoned, of course, because he is a child."*

The following principles, then, appear to have been already acknowledged in the laws and social economy of our country, and only require a fuller development than now exists, to meet the condition and treatment of the children of the " perishing and dangerous" classes of our community and juvenile delinquents.

Firstly, That all parents are responsible for the maintenance and education of their children, and amenable to punishment when they neglect it through their own misconduct.

Secondly, That where a child has no parents, or where, having them, such parents prove themselves incapable of discharging the duty devolving on them, this duty rests upon society,—the child being, by nature, in a condition in which he is irresponsible. Society cannot neglect this duty without incurring a heavy penalty.

Thirdly, That where a parent, through his culpable neglect, or actual criminality, proves that he cannot retain the guardianship of his child without injury to society, and therefore is deprived of it, he is not thereby freed from the duty imposed by nature of maintaining his child, and must be compelled to do so, while losing his legal right over him.

Fourthly, That when society, embodied in the State, assumes the guardianship of a child, for the reasons above assigned, viz., the non-existence of parents, or their incapacity, it is bound to discharge this duty, so as best to fulfil the end for which God sent him into the world,—namely, that he may become a useful member of society, and prepare for another state of existence. This principle equally applies to orphans, to morally destitute children, and to those who have been legally convicted of breach of the law.

Fifthly, That the State in thus assuming, so to speak, a parental relation towards the child, may consign the care of him, as is done by natural parents, to those who can discharge the duty satisfactorily,—a strict inspection being exercised by the State, to ascertain that this duty is well discharged.

Sixthly, That though it may be necessary, in default of better provision, to employ large government institutions for the maintenance and education of such children, it is important to enlist in these as much individual and voluntary effort as possible, as the best means of supplying to the child the parental relation; but that every inducement should be held out to lead individuals, or individual bodies, themselves to establish such institutions, where the child may be, in a measure, restored to the natural condition of a family, and brought under individual influence. The State should, however, always exercise a close inspection of such institutions.

These principles have a general application to all the children now in our Workhouse Schools,—to all those who are vagabondizing in our streets or in the country, and preparing to be highly injurious to society, if they have not become so, and to those already designated juvenile delinquents. Most instructive examples have been given in various existing institutions, how valuable is the aid afforded when individual exertions can be brought to bear on the parochial establishments for children; and how important would be the help to Christian effort, if government support were afforded to it in the training of the morally destitute. But our present inquiry more particularly regards convicted children; any legislative measure especially intended for *them* should

APPLICATION OF PRINCIPLES.

not only be founded on the foregoing principles, but distinctly recognise the following, which arise from them :

That the child, when by conviction of crime he becomes a child of the State, must still be treated as a child, and be dealt with by corrective training, not by mere punishment, as at present.

That he should for this end be placed in a Reformatory School, where he shall be submitted to such training and discipline as may best prepare him to become a useful member of society.

And that, wherever practicable, such schools should be conducted by individual bodies, with inspection from the State.

Such a measure will have as its object—

1. To give power to magistrates and judges to sentence any young person convicted of offence against the laws, to detention in a Reformatory School for a period not less than a year, or exceeding the term of his minority, the period to be dependent on his reformation, and decided by the managers of the school and the government inspector. A discretionary power to rest with the magistrates and judges to restore the child to his (or her) parents or guardians on the first offence, provided they give satisfactory security for his future good conduct.

2. To give power to magistrates and judges in all cases as aforesaid, to charge the parents of such offender with a weekly contribution in aid of his

(or her) maintenance in the Reformatory School, such amount to be paid by the parish, and in all cases to be recoverable by the parish officers from the parents.

3. To enable the Secretary of State to pay an annual sum from the public funds towards the expense of such Reformatory School, and a sum towards the erection of the same; provided always such School be duly certified by Her Majesty's inspectors, as to be so conducted as to carry out a reformatory discipline calculated to train up useful members of society.

4. To enable magistrates in all districts where such Schools have not been established within a certain specified time, or do not exist in proportion to the wants of the districts, to erect and establish such schools by aid of a local rate.

5. To give sufficient power to the managers or directors of such Schools for the necessary correctional discipline of offenders committed to them, for the detention of the same, and for the recovering them in case of absconding; such managers or directors being responsible for their safe custody.

6. To appoint inspectors who shall frequently examine the working and management of the School and its reformatory effect on the children, the care of the religious instruction being left entirely to the managers of the School.

An act of parliament, founded on such principles,

will, it is believed, be the means of calling into action a large amount of Christian effort in behalf of these " moral orphans ;" an earnest of this is afforded by the fact that during the course of the present year, (1852,) three experimental institutions have been commenced, and it is known that the due support and success of these will lead to the establishment of others.

Our beloved country is surely exceeded by no other in the amount of wisely benevolent exertion, which is made both by individuals and by public bodies, to benefit the poorer members of our community, to excite in them a spirit of independence, and at the same time to aid them by the employment in their behalf of knowledge which they cannot possess. Seed sown in such fields of labour brings forth an abundant harvest; the work itself is attractive to the public eye, and captivates even the casual observer. In this neglected vineyard the labourers are few, the seed sown in stony ground, amid thorns and brambles, scantily springs up, and to the eye of man may appear little worth. But in due time we shall reap if we faint not. It is ours only to work on ungrudgingly, earnestly, and without fainting, leaving the result to the Lord of the Harvest.

Then let each one who "knows these things," respecting the condition and treatment of our poor young delinquents, earnestly endeavour to "do them;" let each strive to rouse others to partake in the work; let it be said of all, they have done what they could, warmed and incited by deep Christian love, and remembering the words of Him who said, "INASMUCH AS YE HAVE DONE IT UNTO ONE OF THE LEAST OF THESE MY BRETHREN, YE HAVE DONE IT UNTO ME!"

BRISTOL, *December* 11, 1852.

APPENDIX.

The following extracts from " Principles of Human Physiology," by William B. Carpenter, M.D., F.R.S., &c., [Fourth Edition, Churchill,] have an important bearing on the principles of treatment to be adopted towards Juvenile Delinquents, advocated in this volume:

" The dominant power of the will, not only over every act of the nervo-muscular apparatus, which is not immediately concerned in the maintenance of the vital functions, but over the course of purely psychical action, is probably the most distinctive attribute of the Human mind in its highest phase of development; and it is that which gives to each individual the freedom of action which every one is conscious to himself that he is capable of exerting. . . . . Now between the complete want of this controlling power of the will, and the most perfect possession of it, every intermediate gradation is presented by the several individuals which make up the human species; some persons being so much accustomed, in consequence of the weakness of their Will, to act directly upon intellectual and emotional suggestions, that they can scarcely be said to be voluntary agents; and others, allowing certain dominant ideas or habitual feelings to gain such a mastery over them as to exercise that determining power which the will alone ought to exert. This gradation may be perfectly traced in children, in *whose education the development of the faculty of 'self-control' should be a leading object.* . . . On this power of self-direction, indeed, all the higher developments of intellectual power almost essentially depend; and we shall hereafter see how largely it is concerned in that progressive exaltation of the moral nature, which, even more than intellectual capacity, tends to bring the human soul into relation with its Creator."—(pp. 672, 673.)

"We are not to look merely at congenital peculiarities of psychical constitution, as the source of *original habits of thought;* for as the external conditions in which every individual is placed, differ to a certain extent from those which affect each one of his fellows, so does it happen that, as the development of every kind of capacity for mental action is augmented (like the nutrition of muscle and nerve) by its habitual exercise, the strength of that capacity, and its tendency to exert an active influence on the course of thought, will partly depend upon the degree in which circumstances call it into play, especially during the period when, in the natural progress of psychical evolution, it is first taking a prominent share in the operations of mind. Hence there is a set of *acquired habits of thought*, which, no less than those dependent upon original constitution, determine the consequences of any particular impression upon the 'ideational consciousness,' and which thus form part of the 'character' of each individual at any one period of his existence."—(p. 794.)

We thus see that even in a child of naturally vicious tendencies, if such there be, a long course of good training, the subjecting him to virtous influences, and the excitement in him of healthy desires, may subdue them.

"Man has been said to be a 'bundle of habits.' Where the habits have been judiciously formed in the first instance, the tendency is an extremely useful one, prompting us to do that spontaneously which might otherwise require a powerful action of the will; but on the other hand, if a bad set of habits have grown up with the growth of the individual, or if a single bad tendency be allowed to become an habitual spring of action, a far stronger act of volition will be required to determine the conduct in opposition to them. This is especially the case where the habitual idea possesses an emotional character, and becomes the source of *desires;* for the more frequently these are yielded to, the more powerful is the solicitation they exert."

Such is peculiarly the condition of the children of the " perishing and dangerous classes." This may, in some measure, be corrected by the introduction into the child's mind of

. . . " notions of right and duty, which, so far as they attach themselves to our actions, give them a *moral and religious character.* These may act simply as *ideas*, whose coercive power depends upon the intensity with which they are brought before the mind; but they obtain a much stronger influence, when they acquire an emotional character from *the association of the feeling of desire, with the idea of obligation; that is, when we feel a wish to do that which we are conscious we ought to do.* This association is one which it is peculiarly within the capability of the will to cherish and strengthen. And still more powerful is the operation of these combined motives, when a constant *habit* of acting upon them has been formed; for the strongest desires are then immediately repressed, the strongest aversions cease to exercise an influence, when once the question is looked at in its moral aspect, and a clear perception has been attained of its right and its wrong side."— (p. 844.)

" From the time when the human being first becomes conscious that he has a power within himself of determining the succession of his mental states, from that time does he begin to be a free agent; and in proportion as he exerts that power does he emancipate himself from the domination of his constitutional or automatic tendencies. It is a principle now recognised by the most enlightened educators, that the development of this power of self-control ought to be the object of all nursery discipline, and the process of its acquirement is very gradual. When an infant is excited to a fit of passion by some unpleasant sensation, its nurse attempts to restore its equanimity by presenting some new object to its attention, so that the more recent and vivid pleasurable impression may efface the sense of past uneasiness. As the infant grows into childhood, the judicious parent no longer trusts to mere sensory impressions for the diversion of the passionate excitement, but calls up in its mind such ideas and feelings as it is capable of appreciating, and endeavours to keep the attention fixed upon these, until the violence of the emotion has subsided; and recourse is had to the same process, whenever it is desired to check any tendency to action which depends upon the selfish propensities, appeal being always made to the highest motives which the child is capable of recognising, and punishment being only had recourse to, for the purpose of applying an additional set of motives when all others fail. For a time, this process of external suggestion may need to be continally repeated, where there are strong impulses whose unworthy character calls for repression; but if it be judiciously adopted, and consistently persevered in, a very slight suggestion serves to recall the superior motives to the conflict. And in further space, the child comes to feel that he has *himself* the power of recalling them, and of controlling his urgent impulses to immediate action. The power of self-control, thus usually acquired in the first instance in regard to those impulses which directly determine the conduct, gradually extends itself to the habitual succession of the thoughts; and in proportion as this is brought under the direction of the will, does the individual become capable of forming his own character, and therefore truly responsible for his actions. It must not be forgotten, however, that the power of self-control may be turned to a bad, as well as a good account; and that the value of its results will entirely depend upon the *direction* in which it is employed. The thoughts may be so determinately drawn away from the higher class of motives, the suggestions of conscience so habitually disregarded, and the whole attention so completely fixed upon the gratification of selfish or malevolent propensities, that the human nature acquires far more of the Satanic than of the Divine character; the highest development of this type (if the term may be permitted) being displayed by those who use their power of self-control for the purposes of hypocrisy and dissimulation, and cover the most malignant designs under the veil of friendship. Such men (whose portraiture is presented by our own great Dramatist in the character of Iago) show us to what evil account the highest intellect and the most powerful will may be turned, when directed by the baser class of motives; and we cannot but feel that they are far more degraded in the moral scale than those, who having never learnt to control their animal propensities, and being unconscious of the very existence of a higher nature within themselves, simply obey the promptings of their automatic impulses, and are rather to be considered as ill-conditioned automata, than as vicious men. Of this latter class, some, from original constitution and early influences of the most degrading kind, seem altogether destitute of anything but a *brutal* nature; such ought to be treated as irresponsble beings, and, as such, restrained by external coercion from doing injury to society. But this class is small in proportion to that of individuals who *act* viciously, simply because they have never been led to *know* that any other course is open to them, or to *feel* any motives that might give them a different impulse. With these, the object should rather be to awaken the higher parts of the moral nature, 'to find out the holy spot in every child's heart,' and to develop habits of self-control in the manner just described, than to subjugate by external restraint; and the success which has attended this method, in the hands of those who have judiciously applied it, is sufficient evidence of its superiority; many of the most apparently debased natures having been thus elevated to a grade, which it seemed at first impossible they should ever attain. From the *Satanic*, or positively and wilfully evil type of Human nature, in which the highest powers are turned to the worst account, we are thus conducted through the *brutal*, or negatively evil type, towards that higher aspect of humanity, which is presented by those who habitually keep before them the *Divine* ideal, and who steadily endeavour to bring their *whole nature* into conformity with it. This is *not* to be effected by dwelling *exclusively on any one* set of the motives already referred to, as those which the truly religious man keeps before his mind. Even the idea of duty, operating alone, tends to reduce the individual to the subservience of a slave, rather than to induce in him that true mastery over himself, which consists in such a regulation of his emotions and propensities, that his course of duty becomes the spontaneous expression of his own higher nature; but it is a most powerful aid in the acquirement of that regulation, by the fixation of the thoughts and affections on 'things on high,' which is the best way of detaching them from all that is earthly and debasing. It is by the *assimilation* rather than by the *subjugation* of the Human will to the Divine, that Man is really lifted towards God; and in proportion as this assimilation has been effected, does it manifest itself in the life and conduct; so that even the lowliest actions become holy ministrations in a temple consecrated by the felt presence of the Divinity. Such was the life of the Saviour, towards that standard it is for the Christian disciple to aspire."—(pp. 848—850.)

INDEX

Aberdeen Prison, 109, 114–115
Adams, Sergeant, 25, 313, 355
Ainsworth, William Harrison, 126
Alfred, King, 373
Anselm, Saint, 316
Auburn (N.Y.) State Prison, 211

Bächtelen Reform School, Berne, 254–255
Baltimore (Md.) House of Refuge, 225–226
Barclay, Sheriff Hugh, 42, 49
Bath Gaol, 139–140, 189
Baumgartner, Joseph, 278, 281
Baxter, Rev. Daniel, 109
Bazin (founder, Mesnil St. Firmin), 245
Beaumont, Gustave Auguste de, 208
Belgian Home Office, 250
Bell, Dr. Andrew, 148
Bellevue Penitentiary, N. Y. (City), 210
Blackstone, Sir William, 158
Boston (Mass.) Asylum for Indigent Boys, 213
Boston (Mass.) Farm School, 213–216, 232, 355–356
ages of inmates, 215
Boston (Mass.) Farm School Society, 213
Boston (Mass.) House of Correction, 136
Boston (Mass.) House of Reformation, 136, 211–212, 232
Brétignères de Courteilles, Viscount, 235
Brown, Rev. William, 174–175
Bulwer-Lytton, Edward, 126
Burns, Robert, 348
Burritt, Elihu, 261

Carpenter, William B., 383–388
Carter, Rev. J., 165
Channing, Dr. William Ellery, 301–302, 305, 344, 370
Children's Friend Society, 30, 355
Citizens' Memorial to Edward VI, 122
Clarkson, Thomas, 65
Clay, Rev. John, 31, 32, 38, 39, 40, 52, 56, 64, 91, 92, 99, 100, 101, 102, 120, 124, 126, 127, 133, 137, 141, 151, 167
Cochin, Dr. Augustin, 239, 305–306
Coldbath Fields Prison, 25
Coleridge, Sir John Taylor, 328
Colonie Agricola de Mettrai. *See* Mettrai
Colquhoun, William J., 375
Common Law of England, 373
Comyns, Sir John, 371, 373–374

389

Conference on Preventive and Reformatory Schools, Birmingham, 167, 180, 230–231, 330–333, 337
  object, 330–331, 333, 334
  resolutions, 332–333
Crime. *See also* Juvenile delinquents
  cause of, 28, 30, 33, 36, 37. *See also* Intemperance
  diminished by education, 332
  expense, 166
  undetected, 3

Davis, Rev. John, 186, 190
Delessert, Gabriel, 238–239
Demetz, Frederic Auguste, 235, 239
Denman, Lord Thomas, 328
Dickens, Charles, 29
District Farm Schools, 190
Domestic Missions, 210
Dublin prisons, 105
Ducpetiaux, Edouard, 251
Durham County Gaol, 140–141

Eadmer, 316
Edinburgh Gaol, 175
Edinburgh House of Refuge, 115
Edinburgh prisons, 106–107
Edward the Confessor, 372–373
Edward II, 374

Farm School System, 241
Farm schools, 300. *See also* Mettrai; Rauhe Haus, Hamburg; Reformatory schools; Wurtenburg schools
  family system, 247, 248, 253, 264
  Flanders, 248–249
  Germany, 248, 322
  labour, 247, 253
  management, 253
  private support, 247, 248, 253, 256–257
  reduce pauperism, 253
  religious management, 244–245, 257
  Switzerland, 248, 252–254, 256–257
  teachers, 245
Fellenburg, Philipp Emanuel de, 252
Female delinquents, 83–117, 359. *See also* Juvenile delinquents; Juveniles in prisons
  degradation, 91
  effect of imprisonment, 105, 108, 111
  lack of intellectual capacity, 85, 88, 90
  training in crime by mothers, 99
Fermes-hospices, 250
Field, Rev. John, 309, 364–365
First Ordinances of Bridewell, 122
Fletcher, Joseph, v–vi, 241, 243, 245, 248–249, 250, 251, 253, 256, 300, 322, 336, 337
Frankpledge, law of, 373
Free day schools. *See* Free schools
Free schools, 11, 207, 337. *See also* Industrial schools; Public schools; Ragged schools
  effect on pay schools, 346–347
  government grants, 11, 331, 334–336, 340
  legislation needed, 331, 333
  teachers, 11, 12
French Penal Code, 236–237, 239–240

Gaols. *See* Juveniles in prisons; Prisoners; *specific gaols*
Gehren, A. W., 259
Gipseys. *See* Vagabonds
Glasgow prisons, 106–107
Gloucester Prison, 57

Hackney Wick Institution for Girls, 30
Hamilton, Rev. George Hans, 140–141
Harty, Dr. William, 105
Hawkers, 31
Hill, Matthew Davenport, 180–181, 356, 360, 365–366
Hofwyl Poor School, Switzerland, 252
House of Refuge
  Baltimore, 225–226
  Edinburgh, 115
  New York, 210, 216, 217, 218–221, 229
  Philadelphia, 210, 220–223
Hume, David, 47–48

Industrial feeding schools. *See* Industrial schools
Industrial schools, 83, 91, 132, 329
  enforced attendance, 331, 333, 340
  legislation needed, 331, 333
Intemperance, 133–140

Jails. *See* Juveniles in prisons; Prisoners; *specific prisons*
James, George Payne Rainsford, 126
Jebb, Joshua, 192
Jury, 47
Juvenile delinquents. *See also* Female delinquents; Juveniles in prisons
  coiners, 24–25
  crimes, 35
  discharged prisoners, 48
  education of, 33, 35
  ignorance of, 29, 30
  judicial treatment, 236–237
  lower classes, 4
  muscular power, 296–297
  pickpockets, 24, 37–41, 51, 54–55, 59, 93–96, 100–101, 358–359
  thieves, 17–18, 20
  training in crime by parents, 121–122, 145–147. *See also* Parental neglect
  upper classes, 3–5, 27, 177–178
Juvenile Felons' Act, 64
Juveniles in prisons, iii, iv, 7, 164–177. *See also* Female delinquents; Juvenile delinquents
  ages, 35, 107, 139
  characteristics, 35
  education, 168–175, 237–238
  employment, 48
  female, 171
  first imprisonment, 175
  imprisonment as deterrent, 175
  separation from adult prisoners, 242
  statistics, 35, 107, 139
  United States, 208–209

Kemble, John Mitchell, 373
Kennedy, Louis, 375–376
Kopf, Berlin, 254
Kuratli (manager, Bächtelen), 254

La Petite Roquette Prison, Paris, 238–239
Lange (master, Rauhe Haus), 277
Law Amendment Society, 366
Leet, law of, 374–375
Liddell, Daniel, 104

Liverpool Borough Gaol, 36, 103, 105, 112, 153–155, 165, 171

Manchester Gaol (New Bailey), 55, 56, 94, 99, 176, 202
Mann, Horace, 260
Manzoni, Alessandro, 122
Mettrai, 13, 235, 240, 242, 244, 299–300, 305, 317,
  established, 235
  private management, 235
Mettrai system, 241
Mettray. See Mettrai
Milbank Penitentiary, 31, 146, 197
Millet (advocate), 236
Murray, Amelia, 30

Negroes, 207
Neuhof, Strasbourg, 244–245, 252
New Bailey. See Manchester Gaol
New York (City) Almshouse, 217
New York (City) Bridewell, 217
New York (City) House of Refuge, 210, 217, 218–221, 229
  characteristics of inmates, 210
  established, 210, 216
  finances, 218–219, 220
  labour, 221
  legal power to commit, 218
  rewards for conduct, 221
Newgate, 186, 190, 287, 354
North Leech Prison, 57
Nuremburg House of Reform, Bavaria, 246

Offences. See Crime
Offenders. See also Juvenile delinquents
  professional thieves, 120

Old Bailey, 185
Order of the Agricultural Brothers of St. Vincent de Paul, 245
Orphans
  treatment, Flanders, 249–250
  workhouses, 186

Parental neglect, 7–8, 12, 26, 36, 37, 41–42, 64, 104, 143–145, 148–160, 165, 182
  legal aspects, 8, 12, 64, 67–69, 102–103, 104, 156–159, 377
Parkhurst Reformatory School, 13, 33, 193–201, 310–312, 354, 356–357
  escapes, 224, 356–357
  fire, 196
  health, 311–312
  recreation, 313
Pauperism. See Paupers; Poor Laws; Poverty
Paupers. See also Poor Laws; Poverty
  school for, 261–262
  treatment, Flanders, 249–250
Penal colonies, 242
Penal School, Hamburg, 261–262
Pennsylvania Society for Promotion of Public Schools, 210–211
Perth Prison, 110, 149, 174, 175
Pestalozzi, Jean Henri, 252
Philadelphia (Pa.) House of Refuge, 210, 220–223
  conduct privileges, 221
  discharged inmates, 221–222
  education, 222–223
  established, 210
  finances, 220, 222
  labour, 221, 222
  religious instruction, 223
  statistics, 210, 221

Philanthropic Farm School, Red Hill (Surrey), 287, 288, 310, 339, 355
Pickpockets. *See under* Juvenile delinquents
Pigot, Chief Baron, 328
Poor Laws, 28, 157, 186, 188–189
Poverty, 190–191. *See also* Paupers; Poor Laws
  Belgium, 251
  cause of demoralization, 265
  not cause of crime, 140–141, 152–153, 156, 161
Power, David, 372
Preston Gaol, 31, 32, 38, 51, 59, 63, 91, 149–151
Prisoners. *See also* Juveniles in prisons
  ages, 107
  characteristics, 140
  statistics, 106–107, 140
Prisons. *See* Juveniles in prisons; Prisoners; *specific prisons*
Prosecute, failure to, 177–180
Public schools. *See also* Free schools
  attendance in Boston, 208
  United States, 206–210
Puffendorf, Samuel von, 158
Punishment. *See also under* Rauhe Haus, Hamburg; Reformatory schools; Sentences
  failure to prevent crime, 364–369

Quatt Industrial School, 191–192

Ragged School
  Bristol, 85, 152–153
  Ipswich, 114
  London, 22, 23, 283–291
Ragged School Magazine, 28

Ragged School Movement, 334
Ragged schools, v, 10, 18, 29, 34, 72, 73, 75, 88, 116, 130–131, 178, 187, 318, 329. *See also* Free schools; Industrial schoo's
  admissions, 186–190
  discharged pupils, 285–290
  fines, 285
  teachers, 335–336
Rathbone, William, 147
Rauhe Haus, Hamburg, 84, 246, 247, 254, 255, 258–281, 299–300, 306–307, 317, 320
  admissions, 263–264
  daily routine, 272–275
  discharged pupils, 255, 272, 275
  education, 267
  escapes, 270
  established, 246, 260
  health, 269
  labour, 267
  management, 264–265
  punishment, 268–269
  statistics, 275
  Swiss House, 276–281
Reading Gaol, 309, 364
Recidivism. *See* Re-committals
Re-committals, 106
  female, 105–106
  juvenile, 166, 174–176
Red Hill. *See* Philanthropic Farm School
Reformation, iii, 105, 138, 174–175, 176, 205, 212, 219, 225, 267, 275, 282, 288–289, 303, 319, 320–321, 364–365
Reformatory schools, 56, 98, 112, 113, 179, 181, 193, 194, 299, 300–301, 302, 327, 331, 332, 333, 366–367. *See also* Farm schools; *specific institutions*

Reformatory schools, *(cont'd)*
  admissions, 319–320
  Belgium, 250–251, 256
  Canada, 226–227
  deterring effect, 360
  expense, 98, 379–380
  family system, 299–301, 321–323
  France, 234–235, 242, 243
  industrial training, 205
  labour, 242, 243, 304–312
  legal power to commit, 13, 332, 333, 379
  length of sentence, 320
  management, 228–229, 380
  objections, 353–369
  private support, 205, 242, 332, 379
  public support, 380
  punishment, 315–318
  recreation, 312–315
  religious instruction, 303
  United States, 308, 320, 321, 355
Rushton, Edward, 103, 147–148
Ruysselede Reformatory Schools, 251–252

St. James Back Ragged School. *See* Ragged School, Bristol
St. Nicholas School, Paris, 243–244, 308
Salford Prison, 51, 52, 100
Scotland
  prisons, 105–107
Sentences, 35
  English law, 237
  French law, 236
  short, 59, 100, 146
Separate system, 170, 174, 192. *See also* Solitary confinement
Sharpe, Granville, 65
Shearman, Rev. J., 130
Silent system, 57

Smith, John, 175
Société panternelle, 239
  object, 235
Society for the Reformation of Juvenile Delinquents, N. Y. (City), 216, 218
Solitary confinement, 58, 63, 128, 149. *See also* Separate system
Stapleton Workhouse, 152
Stretton-on-Dunsmore Asylum, 34–35
Sunday schools, 10
Swiss Society of Public Usefulness, 254
Symonds, John Addington (the Elder), 293–295
Symons, Jelinger Cookson, 190, 303–304

Tasmania, Bishop of (Francis Russell Nixon), 85
Temperance Reformation, 134
Thompson, Alexander, 83, 130, 133
Thompson Island Farm School. *See* Boston Farm School
Tocqueville, Alexis de, 208
Tothill Fields Prison, 354
Travellers. *See* Vagabonds
Truancy, 208, 231–232
Tuckerman, Rev. Joseph, 134, 210, 211, 212, 370n
Turner, Rev. Sidney, 310–311

Vagabonds, 32–33, 122–132
  cities, 130
  compulsory education, 129–130
  Italy, 122–124
  legal restraint, 124
  taught by parents, 132
Van Damme (commissaire, West Flanders), 249
Visiting Society, Hamburg, 259

INDEX

Wakefield Prison, 174
Watson, Sheriff William, 230
Watts, Isaac, 312
Wells, E. M. P., 136, 212
Werhli (director, Hofwyl Poor School), 252, 254, 305
Wesleyan School, Kingswood, 313
Westborough Reform School, 223–225
  escapes, 224
Wethersfield Prison, 211
Whitmore, W. Wolryche, 191
Wichern, Dr. Johann, 84, 258, 261, 262, 263, 264, 265, 266, 306, 319
Wilberforce, William, 65
Williams, Capt. William John, 174
Willoughby de Eresby, Lord and Lady, 375–376
Workhouses
  females, 192
  Gloucestershire, 191
  nurseries of crime, 190
  schools, 117, 378
Wright, Thomas, 99, 100
Wurtenburg schools, 245–246, 247, 256, 308. *See also* Farm schools, Germany

Zellweger, Jean Gaspard, 254

PATTERSON SMITH REPRINT SERIES IN
CRIMINOLOGY, LAW ENFORCEMENT, AND SOCIAL PROBLEMS

1. Lewis: *The Development of American Prisons and Prison Customs, 1776-1845*
2. Carpenter: *Reformatory Prison Discipline*
3. Brace: *The Dangerous Classes of New York*
4. Dix: *Remarks on Prisons and Prison Discipline in the United States*
5. Bruce et al: *The Workings of the Indeterminate-Sentence Law and the Parole System in Illinois*
6. Wickersham Commission: *Complete Reports, Including the Mooney-Billings Report.* 14 Vols.
7. Livingston: *Complete Works on Criminal Jurisprudence.* 2 Vols.
8. Cleveland Foundation: *Criminal Justice in Cleveland*
9. Illinois Association for Criminal Justice: *The Illinois Crime Survey*
10. Missouri Association for Criminal Justice: *The Missouri Crime Survey*
11. Aschaffenburg: *Crime and Its Repression*
12. Garofalo: *Criminology*
13. Gross: *Criminal Psychology*
14. Lombroso: *Crime, Its Causes and Remedies*
15. Saleilles: *The Individualization of Punishment*
16. Tarde: *Penal Philosophy*
17. McKelvey: *American Prisons*
18. Sanders: *Negro Child Welfare in North Carolina*
19. Pike: *A History of Crime in England.* 2 Vols.
20. Herring: *Welfare Work in Mill Villages*
21. Barnes: *The Evolution of Penology in Pennsylvania*
22. Puckett: *Folk Beliefs of the Southern Negro*
23. Fernald et al: *A Study of Women Delinquents in New York State*
24. Wines: *The State of the Prisons and of Child-Saving Institutions*
25. Raper: *The Tragedy of Lynching*
26. Thomas: *The Unadjusted Girl*
27. Jorns: *The Quakers as Pioneers in Social Work*
28. Owings: *Women Police*
29. Woolston: *Prostitution in the United States*
30. Flexner: *Prostitution in Europe*
31. Kelso: *The History of Public Poor Relief in Massachusetts: 1820-1920*
32. Spivak: *Georgia Nigger*
33. Earle: *Curious Punishments of Bygone Days*
34. Bonger: *Race and Crime*
35. Fishman: *Crucibles of Crime*
36. Brearley: *Homicide in the United States*
37. Graper: *American Police Administration*
38. Hichborn: *"The System"*
39. Steiner & Brown: *The North Carolina Chain Gang*
40. Cherrington: *The Evolution of Prohibition in the United States of America*
41. Colquhoun: *A Treatise on the Commerce and Police of the River Thames*
42. Colquhoun: *A Treatise on the Police of the Metropolis*
43. Abrahamsen: *Crime and the Human Mind*
44. Schneider: *The History of Public Welfare in New York State: 1609-1866*
45. Schneider & Deutsch: *The History of Public Welfare in New York State: 1867-1940*
46. Crapsey: *The Nether Side of New York*
47. Young: *Social Treatment in Probation and Delinquency*
48. Quinn: *Gambling and Gambling Devices*
49. McCord & McCord: *Origins of Crime*
50. Worthington & Topping: *Specialized Courts Dealing with Sex Delinquency*

Patterson Smith Reprint Series in Criminology, Law Enforcement, and Social Problems

51. Asbury: *Sucker's Progress*
52. Kneeland: *Commercialized Prostitution in New York City*
53. Fosdick: *American Police Systems*
54. Fosdick: *European Police Systems*
55. Shay: *Judge Lynch: His First Hundred Years*
56. Barnes: *The Repression of Crime*
57. Cable: *The Silent South*
58. Kammerer: *The Unmarried Mother*
59. Doshay: *The Boy Sex Offender and His Later Career*
60. Spaulding: *An Experimental Study of Psychopathic Delinquent Women*
61. Brockway: *Fifty Years of Prison Service*
62. Lawes: *Man's Judgment of Death*
63. Healy & Healy: *Pathological Lying, Accusation, and Swindling*
64. Smith: *The State Police*
65. Adams: *Interracial Marriage in Hawaii*
66. Halpern: *A Decade of Probation*
67. Tappan: *Delinquent Girls in Court*
68. Alexander & Healy: *Roots of Crime*
69. Healy & Bronner: *Delinquents and Criminals*
70. Cutler: *Lynch-Law*
71. Gillin: *Taming the Criminal*
72. Osborne: *Within Prison Walls*
73. Ashton: *The History of Gambling in England*
74. Whitlock: *On the Enforcement of Law in Cities*
75. Goldberg: *Child Offenders*
76. Cressey: *The Taxi-Dance Hall*
77. Riis: *The Battle with the Slum*
78. Larson et al: *Lying and Its Detection*
79. Comstock: *Frauds Exposed*
80. Carpenter: *Our Convicts.* 2 Vols. in 1
81. Horn: *Invisible Empire: The Story of the Ku Klux Klan, 1866-1871*
82. Faris et al: *Intelligent Philanthropy*
83. Robinson: *History and Organization of Criminal Statistics in the United States*
84. Reckless: *Vice in Chicago*
85. Healy: *The Individual Delinquent*
86. Bogen: *Jewish Philanthropy*
87. Clinard: *The Black Market: A Study of White Collar Crime*
88. Healy: *Mental Conflicts and Misconduct*
89. Citizens' Police Committee: *Chicago Police Problems*
90. Clay: *The Prison Chaplain*
91. Peirce: *A Half Century with Juvenile Delinquents*
92. Richmond: *Friendly Visiting Among the Poor*
93. Brasol: *Elements of Crime*
94. Strong: *Public Welfare Administration in Canada*
95. Beard: *Juvenile Probation*
96. Steinmetz: *The Gaming Table.* 2 Vols.
97. Crawford: *Report on the Penitentiaries of the United States*
98. Kuhlman: *A Guide to Material on Crime and Criminal Justice*
99. Culver: *Bibliography of Crime and Criminal Justice: 1927-1931*
100. Culver: *Bibliography of Crime and Criminal Justice: 1932-1937*

Patterson Smith Reprint Series in Criminology, Law Enforcement, and Social Problems

101. Tompkins: *Administration of Criminal Justice, 1938-1948*
102. Tompkins: *Administration of Criminal Justice, 1949-1956*
103. Cumming: *Bibliography Dealing with Crime and Cognate Subjects*
104. Addams et al: *Philanthropy and Social Progress*
105. Powell: *The American Siberia*
106. Carpenter: *Reformatory Schools*
107. Carpenter: *Juvenile Delinquents*
108. Montague: *Sixty Years in Waifdom*
109. Mannheim: *Juvenile Delinquency in an English Middletown*
110. Semmes: *Crime and Punishment in Early Maryland*
111. National Conference of Charities and Correction: *History of Child Saving in the United States*
112. Barnes: *The Story of Punishment*. 2d ed.
113. Phillipson: *Three Criminal Law Reformers*
114. Drähms: *The Criminal*
115. Terry & Pellens: *The Opium Problem*
116. Ewing: *The Morality of Punishment*
117. Mannheim: *Group Problems in Crime and Punishment*
118. Michael & Adler: *Crime, Law and Social Science*
119. Lee: *A History of Police in England*
120. Schafer: *Compensation and Restitution to Victims of Crime*. 2d ed.
121. Mannheim: *Pioneers in Criminology*. 2d ed.
122. Goebel & Naughton: *Law Enforcement in Colonial New York*
123. Savage: *Police Records and Recollections*
124. Ives: *A History of Penal Methods*
125. Bernard (Ed.): *The Americanization Studies*
    Thompson: *The Schooling of the Immigrant*
    Daniels: *America via the Neighborhood*
    Thomas et al: *Old World Traits Transplanted*
    Speek: *A Stake in the Land*
    Davis: *Immigrant Health and the Community*
    Breckinridge: *New Homes for Old*
    Park: *The Immigrant Press and Its Control*
    Gavit: *Americans by Choice*
    Claghorn: *The Immigrant's Day in Court*
    Leiserson: *Adjusting Immigrant and Industry*
126. Dai: *Opium Addiction in Chicago*
127. Costello: *Our Police Protectors*
128. Wade: *A Treatise on the Police and Crimes of the Metropolis*
129. Robison: *Can Delinquency Be Measured?*
130. Augustus: *A Report of the Labors of John Augustus*
131. Vollmer: *The Police and Modern Society*
132. Jessel: *A Bibliography of Works in English on Playing Cards and Gaming*. Enlarged
133. Walling: *Recollections of a New York Chief of Police*
134. Lombroso: *Criminal Man*
135. Howard: *Prisons and Lazarettos*. 2 vols.
136. Fitzgerald: *Chronicles of Bow Street Police-Office*. 2 vols. in 1
137. Goring: *The English Convict*
138. Ribton-Turner: *A History of Vagrants and Vagrancy*
139. Smith: *Justice and the Poor*
140. Willard: *Tramping with Tramps*

Carpenter, M.
    Juvenile Delinquents

HV
9069
.C296

57375